God and the Green Divide

The publisher gratefully acknowledges the generous support of the Ralph and Shirley Shapiro Endowment Fund in Environmental Studies of the University of California Press Foundation.

God and the Green Divide

Religious Environmentalism in Black and White

Amanda J. Baugh

UNIVERSITY OF CALIFORNIA PRESS

University of California Press, one of the most
distinguished university presses in the United States,
enriches lives around the world by advancing scholarship
in the humanities, social sciences, and natural sciences. Its
activities are supported by the UC Press Foundation and
by philanthropic contributions from individuals and
institutions. For more information, visit www.ucpress.edu.

University of California Press
Oakland, California

Library of Congress Cataloging-in-Publication Data

Names: Baugh, Amanda J., 1981- author.
Title: God and the green divide : religious
    environmentalism in black and white /
    Amanda J. Baugh.
Description: Oakland, California : University of
    California Press, [2017] | Includes bibliographical
    references and index.
Identifiers: LCCN 2016017202| ISBN 9780520291164
    (cloth : alk. paper) | ISBN 9780520291171 (pbk. : alk.
    paper) | ISBN 9780520965003 (electronic)
Subjects: LCSH: Environmentalism--Religious aspects—
    Case studies. | Environmentalism—United States. |
    Environmentalism--Moral and ethical aspects--United
    States.
Classification: LCC BL65.E36 B37 2017 | DDC 201/.77—
    dc23
LC record available at https://lccn.loc.gov/2016017202

Manufactured in the United States of America

25   24   23   22   21   20   19   18   17   16
10   9   8   7   6   5   4   3   2   1

Contents

Acknowledgments

This book would not have been possible without the generous support of many people. First and foremost, I would like to thank the tireless leaders of Faith in Place, especially Clare Butterfield and Veronica Kyle, without whom this project could never have materialized. In addition to instigating the religious environmental activism that provided material to study, they kindly gave their time and support, candidly sharing some of their innermost beliefs and aspirations. These women made me feel comfortable in their worlds, inviting me to visit places I could never have found on my own (and often transporting me to those places!), and generally made my research experience a pleasure. I am also grateful to the other staff members, board members, volunteers, and participants at Faith in Place who were generous with their time and enthusiastically contributed to my research.

My professors and colleagues at Northwestern University guided this project from its earliest stages. Sarah McFarland Taylor encouraged my research from the beginning, training me in the art of fieldwork and reminding me of the bigger implications of my research and teaching. Robert Orsi challenged me to push my theoretical analysis, pursuing the difficult, sometimes uncomfortable questions. Sylvester Johnson helped me navigate the complicated terrain of racial politics that was evident throughout my fieldwork. Cristina Traina, Henry Binford, and Michelle Molina provided insights and encouragement. Northwestern University's Graduate School funded essential travel through a Research Travel

Grant. This project also received generous funding from the Andrew W. Mellon/American Council of Learned Society Dissertation Completion Fellowship Program.

Members of Northwestern's North American Religions Workshop contributed compelling ideas and questions that have shaped this project. I especially want to thank Brian Clites, Matthew Cressler, and Hayley Glaholt. Abdoulaye Sounaye, Anne Koenig, and Abby Trollinger offered critical feedback, guidance, and motivation in the dissertation-writing phase. Michal Raucher and Tina Howe provided unparalleled insight and support throughout our days at Northwestern and as the project developed into a book. These brilliant women also made graduate school a pleasure. I value their lifelong friendships.

My colleagues at California State University, Northridge have also provided encouragement and intellectual engagement. I especially want to acknowledge Rick Talbott, Claire White, Xochitl Alviso, and Linda Lam-Easton. Lindsay Gonzaba provided excellent assistance in compiling the index. I am grateful for a wonderfully supportive dean, Elizabeth Say, who provided writing space, coffee, and the best gift of all, time to pursue my writing. I would not have been able to complete this project without the generous funding from several CSUN sources, including the College of Humanities, the Office of Research and Sponsored Projects, and Faculty Development.

I'm deeply indebted to Sarah Pike for her brilliant guidance as I revised my dissertation into this book. Sarah challenged me to employ precision and nuance, make difficult decisions about content, and pursue areas of inquiry that I had not previously considered. At the University of California Press, Eric Schmidt offered direction and encouragement as the project went through various stages of development. Thanks also to Maeve Cornell-Taylor for her assistance in preparing the book for production.

On a personal level, I wish to acknowledge the wonderful support of my family. Josh Baugh and Ashley Cash have provided encouragement, friendship, and editorial assistance. They also produced two amazing and delightful nieces, Emma and Katelyn Baugh. My parents, George Baugh and Alissa Levey Baugh, have been my most enthusiastic supporters, always ensuring that I had the material resources to achieve my goals and pushing me to make my mark in the world. Without my mother's insistence that I take Introduction to Judaism as an undergraduate, I might never have found my way to religious studies. My father has been a unique conversation partner as I explore the inner workings of religious worlds. He has encouraged me to find a vocation that is meaningful and rewarding, working hard but also injecting my work with humor and play.

More than anyone else, Jason Lee has lived with the trials, tribulations, and joys that accompany the academic life. He has been a wonderful sounding board as I have tried to develop ideas, has accompanied me on several fieldwork excursions and conference trips, and has offered an impressive editorial eye. He and our son, Zachary Lee, are sources of boundless joy and provide perspective on the important things in life. Together they make me feel like I have it all.

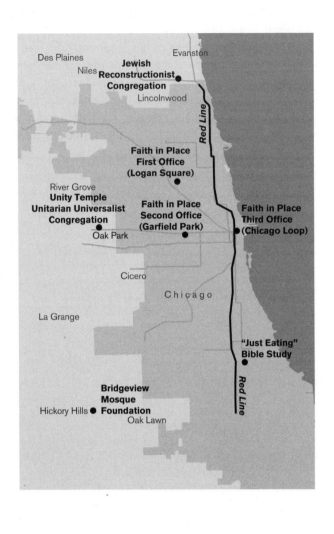

Des Plaines

Evanston

Niles

Jewish Reconstructionist Congregation

Lincolnwood

Red Line

Faith in Place First Office (Logan Square)

River Grove

Unity Temple Unitarian Universalist Congregation

Faith in Place Second Office (Garfield Park)

Faith in Place Third Office (Chicago Loop)

Oak Park

Cicero

Chicago

La Grange

"Just Eating" Bible Study

Red Line

Bridgeview Mosque Foundation

Hickory Hills

Oak Lawn

Introduction

In the warmth of a long hoop house on a crisp fall Chicago afternoon, I listened as Veronica Kyle, an outreach worker for the interfaith environmental nonprofit Faith in Place, delivered a galvanizing speech about the blessings and opportunities of environmental activism.[1] She spoke to a group of thirty fellow African American churchwomen and men who were gathered for an environmental workshop at Eden Place, an urban nature center created in a former illegal dumping ground on Chicago's south side. As part of a weatherization project initiated by the city's Department of Environment and implemented through Faith in Place, the church representatives were learning to install the contents of a low-cost weatherization kit: weather stripping, plastic film, caulk, and foam insulation. After the workshop they would teach these weatherization techniques to youth in their own congregations. In turn the youth would weatherize the homes of elderly neighborhood residents, earning five dollars from the city for each kit they installed and receiving praise from their pastors as a new generation of environmental heroes.

While the Department of Environment's main objective for the project was to improve energy efficiency in Chicago homes, Faith in Place had additional goals. Its leaders hoped the program simultaneously would increase awareness about "green" practices in a geographical region where such knowledge was not widespread, would deliver a cost-saving service, would put well-earned money in the hands of minority teens, and would give them knowledge and skills that could translate into opportunity within the emerging green economy. Kyle's speech highlighted the project's many benefits beyond environmental protection. In addition to conserving energy, she explained, the weatherization project would contribute to overcoming the "eco-divide," a concept she employed to describe lost opportunities in the African American community resulting from a lack of knowledge about the environment.[2] Comparing the situation to the digital divide that had excluded African Americans from employment opportunities a decade earlier, Kyle wanted to ensure that her community was not left behind as new, green opportunities emerged.

After making these points Kyle summarized her goals for the project. "This is about opportunity. It's about role models," she declared to the attentive crowd. Participants responded with an affirming chorus of "Umm hmm!" and "Yeah!" Kyle suggested the weatherization project presented a positive opportunity for south-side youth, providing them with skills, experiences, and knowledge that would enable them to speak the language of environmentalism that was common parlance among white teens. "These kids can be anything," she elaborated, and by helping implement the weatherization project "you can change a person's life." "Yeah!" the churchwomen and men cheered. Energized and motivated to learn, they pulled out their new caulk guns and tape and began to practice sealing windows and doors.

By enlisting self-identified religious groups in the cause of environmental protection, under the assumption that their religions compelled them to protect the earth, this workshop offered one manifestation of what scholars have identified as "religious environmental" involvement.[3] Situating environmental concern at the heart of every religion, religious environmental activists in cities across the United States have formed "green teams," taken measures to save energy, served fair trade coffee, planted gardens, lobbied for improved environmental policies, and taken numerous other measures to protect the earth, all based on the idea that their religions demand concern for the planet.[4] In contrast to the overwhelmingly white and affluent coalition associated with the mainstream environmental movement, religious environmentalism has been more successful at building racial and ethnic diversity.[5] Many of the movement's participants prefer to distance themselves from the secular and political associations of mainstream environmentalism, employing instead the concept of "earth stewardship" to connote that God assigned humans the special role of stewards, or protectors of creation. Although not directly mentioned in the Bible, earth stewardship derives primarily from Genesis 2:15, "The Lord took the man and put him in the Garden of Eden to work it and take care of it."[6] Under the auspices of protecting God's creation, thousands of congregations have made fundamental changes to opt for a more sustainable way of life.

Early scholarship examining the connections between religion and environmental concern tended to celebrate the promise of religion for addressing the environmental crisis. Through texts such as *Religions of the World and Ecology,* which followed a series of conferences held at Harvard University in the 1990s, scholars have examined the scriptures, theologies, doctrines, and traditions of various "world religions" in an effort to demonstrate that all religions advance positive environmental values. Religious studies professors Mary Evelyn Tucker and John Grim, who organized the conferences and served as the general editors for the subsequent book series, have explained, "A major goal of the series was to begin a process of retrieving, reevaluating, and reconstructing the ecological dimensions of the world's religions so as to contribute to a sustaining and flourishing future for the earth community."[7] American religious communities have referenced those "ecological dimensions" as they have developed "environmental ministries," and religion-and-ecology scholars in turn have cited such developments to support their contentions that all religions teach their adherents to become good stewards of the earth.[8]

This book contributes to a growing body of scholarship that urges a more critical approach to understanding the potential connections between religious worldviews and beliefs, attitudes, and behaviors related to the environment.[9] Through my in-depth case study of Faith in Place, an interfaith environmental nonprofit in Chicago that has partnered with over nine hundred congregations and is notable for the racial and ethnic diversity of its coalition, I offer critical analysis of the religious environmental movement. Drawing from participant observation and ethnographic interviews, I uncover varied agendas and motivations that participants brought to their religious environmental involvement. Faith in Place leaders embraced the broad category of religion to encompass diverse groups into their cause, suggesting that every religion supported concern for the earth and that consequently all people of faith ought to take measures to protect the planet. Yet in practice the shape and meaning of religious environmentalism varied by race, ethnicity, and class, pointing to a central paradox underlying the movement. While the liberal white Protestant leaders at Faith in Place endeavored to diversify environmentalism by freeing it from its reputation as a movement for white elites, minority communities participated in part because of the images they thought environmental involvement conveyed—affluence, education, respectability, and positive civic identity.

On the basis of these observations I argue that the spread of religious environmentalism in the United States has relied not simply on the "ecological dimensions" of scriptures, theology, and religious traditions but also on latent assumptions about race, ethnicity, and class. Faith in Place offers a window for examining how such assumptions have contributed to religious environmentalism's development.

RELIGIOUS ENVIRONMENTALISM IN AMERICAN CULTURE

Faith in Place's religious environmental activism was one manifestation of a much larger movement that developed in cities across the United States in the twenty-first century. By 2010, Web of Creation, a website of the Lutheran School of Theology at Chicago (LSTC), listed official statements in support of earth care from twelve Christian denominations, including the Roman Catholic Church, the Presbyterian Church (USA), the Church of the Brethren, and the Evangelical Lutheran Church in America.[10] The website also included published statements or resolutions on climate change from fourteen Christian denominations, as well as denominational resources on earth care for Buddhists and Jews. Likewise, the website of Yale University's Forum on Religion and Ecology (FORE), an international project promoting understanding of the connections between religious worldviews and environmental concerns, listed denominational statements and resources for Hinduism, Jainism, Buddhism, Confucianism, Daoism, Shinto, indigenous religions, Judaism, Christianity, and Islam.[11] Prominent religious leaders publicly supported environmental protection as well. In 2008 Pope Benedict attracted international media attention for installing solar panels at the Vatican, and in 2015 Pope Francis issued a historic encyclical on climate change.[12] The Dalai Lama similarly called on world leaders to prioritize issues related to global warming prior to the 2009 UN Climate Change Conference in Copenhagen.

An outpouring of popular literature and documentary films emerged in the twenty-first century to further support environmental concern among religious communities. For interfaith audiences, *Love God, Heal Earth* (2009) offered a collection of twenty-one essays written by religious leaders (including Faith in Place's director, Clare Butterfield) who argued for a "sacred duty" to protect the environment. *Tending to Eden: Environmental Stewardship for God's People* (2010) provided Christians a "practical guide" to caring for creation, and *Serve God, Save the Planet: A Christian Call to Action* (2007) presented a medical doctor's account of his turn to Jesus to cope with alarm about the growing incidence of pollution-related diseases. In *For the Beauty of the Earth: A Christian Vision of Creation Care* (2010), religious studies professor Steven Bouma-Prediger constructed a theology of creation care for evangelicals. Besides these secondary sources that supported religiously based earth stewardship, *The Green Bible* (2008) offered a resource for those who wanted to locate biblical references to nature. A "green-letter" edition of the Bible, this text highlighted more than one thousand references to the earth by printing them in green ink. Moreover, the documentary film *Renewal* (which featured Faith in Place among its eight stories of religious environmentalism in action) and a PBS special titled "Ethical Eating" contributed additional support for the viewpoint that people of faith should care about the environment. Susan Drake Emmerich's documentary film *When Heaven Meets Earth: Faith and Environment in the Chesapeake Bay* (2008) recorded Emmerich's use of Christian scriptures to convince commercial fishers to become better earth stewards.[13]

Numerous other organizations joined Faith in Place in working to inculcate environmental concern in religious communities. Some, such as Presbyterians for Earth Care, Lutherans Restoring Creation, and the Reformed Church in America's "Caring for Creation" ministry, promoted environmental awareness and activism within particular denominations. The Coalition on the Environment in Jewish Life (COEJL) encouraged earth stewardship among all branches of Judaism, and the Buddhist Peace Fellowship listed environmentalism among its top three concerns.[14] In addition to these environmental groups formed within individual religious traditions, several other organizations joined Faith in Place in working on environmental issues in interfaith settings. New Jersey–based Green Faith worked across the country to "inspire, educate and mobilize people of diverse religious backgrounds for environmental leadership," according to its mission statement.[15] Beginning in 1992, Green Faith worked to encourage environmental activism among religious communities, focusing especially on training environmental leaders through its national leadership certification program.[16] Likewise, Interfaith Power and Light (IPL) was a San Francisco–based interfaith environmental group with affiliates in forty states.

Religious Environmentalism's Academic Roots

Some people of faith have sensed a connection between their religions and concern for the earth for decades, even centuries. But contemporary religious environmental activism in the United States has built on language and scriptural resources that developed among scholars and religious leaders in the academic field of "religion and ecology." Although this academic field was consciously formed in the 1990s, religion-and-ecology scholarship traces its roots back to earlier decades. The 1967 publication of "The Historical Roots of Our Ecological Crisis," a now famous essay written by medieval historian Lynn White Jr. and published in the journal *Science,* marks for many the beginning of the field.[17] In that essay, White argued that the world's environmental crisis was at root a religious problem. Although he used the more general term *religion,* he implicated Western Christianity as the real culprit for having engendered a mind-set that justified, or even encouraged, the exploitation of nature.[18] Western Christianity, according to White, had been interpreted to offer an anthropocentric understanding of the world that taught humans they were masters over nature.[19] White recognized that humans had exercised power over nature for centuries, polluting the air and cutting down forests. Combined with twentieth-century advances in science and technology, White argued, this mind-set resulted in a catastrophic assault on the natural world. White concluded that science and technology alone would be unable to solve the ecological crisis. Instead, he wrote, "Since the roots of our trouble are so largely religious, the remedy must also be essentially religious, whether we call it that or not."[20]

Academics and religious leaders reacted to White in the ensuing decades, returning to the roots of religious traditions in search of resources that could support an environmental ethic. One response was to turn to romanticized versions of Asian religions considered to be ecologically superior to Christianity. Philosopher J. Baird Callicott, a pioneer in environmental philosophy, agreed with White's critique of Christianity and suggested that Asian and indigenous religions were better suited to support an environmental ethic.[21] Others, such as Jay McDaniel and Dieter Hessel, reinterpreted Christian traditions and scriptures to support environmental sustainability.[22]

Besides those individual scholarly efforts, a series of conferences beginning in the 1980s systematically brought institutional religions into dialogue with the environmental movement. In 1986, the World Wildlife Fund (WWF) invited leaders of five religions to participate in an interfaith ceremony to observe the WWF's twenty-five-year anniversary at the Basilica of St. Francis in Assisi, Italy.[23] As part of the event, the religious leaders issued official declarations affirming their religions' support of nature conservation. In turn, several other religious leaders issued conservation declarations of their own.[24] While these statements did not immediately inspire widespread environmental activism at the level of congregations, they were available to authorize environmental ethics when congregations were ready to "go green" in the twenty-first century. Following the Assisi event, religious studies scholar Steven Rockefeller organized a "Spirit and Nature" conference at Middlebury College in 1990, bringing together academics and religious leaders. The conference proceedings were published in a book and contributed to a Bill Moyers PBS special, advancing the conference organizers' goal of stimulating dialogue about religiously based environmental ethics within broader American culture.[25]

The Harvard "Religions of the World and Ecology" conferences held between 1996 and 1998 were perhaps the most influential set of events for shaping both the emerging academic study of religion and ecology and the practice of religious environmentalism. The ten conferences brought together over eight hundred international scholars and theologians, religious leaders, and environmental activists, who discussed the ecological merits of ten world religions.[26] They searched for a common religious ground that could contribute to an environmentally sustainable future, working to build a case that environmental stewardship was an important ethic in all the world's religions. Even if Lynn White was correct that religions in the past had contributed to environmental degradation, these scholars wanted to locate resources within world religions that could be harnessed to bring about a sustainable future.

Organizers of the Harvard conferences intended for the meetings to be constructive, setting forth resources that could support positive human-environmental relations. Conference participants contributed to a ten-volume series titled Religions of the World and Ecology. The series provided a foundation for the emerging academic field of religion and ecology and also became an important resource for clergy and laity interested in religiously based environmental ethics and activism.

Notably, the Assisi ceremony, the "Spirit and Nature" conference, and the Harvard conferences all took place in multireligious settings, drawing from the perspectives of Christians, Muslims, Jews, Hindus, Buddhists, Native Americans, and adherents of other "world religions." Moreover, the "Spirit and Nature" and Harvard conferences brought together academics and religious leaders. This type of shared agenda has continued into the twenty-first century. A 2008 conference at Yale Divinity School, "Renewing Hope: Pathways of Religious Environmentalism," included panels with presenters from both academic and activist circles.[27] Religious environmental leaders from Faith in Place, Green Faith, and other similar organizations presented alongside scholars from major research universities. Faith in Place's executive director also has presented on a "Religion and Ecology" panel at the American Academy of Religion.[28] Moreover, Green Faith is making its presence felt within the academic world. Through its Green Faith Fellowship Program, the organization has educated numerous religious environmental leaders, including some who have pursued training in academic settings. Mallory McDuff, a former Green Faith fellow, acknowledges the financial support of that organization in her research for *Natural Saints,* her 2010 monograph published by Oxford University Press.[29]

Hence, the assumption that all religions share a basic environmental ethic, an assumption that underlies interfaith environmental work today, was forged through alliances among religious leaders and a branch of religion-and-ecology scholars engaged in normative, constructive scholarship. In turn, that assumption has become an accepted fact for that branch of scholars and religious practitioners. Major strands of religious environmental activism and religion-and-ecology scholarship since the early 1990s have relied on the assumption that environmental concerns are important issues for every religion. Further, they assume that religious environmental solutions must be multifaith.

RELIGIOUS ENVIRONMENTALISM AT FAITH IN PLACE

During the time of my fieldwork between 2006 and 2011, Faith in Place was one of many organizations across the United States dedicated to putting religious environmental beliefs into practice. Established in 1999 as a project of the Center for Neighborhood Technology (CNT), an urban sustainability think tank, Faith in Place had the stated aim "to help religious people become good stewards of the earth."[30] Cofounded by Rev. Clare Butterfield, a white Unitarian Universalist minister, the organization was expressly interfaith, listing Protestants, Catholics, Muslims, Jews, Hindus, Buddhists, Baha'is, and Zoroastrians among its congregational partners. During my fieldwork its small full-time staff included two African American women and one Latina, and it offered programming both to predominately white and predominately black congregations. Faith in Place aimed to help congregations develop a "culture of conservation" where people across the congregation would understand earth stewardship as an important issue that was also a matter of faith.[31] Focusing on food, energy, water, and policy, it offered worship resources, educational programming, and practical support for green infrastructural projects. Faith in Place leaders wanted participants to make the environment a fundamental concern for their congregations throughout the year—not just on Earth Day—by connecting environmental degradation to matters of faith and presenting earth stewardship as central to religious life.[32]

Faith in Place offered a productive site for analyzing religious environmentalism in action for several reasons. First, it provided one example of a broader movement that was developing within American religious culture in the first decade of the twenty-first century, a movement Faith in Place helped to shape. Between 1999 and 2011 Faith in Place worked with over nine hundred congregations in Illinois to increase environmental awareness among thousands of people of faith. It was one of forty state affiliates of IPL. Because Faith in Place had been established earlier than many other similar organizations, it served as a model for and offered support to newly forming religious environmental groups. Thus Faith in Place's work represented an important cultural trend in American religious communities.

But Faith in Place also was exemplary because it built a diverse coalition, noteworthy especially for the significant involvement of African Americans. Historically, African American communities did not participate widely in mainstream environmentalism, in large part because the movement was associated with the concerns of white elites. However, religious environmentalists generally, and Faith in Place leaders in particular, concertedly framed environmental issues as matters of social justice that affected *people,* especially the poor. By talking about the environment using the language of social justice, Faith in Place recruited a broad coalition of concerned citizens who had not previously participated in environmentalism. At a time when other religious environmental groups and mainstream secular environmental coalitions aspired to develop racial diversity, Faith in Place was noteworthy for its successful minority recruitment.

THEORETICAL CONTRIBUTIONS

This book grew from a set of questions about the ways American environmentalism—a movement historically associated with the concerns of white elites—has entered new communities and been embraced by populations more racially, ethnically, and economically diverse than ever before. I wanted to understand what motivated people from populations not historically associated with environmentalism to conserve energy by tolerating warmer homes in the summer and cooler homes in the winter, to lobby for improved environmental policy, and to factor "carbon footprints" into their decisions about how to travel and what to eat. Through the religious environmental movement, religious communities diverse in race, ethnicity, and class came to support these and other related practices as a central part of religious life.

In some ways, I discovered, the environmental activities of Faith in Place participants looked quite similar to those of other American environmentalists. They conserved water and energy, purchased organic and local food, and signed petitions to support environmental legislation. Moreover, some were long-term members of other environmental organizations besides Faith in Place, such as the Sierra Club and the Natural Resources Defense Council. However, many participants were involved with environmentalism solely through Faith in Place. The nonprofit tailored its messages and programming to attract those who were "people of faith first, environmentalists second," a strategy I discuss in chapter 1. They expressly sought to work as a "bridge-builder, bringing new individuals and communities into dialogue with the environmental efforts in our state."[33] This strategy resulted in a coalition whose members tended to maintain moderate environmentalist positions. In contrast to radical environmentalists, who accorded great value to nonhuman nature, Faith in Place encouraged faith communities to prioritize the interests of humans. For that reason its participants tended to exhibit what ethicist Patrick Curry calls a "light green" or "shallow" ecological ethic, expressing concern for nature exclusively in terms of its value for humans.[34] By framing environmental issues in the context of social justice, Faith in Place attracted participants who did not identify with, and in fact may have actively rejected, more radical branches of the environmental movement.[35]

The religious environmental movement grew in popularity only in the first decade of the twenty-first century, but scholars have noted a much longer history of earth-centered beliefs and practices that contribute to religious worlds. In *Dark Green Religion* Bron Taylor identifies spiritual dimensions in the life and work of well-known environmental "saints" such as John Muir and Rachel Carson, and he also builds a case for the religious dimensions of nonreligious groups engaged in radical environmentalism, surfing, and other earth-centric endeavors. Rebecca Kneale Gould's *At Home in Nature* similarly points to a nature-oriented spirituality held by modern American homesteaders who have rejected affiliation with traditional religion and find spiritual meaning through a life lived closer to nature.[36] Works such as these focus primarily on ways nature-oriented religions emerge to *replace* older forms of institutional religion, but they offer little understanding of how environmentalism makes sense to those who still participate in institutional religious worlds.

By contrast, I found at Faith in Place a group of environmentally concerned citizens who endeavored to integrate their concerns about the planet into their inherited religious worlds. In addition to liberal, white Protestants, Faith in Place's coalition included Muslim immigrants from Palestine, Syria, and Lebanon, Zoroastrian immigrants from Pakistan, and African American Protestants connected to the Great Migration through personal experience or the stories of a close relative. Many of the women and men I met through Faith in Place found a meaningful connection to environmentalism, not through the Nature Conservancy or the Sierra Club, but through their religious congregations. Unlike environmental activists who might be "spiritual but not religious," Faith in Place participants were active in institutional religious life and identified as members of a distinct religious tradition, often resulting in moderate environmental positions. While the radical environmentalists described by Taylor and the homesteaders described by Gould placed nature at the center of their spiritual lives, Faith in Place participants tended to understand environmental concern as supplementing and perhaps augmenting their other religious priorities. For them nature religion emerged not to replace, but to exist alongside and within institutional religious forms.

Constructive theological and ethical scholarship in the field of "religion and ecology" supports the work of organizations such as Faith in Place, defining normative values of environmentalism deemed to be present in every religion. Most prominently, the Religions of the World and Ecology book series draws from scriptural resources, theological reflections, and religious ethics and traditions to suggest ways that religions can contribute to solving the environmental crisis.[37] While this body of literature suggests that people of faith *should* care about the earth, scholars have offered little understanding of how theological and ethical reflections about earth stewardship play out in the lives of ordinary people. Ethnographic studies documenting religious environmental involvement often replicate insider language about the universality of ecological teachings in every religion and celebrate the movement's promise for addressing the environmental crisis.[38] In *A Greener Faith*, Roger Gottlieb provides an overview of religious environmental ideals and leaders in order to "cheer us up," he explains, because he is "deeply heartened by the astonishing new movement of religious environmentalism."[39] In *Natural Saints*, Mallory McDuff documents Christian environmental ministries based on a summer of fieldwork, also repeating insider language throughout, such as her contention that religion offers the environmental movement hope.[40] The constructive aims of much scholarship focusing on the ties between environmental concern and institutional religions have led scholars to overlook the messiness of religious environmentalism in practice, limiting the scope of present knowledge about the ways theologies and religious ethics of earth stewardship inform the daily life of modern Americans.

This book contributes to overcoming such oversights, as I consider how ordinary adherents of religious congregations understand their obligations to protect the earth and how such understandings contribute to changing forms of religion in American life. Throughout my research I heard theological reflections such as those from the Harvard series during sermons and discussions at meetings when people wanted to convince others that earth stewardship was a central religious value. Yet such well-defined theological viewpoints rarely offered the definitive motivating factor for people's encounters with religious environmentalism in daily life. Instead, other interests and motivations contributed. For some, environmental programming presented an opportunity to instill new life into the church. One pastor told me he did not really care about the environment but that he worked with Faith in Place because it offered new life and opportunities to revitalize his dying church.[41] Members of a Catholic "peace and justice" committee remarked after a Faith in Place presentation that starting an environmental ministry could bring more people into their church, especially those who were "scientifically minded" and under age thirty-five.[42] Others embraced Faith in Place events as opportunities to promote their own causes. A man that the staff members had never seen hijacked the Q&A portion of one Faith in Place event as he tried to sell copies of his new book.[43] Another man frequently appeared at Faith in Place events during his time of unemployment, trying to recruit participants for his own neighborhood organization.[44] When Kyle joined Faith in Place's staff to conduct outreach among African American congregations, she connected environmentalism with other concerns as well, initiating a conversation that linked environmental practices with a discourse of opportunity.

Encounters such as these served as ever-present reminders that participants brought all kinds of agendas to their involvement with religious environmentalism. By closely examining these diverse motivations and agendas not as peripheral matters but as a central to the story of religious environmentalism, this book complicates ideas about religious environmentalism as direct expressions of religious scriptures, doctrines, and beliefs. Instead, as I demonstrate throughout the following chapters, religious environmentalism is an ideology that is constructed and contested. Its maintenance in daily life relies on diverse motivations and negotiations that proponents of religious environmental ideology may prefer to overlook.

More broadly, this book addresses a set of questions about the role and place of religion in the modern world. It contributes to understanding changing forms of religion in American daily life, providing insight into how religion happens, day to day, as women and men make sense of the worlds they inhabit. I employ the hermeneutic of "lived religion," which points toward religion as it is negotiated and practiced in everyday experience. Through the lenses of lived religion, Robert Orsi explains, we recognize that "something called 'religion' cannot be neatly separated from the other practices of everyday life. . . . Nor can 'religion' be separated from the material circumstances in which specific instances of religious imagination and behavior arise and to which they respond."[45] Lived religion helps us see "the human at work on the world."[46]

My study of religious environmentalism among Faith in Place participants points to the shifting religious imaginations of women and men as they respond to a set of material circumstances that Americans face in the twenty-first century: the environmental crisis. With the threats of climate change, air and water pollution, and global water shortages, religious environmentalists find new ways of living and relating to others. For Faith in Place participants, religion happened in the bathroom (taking shorter showers and flushing the toilet less frequently), on the streets (deciding to walk or ride public transit even when it was easier to drive), and in the kitchen (taking the time to prepare, and enjoy, locally grown food). Looking for religion in the spaces of trains, bathrooms, and community gardens reveals ways that environmental concerns shape the religious worlds of Americans in the twenty-first century.

WOMEN PROTECTING THE ENVIRONMENT

I was drawn to study Faith in Place's work in part because of the preponderance of women in the organization. When I first encountered Faith in Place I noticed that the entire staff and the majority of the board members, volunteers, and participants were women. A 2014 analysis of the organization's network confirmed my observations, finding that female supporters outnumbered males by a ratio of 2:1.[47] This female majority was constant throughout my fieldwork, but my observations suggested that gender was not the most pertinent category of analysis for understanding the organization's work. After all, religious involvement, charity work, and grassroots environmental organizing all tend to draw female majorities, as does the low pay of employment in the nonprofit sector.[48] Faith in Place leaders were much more vocal and intentional about their efforts to involve racial and ethnic minorities than they were about advancing the rights of women, and I have followed their priorities as I have focused primarily on race, ethnicity, and class as categories of analysis throughout this text.

Nevertheless, the dominance of women at Faith in Place did shape the contours of the organization in particular ways. Several of the women I interviewed came of age during the 1960s and 1970s and mentioned that they were influenced by the feminist movement, although few explicitly linked their feminist commitments to their environmental ones. Butterfield mentioned that both environmentalism and feminism were critical movements in her teenage years and had really stuck with her. "So here we are at an organization with five women and one man, and we're doing environmental stuff," she said matter-of-factly, indicating that Faith in Place's hiring practices were an expression of her feminism.[49] Like Butterfield, the other staff members quietly celebrated the organization's lack of diversity in terms of gender.[50] When they were hiring a new staff member in 2007, Emily Eckels, the deputy director, remarked in a casual conversation, "We're not hiring a *man* for that position!"[51] Discussing board recruitment at a staff meeting two years later, Eckels suggested they might aim for greater gender parity given that only three of the ten current board members were men and the entire staff was female. Butterfield disagreed. "Can't we [women] have at least *one* organization of our own?" she asked with a smile, pointing out that men dominated so many other organizations.[52] When Faith in Place finally did hire its first male staff member in 2010, an outreach worker for the new office in central Illinois, Butterfield joked that she was slowly allowing men on board but was keeping them a few hundred miles away from the main office.[53]

Veronica Kyle, who held a bachelor's degree in religion and women's studies and master's degree in gender studies, spoke the most frequently about women's empowerment and women's rights. Apart from her work at Faith in Place, Kyle participated with Girls in Green, an environmental education and leadership program designed to inspire and empower African American girls.[54] Prior to a Faith in Place awards ceremony for African American youth who participated in a weatherization project, she pointed out proudly that the youth who installed the most weatherization kits were all girls, although she did not share that information publicly since she did not want to discourage the boys.[55] Reporting on her first nine months at Faith in Place in a presentation for the board, Kyle wrote a poetic reflection in which she compared her work at the organization to the work of gestating a child. She told me she found it important to use female imagery whenever possible, "because we live in a male-dominated world and are dominated by their imagery."[56] I seldom heard Faith in Place leaders speak publicly about women's rights, but in the private spaces of the office they were more likely to reveal their feminist leanings.

During the early years of my fieldwork, I watched as staff members learned to navigate certain challenges that they faced as a female-dominated organization. Shireen Pishdadi, the first coordinator for Muslim outreach, told me she had had a difficult time getting respect from men when she made presentations about Faith in Place's organic meat cooperative, so she had learned to approach the women instead. This proved much more effective, she said, because the women listened to her more, and they were the ones in charge of shopping for their families' food anyway. Butterfield similarly learned that switching to reusable coffee mugs was a poor first step for congregations wanting to start environmental ministries because someone has to wash those mugs and that work invariably fell to women. It was important to Butterfield that the burden of environmental practices did not fall disproportionately on women. Faith in Place's feminist tendencies also became apparent in its accommodations for working mothers. In the organization's early years two part-time staff members frequently brought their young children with them to work, resulting in an environment that was chaotic at times. The presence of noisy children crashing blocks, pushing toy cars, and smashing raisins around the organization's shared workspace was not necessarily celebrated by the other staff members trying to accomplish their own work, but it was at least tolerated. From subtly celebrating women's empowerment to protecting the rights of women, Faith in Place leaders expressed a tacit feminism through their religious environmental work. The distinctively feminist undertones of the organization shifted, however, as Faith in Place became more professionalized and additional men joined the leadership team. I discuss this shift in the context of Faith in Place's grassroots identity in chapter 7.

PROTESTANT ASSUMPTIONS AND THE "GREEN CEILING"

"The State of Diversity in Environmental Organizations," a 2014 study of more than three hundred environmental groups in the United States, concluded that the state of racial diversity among those organizations was "troubling," with racial minorities constituting a scant 12 percent of leadership positions and 16 percent of board members and general staff.[57] While the study found the organizations had made significant progress on diversity in terms of gender, most of the gains went to white women, and men were still significantly more likely to hold the most powerful positions.[58] In terms of membership and volunteers, the organizations remained "predominately white."[59] The report concluded that people of color had been unable to break the "green ceiling" that had barred minorities from leadership positions over the previous fifty years, despite the fact that minority communities demonstrated greater support for environmental protection than whites.[60]

Developing initiatives to chip away at the "green ceiling" was a central goal at Faith in Place. A report the organization's leaders submitted to the nonprofit reporting service GuideStar stated that their long-term success would be measured by the degree to which environmental activities became mainstream among faith communities and "the degree to which our efforts bring new voices and new faces (especially those of people of color) into the overall environmental movement."[61] The weatherization project featured in this introduction's opening was specifically designed to contribute to that goal by involving African Americans in the work of Faith in Place. As coordinator of African American outreach, Kyle developed new tactics and programs intended to meet the needs of African Americans while simultaneously advancing the goals of Faith in Place. To that end, she developed the weatherization project to promote environmental literacy, provide immediate (albeit short-term) employment, and offer experiences that would lead to greater opportunities in the future. Kyle fundamentally changed the work and demographics of Faith in Place, seeming to overcome challenges of diversification that environmental leaders had struggled with for five decades. In this book I set out to understand how that happened.

I do not anticipate that readers will disagree with my contention about the importance of race, ethnicity, and class in our understandings of religious environmentalism. The dearth of people of color in the mainstream environmental movement is an important issue that has been discussed by scholars and activists alike.[62] It is clear that a more effective and equitable form of environmentalism must include the perspectives of communities diverse in terms of race, ethnicity, and class, and my research at Faith in Place contributes to understanding some of those diverse perspectives.

But Faith in Place enacted a different kind of power dynamic that was not included in the "Green Ceiling" report or in studies of environmental or religious environmental organizations more broadly. Ironically, that dynamic had to do with religion.[63] Faith in Place's work, and interfaith environmentalism more broadly, entailed certain assumptions about the role and place of religion in the modern world, the nature of humans' relationship with the divine, and explanations of cause and effect. These assumptions have been shaped by a secularized liberal Protestant culture, whether those who hold those viewpoints identify as Protestants or not.[64] Faith in Place offered a distinctively modern, progressive Protestant way of being religious. Its leaders unknowingly enforced boundaries that designated "good" religion, while excluding religious beliefs and behaviors that did not adhere to their liberal Protestant norms. I provide examples of these distinctions in chapters 5 and 6.

Liberal Protestant domination within religious environmentalism has manifested at two levels, one very concrete and the other less quantifiable but nevertheless quite real. First, mainline Protestants have dominated the leadership positions of interfaith environmental organizations in the United States. IPL, the umbrella organization hosting state chapters in forty states, was founded by an Episcopal priest. Green Faith's founding director was Episcopal as well. State IPL chapters recruited Jews, Muslims, Catholics, and other religious minority groups to their steering committees and boards of directors, but mainline Protestants filled nearly two-thirds of those positions in 2015 (table 1). Among the forty-four staff members who provided their religious affiliations on their state IPL's websites in the same year, thirty-six, or 82 percent, were

TABLE I   INTERFAITH POWER AND LIGHT BOARD AND STEERING
COMMITTEE MEMBERS BY RELIGIOUS AFFILIATION, BASED ON
SELF-REPORTING ON STATE CHAPTER WEBSITES, 2015

Episcopal	28
Catholic	24
Lutheran	23
Jewish	20
Methodist	19
Baptist	19
Unitarian Universalist	17
Presbyterian	15
United Church of Christ	15
Protestant	10
Buddhist	9
Quaker	6
Baha'i	5
Muslim	5
Mennonite	3
AME	2
Disciples of Christ	2
Hindu	2
Greek Orthodox	1
Interfaith	1
Jain	1
Moravian	1
Mormon	1
Pentecostal	1
Seventh Day Adventist	1
TOTAL:	231

mainline Protestants (table 2). While purporting to represent the viewpoints of every faith, interfaith environmental coalitions in the United States were shaped strongly by mainline Protestants.

Second, whether liberal Protestants or not, those involved with religious environmental projects in the United States tend to maintain progressive religious values and secular understandings of the world. In the past several decades, scholars have identified ways that Protestant understandings of the world—understandings of relations between the human and divine, the natural and the supernatural, that developed from Enlightenment thought and contributed to the Protestant Reformation—have shaped what we now identify as secularism. Rejecting the notion that the secular is merely the absence of religion, scholars

TABLE 2   INTERFAITH POWER AND LIGHT STAFF
MEMBERS BY RELIGIOUS AFFILIATION, BASED ON
SELF-REPORTING ON STATE CHAPTER WEBSITES, 2015

Lutheran	9
United Church of Christ	7
Presbyterian	6
Episcopal	5
Methodist	4
Catholic	3
Jewish	2
Unitarian Universalist	2
Baptist	1
Disciples of Christ	1
Hindu	1
Mennonite	1
Muslim	1
Quaker	1
TOTAL:	44

now assert that secularism itself is a religious project and offers a particular way of being religious. Secular moderns inhabit what philosopher and political theorist Charles Taylor calls the "immanent frame," a worldview in which cause-and-effect relationships are assumed to be this-worldly, rather than resulting from actions of the divine.[65] Taylor contends that this secular way of understanding the world is a defining feature of modernity, and he joins scholars such as anthropologist Talal Asad as he disputes the supposedly clear distinction between the religious and the secular.[66] The religious and the secular are always defined in relation to each other, these scholars point out, and in the context of the West ideas of the secular are informed by liberal Protestant Christianity.[67] A defining characteristic of what we might call secular religion is that its assumptions are taken for granted, so leaders at Faith in Place would not recognize the ways in which their organization enforced particular ideas about what counts as "good" religion. The religious power and authority they assert, in other words, are unmarked.

The women and men I met at Faith in Place brought to the organization modern religious worldviews in which they understood their actions within the immanent frame. In other settings they may have expressed belief in a transcendent God. But at Faith in Place they learned to deal with the global water crisis by incorporating native plants and permeable surfaces outside their churches, not by praying to God for relief. They learned to address food injustices by building community gardens, not by looking forward to a better world with the coming of the Kingdom of God. And they learned to curb climate change through policy advocacy, not petitionary prayer. These steps may seem like perfectly reasonable actions to take in light of modern, secular understandings of the world, and as such they seem like logical measures to prescribe to Faith in Place's intended audience: *all* people of faith. Yet as scholars such as Taylor and Asad insist, modern secular assumptions are shaped in relationship to particular religious views, and in the Western context inhabited by Faith in Place those particular religious views rely heavily on liberal Protestant thought.

Faith in Place offered one way of being religious, a way that conformed to the dictates of liberal modernity. It offered a "welcoming space" for adherents of what was deemed "good" religion and excluded others by not recognizing their beliefs and practices as properly religious. Religious viewpoints that entailed belief in a supernatural God and allowed for the possibility of God's intervention in human history were not especially welcome at Faith in Place, where the Unitarian Universalist executive director's theological outlook was grounded in a rejection of the supernatural. The organization claimed to represent people from "every faith," but it did not involve representatives of different faiths whose religious outlooks acknowledged the existence of a "transcendent frame," a contradiction I examine in chapter 6. Just as it is important to underline ways that constructions of religious environmentalism are always racially marked, it is important to notice how constructions of religious environmentalism are shaped by particular religious understandings. I set out to understand those assumptions, and the ways they shaped Faith in Place's religious environmental activism, in the following pages.

METHODOLOGY

I learned about Faith in Place in 2006 through a lunchtime discussion hosted by the Religion and Environment Initiative, a student group at the University of Chicago. As I listened to Faith in Place's director and its Muslim outreach worker discuss their environmental efforts among religious communities across Chicago, I was intrigued. After the discussion I e-mailed two of Faith in Place's staff members to ask if I might volunteer in the office, potentially as part of my research on whether, how, and to what extent American religious communities were "going green." The women I contacted warmly welcomed my involvement and quickly put me to work alongside another volunteer, an undergraduate from the University of Chicago, who also had learned about Faith in Place through the Religion and Environment Initiative.

During the summer of 2006 I volunteered at Faith in Place two to three days each week, going on field trips with the youth program, helping pack orders for the organic meat cooperative, and calling local businesses to solicit donations for the silent auction at its annual fall fund-raiser. Having determined that Faith in Place was an ideal site for conducting my research, I continued spending time with the organization over the next five years. I volunteered in the office two to three days each week in the summers of 2006, 2007, and 2008. My primary task in those months was to prepare for the annual fall Harvest Celebration dinner and fund-raiser, mostly by soliciting donations for the silent auction from restaurants, museums, arts organizations, and businesses. I also helped with other office tasks as needed, answering the phone, organizing the membership database, preparing thank-you notes, filing documents, and packaging meat orders. Besides my volunteer work, I attended staff and board meetings, clergy group discussions, and meetings between Faith in Place staff and other collaborators. Each fall my attention returned to duties of the academic year, but I periodically attended Faith in Place events throughout the fall, winter, and spring, including workshops, fund-raisers, meetings of its clergy group, and training sessions for seminary students.

Besides giving me insight into the organization's daily operations, my long-term volunteer work enabled me to develop at least a small measure of reciprocity with Faith in Place leaders. Staff members often expressed gratitude for my help and wanted to return the favor by helping me, but they also saw my research as beneficial to their work. Faith in Place's development director introduced me to a new seminary intern by saying, "Amanda's a PhD student and we're the apple of her eye." She told him that I had full access to Faith in Place materials, and programs because I continued to "come in and do grunt labor for free."[68] Similarly, when Faith in Place hosted an event for "major donors," the executive director welcomed me to attend as a guest because she considered me a "major donor" even though my contributions were not financial. While these relationships enabled me to develop an intimate understanding of Faith in Place, they also weighed heavily on my mind as I sat down to write this work and considered how Faith in Place leaders would react to my analysis.

Beginning in June 2009, I conducted twelve consecutive months of fieldwork at Faith in Place. I continued volunteering in the office regularly but also conducted extensive fieldwork outside the office, attending worship services and meetings of "green teams" at Faith in Place partner congregations, participating in earth-themed Bible studies, visiting community gardens, and joining Faith in Place staff at every meeting and event where I was welcome. When I felt it was appropriate I requested permission to record conversations and meetings. For example, I began recording meetings of the clergy group once I had attended several times and the group seemed comfortable with my presence. I also recorded meetings of the Bible study group that I discuss in chapter 4. In that case, the group wanted the sessions recorded for their own purposes, so I gave them both audio files and my own transcriptions. However, I felt it would be disrespectful to bring my audio recorder to green team meetings and other events at congregations where I was an infrequent guest, so in those cases I took written notes during the events and recorded my observations in greater detail immediately afterwards.

My research also included recorded, semistructured interviews with thirty-six individuals, including four Faith in Place staff members, four interns, twenty-six congregational participants (both clergy and lay), and two staff members of other environmental organizations that collaborated with Faith in Place. Interviews lasted approximately one hour and took place in participants' offices, congregations, or homes. Clare Butterfield, Faith in Place's executive director, sat down for two separate interviews and was always forthcoming as she answered my questions in informal settings. I have chosen to change names to respect the privacy of most Faith in Place participants and volunteers even though few of them requested anonymity, but I kept their pseudonyms consistent throughout and did not combine their stories to create composite figures. Clare Butterfield and Veronica Kyle were public figures whose identities would be impossible to conceal. Both gave me permission to use their real names, as did a few other public figures that I discuss in the text.[69]

In addition to conducting participant observation and interviews, I collected every newsletter, invitation, and e-mail that Faith in Place sent to its membership between 2006 and 2015, as well as programs and brochures distributed at events. Butterfield granted me full access to all of the documents on Faith in Place's computer network, which included internal correspondence, strategic plans, promotional materials, sermons, presentations, educational curricula, and worship resources that Faith in Place staff had written over the previous ten years. These documents gave me insight into Faith in Place's development over the years, revealing shifts in the organization's methods and messages.

From the beginning of my time among the staff, I felt at home in the laid-back office environment. Unlike the staff and most of the volunteers, I was not involved with a religious congregation. However, my own middle-class background, educational attainment, and liberal politics aligned with those of the women in the office. Most importantly, I shared their commitment to environmental values, parking my bicycle next to theirs outside the office, packing my vegetarian lunches in reusable containers, and engaging in conversations about pressing environmental issues. The staff interpreted my academic interest in religious environmentalism as developing from a personal commitment to sustainability, and through informal conversations they learned about my previous involvement in other environmental organizations. I was always clear that my goals for volunteering at Faith in Place had to do with my research, but in the office I easily blended in as a fellow environmentalist, a "major donor," and a volunteer. My gender, race, and class status were also held in common with most of the people in the office. College and seminary students along with other supporters of Faith in Place were always working in the office, so my presence was unremarkable. While my purposes for volunteering were different, my actions looked the same. At staff meetings I was not the only participant who was not technically part of the staff, and at board meetings I was not the only one who was not on the board. Staff members periodically made comments that revealed their ongoing awareness of my research agenda, saying things like "You can go write that up now. I know you're dying to!"[70] But in general I was such a regular presence in the office that I was able to observe Faith in Place's daily operations as an insider, witnessing the sometimes tense (but always cordial) negotiations involved with cultivating a usable environmentalism.

When I conducted fieldwork among partner congregations that endeavor became much more challenging. Outside the office, the line between observer and observed became more starkly drawn. There was no established role for me to fill, and that made it challenging to gain access to congregations for research. When I approached clergy, they often suggested that their congregation was not very "environmental." They might have organized a green team or utilized Faith in Place worship resources, but several clergy expressed concern that they were not doing enough environmental programming to serve as a model Faith in Place partner. Even as I assured them that I was interested in spending time with congregations that had varying levels of involvement with Faith in Place, clergy often suggested that their congregations could not offer me much to study. Over time I learned that attending events such as meetings, workshops, Bible studies, and worship services at congregations when Faith in Place staff were present was a much more fruitful approach, because at those times conversations were sure to focus on environmental issues. Through these events I met people who were willing to participate in formal interviews about their environmental attitudes, values, programs, and beliefs and who also invited me to attend periodic meetings and events at their congregations even when Faith in Place staff members were not present.

This approach offered a window for observing extensive environmental programming in action, but it also shaped the focus on my research in particular ways. Through my fieldwork I was able to observe many of the complex negotiations involved with putting religious environmentalism into practice, but I did not conduct research that would lead to understanding why some people choose *not* to become religious environmentalists. My access to congregations and individuals was shaped by relationships Faith in Place had built, so when people had brief encounters with Faith in Place but never returned, I was not able to find out why.

The strength of Faith in Place's partnerships also shaped my pool of research participants. When I was more than halfway through my full year of fieldwork at Faith in Place, I looked through my interview log and saw that my interview subjects were almost entirely Protestant. Over the previous months I had followed Faith in Place staff members to religious environmental events across the city, setting up interviews with people I met. Although Faith in Place emphasized that it was interfaith, my interview log suggested a racially diverse coalition of Protestants. Because I was researching an interfaith organization, I wanted to hear from non-Christian participants, so I asked Butterfield to suggest people whom I might contact. She was eager to help and recommended people whom she considered "good friends" of Faith in Place. But the women and men I contacted at her suggestion often declined my interview requests, saying they were not really associated with environmentalism or Faith in Place. While at the time this seemed like a limitation, it turned out to be important data for my research, contributing to my central point that religious environmental ideology in general, and Faith in Place's work in particular, were strongly shaped by attitudes and assumptions of liberal Protestants. My challenges in connecting with participants who were not Protestant were indicative of Faith in Place's challenges in connecting with them as well, and I learned that this was a limitation that Butterfield did not perceive when I discovered that her ideas of who had close connections with Faith in Place were not always based on mutual feelings of camaraderie.

This work, then, offers a portrait of religious environmentalism as it was actually lived in Chicago through the work of Faith in Place. While religious environmental leaders might point out the universal appeal of the work, in this book I examine the negotiations involved with those groups and individuals as they encountered it.

Veronica Kyle joined Faith in Place's staff during the third summer that I conducted participant observation, an addition that fundamentally shifted the contours of Faith in Place's work and also my research. Suddenly Faith in Place was forging partnerships with African American congregations hitherto absent from their coalition, and participants from these congregations were willing to participate in my research. Because of Kyle's work I traveled to parts of Chicago I had never seen in my previous four years of living in the city, embarking on long public transit rides where I turned into a minority as the only white person in what seemed like miles. If I stuck out as a researcher among some of the white congregations where I conducted fieldwork, I became even more plainly visible at African American churches, where people that I had not met immediately wondered why I was there. Although some participants initially seemed wary of my involvement in their communities, they seemed impressed that I continued to take public transit and show up at their events week after week. Several women came to welcome me and took caring, protective roles. They offered their hospitality, friendship, and rides to the train station and seemed enthusiastic about sharing their experiences and insights. I even received a few proselytizing invitations to attend church.

My relationship with Kyle, on the other hand, was always complex. Kyle's attitude toward my research seemed to vacillate between encouraging and suspicious, as she sometimes went out of her way to invite me to her meetings and events but other times did not seem so welcoming of my presence. Kyle was very aware of the close connections between her work and the advancement of my own career, and shortly after she joined the staff she frankly described her concerns about white scholars who build their careers by studying "the ghetto." Perhaps as a small way of countering that dynamic Kyle would sometimes treat me as her assistant when others were present, asking me to fetch coffee or supplies for her guests in the office. She was the least forthcoming of Faith in Place's leaders, willing to sit only for one short interview. Understanding her work involved a constant process of reading between the lines.

Ethnographers since the 1960s have reflected on the partiality of ethnographic truth, pointing out that all knowledge is situated.[71] Nowhere was this more apparent for me than in my research among African

Americans. I had important differences with my white interlocutors, but these were not as visible and perhaps were easier to ignore. The white Protestants I encountered seemed to assume that I shared their religious worldviews even if I did not share their particular religious affiliation, and in one case a woman interpreted my research at Faith in Place as tantamount to religious involvement. The African American churchgoers I met made a much greater effort to give me details and explanations about their history and culture, with more awareness that I might not share their experiences or assumptions. I often felt as if Kyle considered me to be a privileged, naive, white girl, but whatever accommodations she made for me she also made for other members of Faith in Place's overwhelmingly white cadre of staff and volunteers. I have done my best to understand the experiences of my interlocutors, but this is the provisional account of a white middle-class scholar, and I hope other scholars will fill out the picture from their perspectives.

A final note on provisionality as it relates to my time "in the field." As I was writing this work in 2013 I received an e-mail announcement that executive director Clare Butterfield was leaving Faith in Place for a new job, and in many ways that has eased my anxieties about the impact of my analysis on the work of Faith in Place. Butterfield's departure provides a logical place to consider this the end of a chapter in the life of Faith in Place and in some ways resolves the fact that this ethnographic work in a sense is a work of history. Now each of the four women who ran Faith in Place when I began fieldwork has gone on to new places, and Faith in Place is taking new forms that are profoundly shaped by the new leadership. This book documents key moments in the first ten years of an organization that does not really exist in the same way as it did during my fieldwork. These stories offer an intimate portrait of religious environmental involvement as it was worked out among some of the earliest "converts" in Chicago. The movement continues to grow and develop, and this book provides insight into the complex negotiations and challenges facing the "greening" of religion in the contemporary United States.

WHAT LIES AHEAD

In the following pages I examine ways that assumptions about race, ethnicity, and class have shaped religious environmentalism through an analysis of daily operations at Faith in Place. In chapter 1 I describe Faith in Place's origins and development within the context of the American environmental movement, highlighting how measures to diversify helped the organization survive and ultimately flourish. Although Faith in Place originated with priorities, activities, and participants that resembled those of numerous other environmental groups, attracting mainly affluent white supporters, Faith in Place's first ten years involved a series of strategic decisions in which leaders differentiated their work from mainstream environmentalism. In chapter 2 I discuss the organization's daily activities in the context of a movement the organization's leaders did embrace, the green cities movement. Faith in Place contributed to reimagining urban spaces in a more positive light but could not entirely overcome environmentalism's legacy of celebrating wild nature as an ideal site for leading the good life and experiencing the divine.

While the first two chapters focus primarily on the leaders of Faith in Place, chapters 3 and 4 consider the perspectives of individuals and groups who became involved with the organization's religious environmental work. Based on fieldwork and ethnographic interviews among Faith in Place interns, Bible study participants, and congregational partners, I uncover ways that considerations of racial and ethnic identity factor into decisions to "go green."

Building on those stories of different communities' pathways to religious environmental involvement, chapter 5 discusses the role of race and ethnicity in the organization's commitment to religious diversity. Faith in Place's many interfaith partnerships were central to its public persona, but in practice Faith in Place was overwhelmingly populated by Protestants. On the other hand the racial diversity of Faith in Place's coalition was noteworthy, but this was a distinction Faith in Place's leaders seemed hesitant to discuss directly. In chapter 5 I consider ways that these commitments played out in the daily life of the operation, contributing to the allure and spread of religious environmentalism. Chapter 6 delves into the specifics of Faith in Place's religious message, intended to be universal, and identifies ways that racial assumptions have played a limiting role. Although intending to represent every faith, Faith in Place enforced a particular theological outlook, based on the model of liberal white Protestantism, within its purportedly universal interfaith message.

Taking into consideration the details of Faith in Place's changing coalition and religious message, chapter 7 steps back to examine the ways those details factored into the organization's growth, development, and shifting identity in its first fifteen years. Having initially distanced itself from negative associations with mainstream environmentalism, Faith in Place gradually realigned itself with mainstream environmental agendas as the organization built partnerships in the diverse communities it had always aspired to serve. The conclusion highlights tensions and inconsistencies that emerged throughout my research, pointing to complex factors that have accompanied the "greening" of American religious worlds.

People, Not Polar Bears

Faith in Place's First Ten Years

"It's about people, not polar bears," Faith in Place spokespeople pronounced as part of their standard talk on developing environmental ministries. "By all means, love nature, take your kids outside, and make interaction with the natural world part of your spiritual life. But when it comes to environmental issues in church, talk about people and where people live."[1] While popular associations with environmentalism might evoke images of backpackers hiking the Sierra Nevada, Greenpeace activists defending whales, or Al Gore warning about melting polar bear habitats, Faith in Place leaders wanted to convey that their work was about something else: the human faces of environmental disasters and the growing challenges that regular people confront, day to day, as a result of environmental degradation.

Although Faith in Place leaders shared other environmental organizations' concerns about natural places, endangered species, and climate change trends, Faith in Place looked fundamentally different in its coalition, activities, and priorities. Each year when several Chicago environmental organizations traveled to the state capitol for Environmental Lobby Day, Faith in Place's was the only coalition that included a Zoroastrian and several African Americans. Whereas other nonprofit organizations' donor events involved gourmet food and bountiful wine, Faith in Place raised funds over a spread of fried chicken and homemade pie. And while the Sierra Club's mission statement talked about protecting wild places, using resources responsibly, and restoring the quality of the natural environment, Faith in Place's mission statement focused on love, care, and faith.[2]

Like many other participants and observers of Faith in Place, I was initially absorbed by the organization's distinctive approach. Shortly after I began my fieldwork, Faith in Place received a *Chicago Magazine* "green award." The accompanying magazine article included a full-page color photograph of Faith in Place's executive director and the coordinator for Muslim outreach, who was wearing a black hijab that revealed only her hands and face. The story began by contrasting Faith in Place's "small and fair" Unitarian Universalist director with its "tall and dark" Muslim outreach coordinator before describing how the women overcame their seeming differences.[3] The article and photograph, like much of Faith in Place's own promotional material highlighting its ability to unite diverse communities through environmental involvement, signaled Faith in Place's distinctive approach and priorities. As my time at Faith in Place progressed I never saw reason to doubt the sincerity of their message, yet I did come to understand how these dichotomies played into constructions of fantasy and desire among Faith in Place participants and supporters.

In this chapter I describe Faith in Place's origins and development within the context of the American environmental movement and with attention to strategic decisions its leaders made to help their organization survive and ultimately flourish. Although Faith in Place originated with priorities, activities, and participants that were quite similar to those of numerous other environmental groups, its first ten years involved a series of strategic decisions in which leaders developed measures to differentiate their work from mainstream environmentalism. The environmental movement historically has been associated with the interests of white elites, and despite the best efforts of white environmental leaders most mainstream organizations have had difficulty attracting minority audiences.[4] Faith in Place became much more successful in that endeavor in part because it rejected its own place within the history of American environmentalism. Instead it positioned itself as an authoritative leader within a new movement, *religious* environmentalism, which offered its own set of priorities and concerns. Placing itself outside the community of mainstream environmentalists and inside the broad community of "people of faith," Faith in Place was able to attract minority communities who previously had discounted the environmental movement.

IN THE BEGINNING . . .

"In 1999 a light bulb (compact fluorescent, of course) goes off in Steve Perkins' head and Faith in Place is launched to create a welcoming land-scape for dialogue and action on environmental sustainability."[5] So goes the origin story of Faith in Place as recorded in the organization's ten-year report. As this story suggests, Faith in Place began with the vision of Steve Perkins, vice president of a Chicago environmental non-profit, the Center for Neighborhood Technology (CNT). Having worked at CNT for nearly two decades, Perkins was struck by the overwhelm-ing absence of religious communities from environmental efforts in Chi-cago, and he sought to redress that problem at CNT. He organized an advisory group of theologians, religious leaders, and activists to help develop the idea. In 1998 the group published a statement, "One Crea-tion, One People, One Place," intended to initiate conversations about the environment among religious communities across the region.[6] After declaring the unity of the Chicago religious community despite differ-ences in languages and styles of prayer (the "one people" who shared the "one place"), the statement called on congregations to "act as responsible citizens of Creation." To implement that vision, the group advised CNT to develop an "Interreligious Sustainability Project" (ISP) where participants could reflect and take action on the religious man-date to protect creation. Perkins established an "interreligious sustain-ability circle" that drew members from congregations in the affluent suburb of Evanston in 1999, and CNT obtained foundational support to hire Rev. Clare Butterfield, a Unitarian Universalist minister who had interned for CNT as a seminary student, to lead the project full time. Under Butterfield's leadership the ISP established sustainability circles in six other regions across Chicagoland over the next year.[7]

With varying levels of involvement the groups engaged in interfaith reflection on environmental teachings and initiated local environmental projects. Although CNT staff chaired the circles' monthly meetings, each group had significant leeway for determining its structure, activities, and programming. Activities ranged from developing sustainable food initia-tives and an urban agricultural program for neighborhood youth, to engaging in local political organizing for improved public transit and helping the city invest in energy-efficient streetlights. ISP leaders intended to cultivate religious diversity by creating interfaith circles, but in prac-tice the groups were mostly Protestant with a mix of liberal Jews and

Catholics. A 2003 evaluation report notes the membership of a single Sikh and a single Zoroastrian in one of the suburban circles. Like most other environmental organizations the circles drew participants who were almost entirely white, affluent, and highly educated.[8]

The ISP began to change its focus in 2002. First, Butterfield changed the organization's name to Faith in Place because she thought the previous name "was just nasty from a marketing perspective" and did not adequately convey the organization's focus.[9] Second, she initiated two regional projects independent from the sustainability circles as a way to cultivate increased participation and support. This shift marked the beginnings of Faith in Place's transition away from CNT. The first regional project, Twenty Percent for Creation, promoted alternative energy by encouraging congregations to purchase wind power and contribute to building the necessary infrastructure in the region. The second, Taqwa Eco-Halal, provided a source of sustainable meat slaughtered according to Muslim dietary requirements. Shireen Pishdadi joined the staff to oversee that project and recruit Muslim communities to Faith in Place.

With its expanding staff and programming, Faith in Place was experiencing growing pains as it struggled to compete for funding with other CNT projects. In 2003 the project's leadership determined it would be best for Faith in Place to separate from CNT, and the following year Faith in Place incorporated as an independent nonprofit. With the addition of a development director, a youth program coordinator, and its own office suite inside a church on Chicago's northwest side, Faith in Place began to move away from its work with the sustainability circles to focus more on regional projects and direct interaction with congregations.

RACE, CLASS, AND AMERICAN ENVIRONMENTALISM

As Faith in Place expanded its outreach efforts, its leaders began developing measures to address a challenge confronting the environmental movement: attracting minority participants. Scholars and activists alike have long noted the absence of people of color in the environmental movement and have offered several explanations to account for minority communities' seeming lack of environmental concern.[10] A dominant explanation in the 1970s and 1980s suggested that poor minority populations were too overwhelmed with the pressing concerns of daily life to consider less urgent problems such as the long-term health of the environment.[11] While this theory remains influential in popular understandings of the gap between the environmental concerns of whites and minorities, more recent scholarly explanations have shifted to emphasizing the social locations of those empowered to define what constitutes an environmental problem. Revisionist accounts of environmental history contend that environmental concern transcends lines of race and class once we expand the definition of environmentalism. Both Robert Gottlieb and Carolyn Merchant offer comprehensive environmental histories along that model, integrating urban, public health, and industrial themes as well as examples of minority populations' interactions with the environment through subsistence farming and slavery. Both point out that poor and working-class urban populations engaged in environmental activism throughout the twentieth century but that their efforts have not historically been considered "environmental."[12] Scholars have also noted that the Congressional Black Caucus has a strong environmental voting record and that minority groups were central to the passage of clean air and water legislation.[13] But mainstream environmental organizations fail to attract minority involvement, these studies suggest, because of their wilderness-focused agendas and overwhelmingly white leadership, membership, and image.

Despite a growing body of literature suggesting an expansive understanding of environmental history that includes working-class, industrial struggles, American environmentalism in the popular imagination continues to be associated with a legacy of white, middle-class efforts to protect nature for white middle-class enjoyment.[14] The modern environmental movement developed from Progressive Era conservation efforts of powerful figures such as President Theodore Roosevelt, forester Gifford Pinchot, and Sierra Club founder John Muir. As a precursor to modern environmentalism, conservationism entailed efforts to use natural resources wisely. The Sierra Club, the prototypical conservationist group, was founded in 1892 under the leadership of educated, affluent men.[15] Understanding themselves as "moral defenders of the great outdoors," Progressive Era conservationists promoted outdoor experiences such as hiking and camping that were oriented to the upper class. Ancillary to its primary focus on experiencing the outdoors, the Sierra Club also supported efforts to protect wild spaces from the encroachment of civilization through the establishment of national parks. Until the 1950s, conservationism focused almost exclusively on protecting wild areas.

Environmental historian Hal Rothman marks the 1950s battle over Echo Park Dam as a decisive turning point in which conservationism was transformed into the modern environmental movement.[16] Seeking to address growing water needs in the aftermath of World War II, the Bureau of Reclamation proposed the Colorado River Storage Project (CRSP), a chain of dams that would allocate water to support growth in several western states. One particular dam, to be sited at Echo Park in a remote corner of Utah and Colorado, caused widespread controversy because it would submerge Dinosaur National Monument. Through intense lobbying efforts and publicity campaigns—which included direct-mail pamphlets, news features, and even a motion picture—the Sierra Club and the Wilderness Society convinced Congress to eliminate the Echo Park Dam from the CRSP. In the process, they developed methods for a new, politically aggressive form of environmentalism and expanded their constituencies beyond their narrow, elite base. The new constituency's concerns, however, remained narrowly focused on wilderness issues and failed to address pollution, sprawl, or other emerging issues that increasingly affected urban communities.

The growing constituency coalesced after the publication of Rachel Carson's *Silent Spring* in 1962. Ringing alarm bells about the effects of pesticides on human and wildlife populations, *Silent Spring* raised public awareness about the dangers of chemical pollution and contamination and led to major growth for the membership rolls of reform-focused environmental organizations such as the Sierra Club, the National Audubon Society, and the Wilderness Society.[17] Expanded resources helped national organizations persuade government officials to protect the environment and resulted in numerous federal regulations and protections for water quality, scenic rivers, and clean air.[18] Members of the Nixon administration organized the first Earth Day in 1970 to help solidify growing environmental awareness among Americans, and extensive media coverage of that event helped define an emerging environmental movement focused on issues of population growth, pollution, wilderness loss, and the use of pesticides.

Throughout the 1970s and 1980s three distinct branches of environmentalism emerged. First were the centrist national organizations such as the Natural Resources Defense Council, the National Wildlife Federation, the National Audubon Society, and the Sierra Club, who largely defined environmentalism in this time period. These organizations worked on large-scale efforts to bring about reform on national and international issues through legislative and judicial actions. Second, a brand of radical environmental groups such as Greenpeace and Earth First! developed from the tradition of American radicalism and advanced

Centrist env.
Radical env.
Env. Justice

an alternative vision of environmental activism defined by protest and bearing witness. Through direct action campaigns such as sailing ships in nuclear testing zones, Greenpeace attracted former members of the 1960s counterculture who disliked the moderate tactics of mainstream environmental groups. Even more radical was Earth First!, which stood for the absolute defense of nature above all else.[19] Drawing inspiration from Edward Abbey's 1976 novel, *The Monkeywrench Gang,* Earth First! activists interrupted construction and development projects that would destroy wilderness, using such tactics as damaging construction vehicles and occupying ancient trees.

A third branch of activism comprising grassroots efforts to protest toxics and pollution in local neighborhoods also developed in the seventies and eighties. In 1978 Lois Gibbs organized a grassroots network of housewives who successfully held the state of New York accountable for the toxic dumping in their Love Canal neighborhood. Using the expertise she gained with Love Canal, Gibbs established the Citizen's Clearinghouse for Hazardous Wastes to help other communities confront polluting industry forces and government agencies. The antitoxics agenda became explicitly racialized with the Warren County, North Carolina, protests in 1982, when activists challenged the siting of a chemical waste landfill in their poor, predominately black county. Driven by that and other antitoxics protests in minority communities, Reverend Benjamin E. Chavis Jr., a former civil rights leader and the executive director of the United Church of Christ's (UCC) Commission for Racial Justice, sponsored a five-year national study to understand the relationship between race and toxic dumping sites. Issued in 1987, the UCC report identified widespread evidence for environmental racism, a term Chavis coined, determining that hazardous waste sites were overwhelmingly and systematically located in minority communities.[20] The UCC report proved influential in generating the environmental justice movement to protest the disproportionate and deliberate placing of environmental hazards in minority communities.

While grassroots and mainstream environmental groups shared concerns about toxics and pollution, differences in tactics, priorities, and images led each party to resist identifying with the other. Mainstream groups tended to focus on large-scale and policy tactics and were less interested in local issues, just as grassroots organizers tended to resist the label "environmentalist" because they did not want to be associated with mainstream efforts. Environmental justice advocates further resisted partnerships with mainstream groups because justice advocates expressly promoted environmental protections on behalf of people whereas they believed mainstream environmental groups prioritized earth-centric concerns.

Despite a lack of cross-fertilization between these groups in the 1980s, the environmental justice movement raised issues about race and class that mainstream groups could not ignore. On the basis of a survey of environmental groups in the United States since the 1990s, Eileen McGurty claims that the environmental justice movement has "deeply impacted environmentalism in all arenas, including traditional environmental organizations, emerging environmental justice groups, and governmental agencies responsible for implementing environmental legislation."[21] McGurty notes that traditional environmental organizations such as the Sierra Club and the Natural Resources Defense Council administer extensive environmental justice programming and that government agencies such as the Office of Environmental Justice at the Environmental Protection Agency are attuned to the interests of minorities. Yet even into the twenty-first century environmentalism in the popular imagination has continued to be associated with protecting wilderness and advancing the interests of white elites. Even as minority communities have expressed concern for environmental causes, mainstream environmental organizations have failed to attract minorities to their membership rolls.[22]

ENVIRONMENTALISM FOR "PEOPLE OF FAITH"

In its early years Faith in Place attracted participants who were representative of the mainstream environmental movement. Highly educated, affluent, and white, most were longtime environmentalists who could just as easily be involved (and indeed were involved) with other environmental groups. Although they brought their environmental concerns to their religious communities, their involvement tended not to be religiously motivated, and they had deeply entrenched ideas about the environmental crisis and how to solve it.[23] As Faith in Place developed and as its leaders found their footing as an independent organization, however, they began instituting an organizational shift designed to reach a broader audience that would be more receptive to Faith in Place's human-centered environmental approach. In the process, they established clear boundaries between Faith in Place and other environmental groups, defining Faith in Place as a new environmental community that could overcome many of the issues that plagued the old one.

The major change concerned the types of participants Faith in Place wanted to recruit. By creating sustainability circles that brought together environmental leaders from numerous congregations, Butterfield surmised, Faith in Place actually had created a support group for "environmental refugees." Those who joined sustainability circles, she recalled during a conversation years later, were longtime environmentalists who happened to belong to religious congregations and had been trying to awaken fellow congregants to environmental issues for years. These men and women were deeply frustrated by their congregations' lack of environmental concern, and their congregations often were frustrated by them. With polarizing personalities, they tried to convince their congregations to stop using Styrofoam coffee cups, replace old, inefficient boilers, or spend less time in their cars, but their fellow congregants just rolled their eyes.[24]

Concerned that the sustainability circles were functioning primarily as support groups for discouraged environmentalists, Butterfield wanted to find new participants who could advance Faith in Place's work more effectively. Rather than trying to organize environmental initiatives through "people whom the congregation has learned not to hear," Butterfield planned to stage what she called "a gentle coup," removing "environmental refugees" from their positions as the spokespeople for environmental causes.[25] To replace them Faith in Place sought a new population: those who were "people of faith first, environmentalists second." Instead of talking only to the small handful of any congregation's participants who chose to show up at environmental events, Faith in Place wanted to reach entire congregations at the heart of their worship. Thus it developed a set of practices designed to "infiltrate" congregations—encouraging sermons on environmental themes, providing environmental tips in bulletin inserts, and appointing environmental representatives to congregational committees—in order to cultivate a broader culture of earth stewardship, especially among people who did not consider themselves environmentalists. By taking steps to silence those who had always spoken out on behalf of the environment, Butterfield was also silencing the legacy of mainstream environmentalism that those participants represented and creating an opportunity to change the conversation. With a fresh environmental message centering on faith and social justice, Faith in Place started to build a coalition of environmental activists from populations that other environmental groups had failed to reach.

Combining Nature and Social Justice

Whereas CNT's "One Creation" report established Faith in Place's original mission in the context of standard environmental tropes, the new vision more clearly developed from Butterfield's background and aspirations, which combined environmental concern with a priority on social justice issues. Born in a central Illinois farming community in 1960, the daughter of a computer science professor who one year planted nine thousand trees on his property, Butterfield was attuned to the natural environment from early childhood. She recalled hearing her parents engage in heated debates about the potential ecological impacts of a proposed dam on a local river, and she remembered celebrating the first Earth Day in elementary school. As Butterfield recalled during an interview, "That sense that you take care of the land you live on was really ingrained in me from a very early age."[26]

After completing college and law school at the University of Illinois, Butterfield moved to Washington, D.C., where she began working as an attorney for the Internal Revenue Service. But something changed for her during the Reagan administration and led her down an entirely different path. As she described her call to ministry, Butterfield began volunteering at a local soup kitchen some mornings before work and was struck by the growing presence of people who had jobs and places to live but ate at the soup kitchen because they could not afford enough food. That led her to rethink her life's calling over the next decade and eventually to return to the Midwest, where she attended Meadville Lombard Theological School, a Unitarian Universalist seminary. There, Butterfield studied environmental ethics and discovered ways to connect her interest in social justice to her lifelong concern for the environment. As a course field placement she secured an internship with CNT, and when the opportunity for a full-time job arose in 1999 Butterfield immediately seized it. At CNT, and then at Faith in Place, Butterfield sought to implement her combined vision of ecological ethics and social justice. With significant leeway in her new position as executive director of a nonprofit newly independent from CNT, Butterfield was able to align the organization more clearly under her own vision.

Social Justice and "Light-Green" Ethics

The language Faith in Place leaders used to describe their work shifted over time as they developed strategies to mobilize Chicago's religious population. In its early years, Faith in Place leaders routinely invoked nonhuman nature as they rallied support for environmental causes. In 2004 Butterfield included nonhuman animals when she introduced Faith in Place at a community-wide workshop, saying, "We all have teachings that lead us to want to live in loving relationship with our neighbors, including our neighbors the fish and the nematodes and the soil and the trees."[27] A 2006 brochure started with a paragraph about social justice, but it also included a statement of concern for other parts of nature: "The way we relate to the smallest species, to the tiniest stream and to the least powerful of our human brothers and sisters will define our relationship with our world and the One who placed us here. These are serious matters of faith."[28]

By 2008, however, the organization had begun advancing what Patrick Curry calls "light green" ecological ethics, valuing nature but emphasizing human concerns as the primary reasons for protecting the environment.[29] In their standard introductory talk on establishing environmental ministries, Faith in Place leaders included the point that religious environmentalism was "about people, not polar bears."[30] In a 2009 sermon Butterfield also downplayed concern for nonhuman animals. After describing ways that global warming would likely affect Arctic animals, Butterfield said, "But for me this isn't really about polar bears and narwhals. Frankly, where I live, down on the south side of Chicago, those are pretty hard things to argue for. At least until we stop shooting at children. But as a religious person connection is something I can and do argue for all the time. And that's what the carbon crisis is really about."[31] While recognizing that measures to mitigate climate change would benefit animals in faraway places, Butterfield focused the issue on children close to home.

This shift in language parallels the shift in Faith in Place's organizing strategy. The years when Butterfield was talking about tiny streams and nematodes were the years when she worked among long-term, committed environmentalists. Those audiences were receptive to mid- or dark-green environmental ethics that acknowledged nature's intrinsic worth apart from its value to humans. As Faith in Place worked to attract entire congregations rather than just a handful of "environmental refugees" from any single congregation, however, they began to advance a more moderate form of environmentalism. Whereas Butterfield might not have been able to convince entire congregations to shift their behaviors out of concern for nematodes or narwhals, social justice concerns for children on Chicago's south side or people who lost their homes to flooding were less controversial issues that could motivate broader action.

While Faith in Place's focus on social justice may have been effective for motivating new people to join the environmental movement, it was less compelling for more seasoned environmental activists. Daishi, a white convert Zen Buddhist priest whose *sangha* participated with Faith in Place, did not think the organization went nearly far enough in its religious environmental activism. Daishi had been a dedicated social activist for decades. Just before our interview in 2010, he had organized a demonstration in downtown Chicago to protest BP after the oil spill in the Gulf of Mexico. Daishi told me, "I know [Butterfield] has empha-sized conversion of religious institutions, and I think that's good. But it's not going to address the problem. It's just not."[32] Daishi told me he preferred the model of 350.org, an international team of organizers founded by environmental activist Bill McKibben. McKibben's group aimed to build a global grassroots movement that would drastically reduce the amount of carbon dioxide in the atmosphere.[33] As Daishi told me, "There needs to be changes in terms of society and industry. So I really do think that solving and taking care of the environment has to happen on the level of political action. . . . It's not going to happen through people having personal conversations."[34] While Daishi sup-ported Faith in Place's mission, he did not believe its efforts, grounded in moderate environmental ethics, would make a significant impact.

A group of seminary students who participated in a training session at Faith in Place similarly challenged Butterfield on her assertion that religious environmentalism should focus mainly on people. Having par-ticipated in Earth Year at the Lutheran School of Theology Chicago, several of the students had already reflected on the links between the environment and their faith.[35] They considered Faith in Place's message overly anthropocentric and suggested that social justice concerns must be supported by care for *all* of creation because they believed concern for people would not be enough to sustain environmental activism. Nevertheless, Butterfield maintained that when they spoke on behalf of Faith in Place she wanted them to emphasize people. She explained that historically the environmental movement had been white and middle class and that focusing on social justice "makes it more relevant."[36]

Margaret, a professional environmental organizer who had worked with Faith in Place, explained to me that she did not mind Faith in Place's moderate environmental position because it did not really mat-ter what motivated individuals to protect the environment. As long as people were taking measures to lighten their impact on the earth, she said, she did not care whether they were motivated by concern for people or concern for polar bears. "People on the south side of Chicago don't care about the polar bear. Well I don't want them to care about the polar bear!" she said. "But I want us to do something about climate change, because if we don't we're dead."[37] Nevertheless, Faith in Place leaders' choice of language shaped the types of participants the organization could attract. By prioritizing concern for people over endangered species in faraway places, they connected with an audience of new, "light-green" environmentalists. At the same time, long-term environmental activists did not find Faith in Place's messages adequately transformative.

BECOMING MAINSTREAM

Using methods and messages that inscribed clear boundaries between Faith in Place and secular environmental groups, Faith in Place successfully created a place for itself within the environmental community. Secular environmental groups such as the Sierra Club began to recognize Faith in Place as a partner that could effectively recruit religious communities, an untapped resource, to environmental causes. With a little help from Al Gore, Faith in Place found an authoritative place for itself in religious communities as well. In 2005 Faith in Place tied its local efforts to a broader movement when it joined Interfaith Power and Light (IPL), a national organization that mobilized religious communities to fight global warming. The next year, Faith in Place participated in an IPL campaign to host screenings and discussions of *An Inconvenient Truth* at congregations across the country. That campaign became a turning point for Faith in Place, as it recruited 144 Chicago-area congregations to offer free screenings and discussions of the film. Many of those congregations had never before hosted an environmental event. The screenings and facilitated discussions, attended by more than two thousand people from religious communities in Illinois, helped convince people that global warming was an issue of social justice, and thus a matter of faith, that their congregations must address. Dozens of churches and synagogues wanted to start new green teams and build an environmental movement within their congregations, and they knew that Faith in Place was the organization to help them. Prior to *An Inconvenient Truth,* Butterfield told me, she was never sure that her organization would survive.[38] But after the film screenings, enthusiasm and support for Faith in Place's mission swelled.

With a place in both Chicago's environmental community and its (progressive) religious communities, Faith in Place's influence expanded. In 2005, Faith in Place had 120 congregational partners, but that number grew to 450 by 2008.[39] With its growth in membership, other groups advancing environmental projects recognized Faith in Place as an important potential ally. By going to religious congregations, it had connected with a type of audience that largely had eluded the environmental community. And among those congregations, Faith in Place became a widely recognized authority on a matter that it had helped establish as central to every faith.

Religious Instrumentalism and Authenticity

In its strategy of mobilizing religious communities, Faith in Place inherited a long tradition of church-based progressive activism that had begun with Saul Alinsky (1909–72), a secular Jew from Chicago who originated what now is known as community organizing. In the late 1930s, Alinsky founded the Back of the Yards Neighborhood Council (BYNC) on the southwest side of Chicago. The organization worked along with the Congress of Industrial Organizations (CIO) to support union-organizing drives and also to address other problems in the impoverished, largely immigrant community. The collaboration of Catholic Bishop Bernard J. Sheil, who recruited local pastors to support the BYNC's union drives and neighborhood organizing, was crucial to the success of the community organization. Alinsky exported his model of church-based community organizing to other states in the ensuing decades, relying on existing social institutions such as churches, block clubs, and small businesses, to provide resources and a base of followers for initiating social and political action. Although he is known for organizing within churches, Alinsky had little interest in the culture, belief systems, or values of the churches where he worked. Instead of reinterpreting religious traditions to fit his projects, he saw churches simply as resources for community-organizing efforts.[40]

As a group that worked with religious communities to advance progressive causes, Faith in Place seemed to offer a modern-day example of Alinsky's organizing model. However, this was a history that Faith in Place leaders actively rejected, considering their efforts to be more "authentically" based on religion. Butterfield castigated "classic religious organizing" on the model of Alinsky as a kind of "naked instrumentalism," distinguishing Faith in Place as a collection of "religious

intermediaries who can have a more authentic presence in the congregation."[41] More than recruiting churchgoers to a grassroots cause, their
intention was to engage communities in "the work of personal transformation." Faith in Place routinely collaborated with other environmental groups, but its leaders were wary of aiding those who wanted only
to appropriate the religious community.

As it engaged religious communities in projects to protect the earth,
Faith in Place carefully framed its programming to reflect "the teachings
of faith." More than offering basic ecological arguments to people who
happened to belong to religious communities, it called on participants to
act as "people of faith," encouraging them to behave in particular ways
because their religions demanded it. Butterfield wanted Faith in Place to
offer something more than a set of tips for congregations to become
green, she wrote, because "I don't think most people go to church or
synagogue because they want to be 'green.' I think they go because they
want to be better human beings." Faith in Place, then, "[was] intended
to reach toward them there—in that desire to conform the way that they
practice their lives to the beliefs they hold most dear."[42]

The distinctions between Faith in Place's "authentic" religiosity and
the "merely instrumental" interests of some secular environmental groups
were central to Faith in Place's identity. The first suggestion of Faith in
Place's "ten tips," which formed the backbone of the basic introductory
talk that Faith in Place staff members presented to congregations, was to
"connect your green efforts to your faith."[43] Staff members elaborated
this point by saying, "We love the Sierra Club, but we're not the Sierra
Club. Changing bulbs is an act of worship. Make the translation—it's an
act of love and faith."[44] Moreover, Butterfield suggested that religious
environmentalism was different from (and more efficacious than) secular
environmentalism because religion offered hope. Butterfield explained
this difference in a book proposal: "In many of the secular environmental
groups I have encountered since beginning this work I have found a kind
of grim hopelessness—activity that is based in a desire to be right rather
than any real expectation that things will change. Hopelessness is an
unhealthy emotion. It does not draw healthy-minded people toward it.
But in the religious community we live in the hope of God's redemptive
initiative. Despair is theologically impermissible."[45] While any number of
progressive and environmental groups could approach religious communities as outsiders, Faith in Place represented itself as a fellow religious
voice that could speak from within religious communities. The category
of "authentic religion" created a boundary between "people of faith" and

those who merely wanted to appropriate them, placing Faith in Place squarely on the side of the faithful.

FAITH IN PLACE AT TEN YEARS

In October 2009 Faith in Place celebrated its ten-year anniversary with a festive benefit dinner and a move to office space in Chicago's downtown. With an annual operating budget of just over $500,000, the full-time staff included the executive director, a deputy director, a congregational outreach worker, a youth coordinator, and a member of the Lutheran Volunteer Corps (LVC) who worked on congregational outreach and administration. Faith in Place was also in the process of obtaining funding to support an additional staff member based in central Illinois to organize congregational outreach in farming communities and provide a regular presence at the state capitol. The Muslim-outreach position had been eliminated after being vacated by two different women, as Faith in Place began to shift its resources toward supporting African Americans. Faith in Place also periodically hired temporary employees to work on particular projects, and each semester had the labor of one or two seminary students completing field training at Faith in Place. A Seminarian Speakers Bureau of students trained to give Faith in Place's two introductory talks also helped with outreach efforts.

In terms of congregational partnerships Faith in Place had worked with over 550 congregations, and the coalition was growing increasingly diverse in terms of race and ethnicity. Major achievements included helping the Bridgeview Mosque Foundation become the first solar mosque in the United States and initiating a clergy conversation about green jobs that included representatives from twenty-five African American congregations. Although numerically the organization was still populated primarily by liberal white Protestants, a series of intentional hiring practices and programmatic decisions helped Faith in Place appear more and more diverse.

Faith in Place carved its own unique niche in the environmental community by identifying an absence—religious communities—and developing methods that would deliver them to the environmental movement. During an interview, Megan, an organizer for Chicago's chapter of the Sierra Club, explained ways that Faith in Place offered something unique. She told me that Faith in Place's ability to engage religious communities brought an entirely new population to local efforts to address environmental problems. The Sierra Club was adept at recruiting young, progressive men and women, Megan suggested, but "There are communities that Faith in Place can talk to that I just feel uncomfortable with, or I'm just not as well equipped to make the right arguments. . . . So I feel like we all contribute in the best ways we can towards the ultimate goal, which is really solving the climate crisis."[46] Although many of Faith in Place's participants also belonged to other environmental groups, the religious environmental group achieved its success by developing methods that differentiated its work from other environmental groups and attracted populations who would not consider participating in environmentalism through other organizations. The Sierra Club might have offered a long history of experience influencing environmental legislation, but Faith in Place offered something a secular group could not: an "authentic" religious voice that promised to speak on behalf of all religious communities.

2

Religious Environmentalism
in the City

When I traveled to Faith in Place's downtown office weekday mornings
to conduct research in 2009 and 2010, I rode the #65 bus east to the
organization's headquarters in the Chicago Loop. From my bus stop I
would head along the freshly swept sidewalks toward 70 E. Lake, a
fifteen-story building a few blocks south of the upscale shops of the
Magnificent Mile, two blocks north of the pristine Millennium Park,
and three blocks east of Daley Plaza and the federal courthouse. Walking past upscale hotels and restaurants catering to the city's financial
elite, I passed through dense crowds of tourists, well-dressed profes-
sionals, vendors distributing placards that promised "LOW LOW
PRICES!" on silver and gold, and college students holding clipboards
and asking, "Do you have a minute for the environment?" Ducking
between slow groups of tourists gazing upward at the tall buildings, in
the very place where the modern skyscraper was conceived, I would
maneuver through the chaotic sidewalks at a pace slightly faster than
the buses that inched along the traffic-ridden block.

When I arrived at 70 E. Lake, I waved hello to the doorman before
heading upstairs to Faith in Place's ninth-floor offices, recently renovated
with reclaimed hardwood floors, an energy-efficient dishwasher, and eco-
friendly paint. The receptionist, a volunteer from the Lutheran Volunteer
Corps, would greet me from her desk in the middle of the bright reception
area. Adjacent to the entryway were the offices of three full-time staff, the
spacious corner office for the executive director, and a fifth office that

housed a rotating cast of seminary interns and volunteers. Around the corner a large open area housed a kitchen, a conference table, and a small library. Office windows overlooked a dark, narrow alley, and adjacent buildings were so close that they seemed almost possible to touch.

This office was the third that Faith in Place had occupied during my five years of fieldwork, and the first that the organization had inhabited in Chicago's downtown. But whether it was headquartered in the gentrifying Latino neighborhood of Logan Square, in the predominately African American area of Garfield Park, or amid the power structures of the downtown Loop, Faith in Place's office location always contributed to its distinctively urban character. Its urban identity also became evident in its priorities, projects, and alliances.

In the previous chapter I discussed Faith in Place's history in the context of American environmentalism, highlighting the ways it distanced itself from constructions of mainstream environmentalism by prioritizing social justice and concerns about humans. Here I discuss its daily activities in the context of a contemporary form of environmentalism the organization did embrace: the green cities movement. Through its work in Chicago and the surrounding areas, Faith in Place helped shape distinctively urban religious worlds. It reconceived the city as a salvific landscape with redeeming qualities for the environment and for the soul, but it could not entirely overcome the legacy of romantic urges toward wilderness. Over the years its leaders invoked a particular vision of the city and the need for green behaviors within it, and their work aimed to realize that vision, with all its tensions and inconsistencies.

THE GREEN CITIES MOVEMENT

The American environmental movement historically focused on protecting natural places far removed from urban centers.[1] But Faith in Place participated in the more recent green cities movement, which focused on ways to reduce the ecological impact of city life.[2] At first glance, cities seem to be ecological nightmares. Residents consume vast amounts of resources and produce masses of waste compared to less densely populated areas of comparable sizes. However, green cities advocates point out that city residents, per capita, actually consume less energy and cause less pollution than their rural and suburban counterparts. Urban homes tend to be smaller and require fewer resources to heat and cool. Dense urban conditions encourage greener forms of transportation such as walking and public transit. The concentration of homes and businesses also makes it cheaper for cities to minimize environmental hazards and enforce environmental legislation.³ While cities may be unappealing to the inheritors of John Muir's legacy, green city advocates want environmentalists to know that cities offer an ideal place to "live lightly on the earth."

Besides celebrating ways that cities make it possible to live more sustainably, green city advocates have worked to make cities even more eco-friendly and more livable.⁴ Many efforts to "green" Chicago were the result of former mayor Richard M. Daley's initiative to make Chicago one of the world's greenest cities. Through this initiative, the city planted over four hundred thousand trees, built rooftop gardens (including one on top of City Hall), constructed green buildings, provided tax subsidies for solar panels, designated hundreds of miles of bike lanes, and created the Chicago Conservation Corps to train and support environmental leaders.⁵ Chicago's Center for Neighborhood Technology (CNT), the organization that originally housed Faith in Place, was a national leader in supporting the development of sustainable urban communities.⁶

Originating as a project of CNT, Faith in Place offered a distinctively urban form of environmentalism. Many of the organization's earth stewardship guidelines pointed to ways of being a better green citizen within the city. Faith in Place focused on problems specific to urban life and offered solutions that were unavailable to rural or suburban communities. Its leaders encouraged participants to use public transit and walk or bike to reduce reliance on cars. They promoted shopping at farmers' markets or joining community-supported agriculture networks (CSAs),⁷ and they developed projects that created healthy food sources in areas where fresh produce was scarce. Through the youth program they educated children about urban nature, and through weatherization projects they provided job opportunities and training in urban areas where joblessness was prevalent. Faith in Place also helped congregations install eco-friendly permeable surface parking lots and held an architectural competition to generate creative ideas for the efficient use of urban building space. Its projects, ethos, and way of being were driven by the resources and needs of a particular construction of the city and its inhabitants.

To attract faith communities to its urban environmental work, Faith in Place's primary service for congregations was to act as a resource, offering concrete guidelines such as recommendations for reducing energy consumption, referrals for green contractors, resources to support environmental policy advocacy, and worship materials to advance faith-based understandings of environmental activism. Butterfield and other Faith in Place leaders offered seminars and guest sermons at partner churches, and they worked directly with congregations to suggest appropriate environmental steps based on their resources, interests, and needs. For some, the process began with switching to energy-efficient lightbulbs. For others, solar panels or geothermal heating systems were viable options. Faith in Place also helped congregations develop sustainable food initiatives: establishing churches as CSA drop sites, switching to fair trade coffee, encouraging shopping at farmers' markets, and growing food in church gardens. Once congregations had developed a "culture of environmental awareness," Faith in Place encouraged them to become active in the arena of environmental policy.

In addition to those general offerings, Faith in Place leaders developed programs to attract specific urban communities to their religious environmental work. The organization's first major program, Taqwa Eco-Foods, was developed in 2001 specifically to recruit Muslims. A cooperative providing humanely raised organic beef, lamb, and chicken, slaughtered according to *zabbeha* guidelines, Taqwa for a time provided Chicago's only source of sustainable meat that fulfilled Muslim dietary requirements. A Taqwa brochure clearly connected the project's mission to Islamic values, suggesting its meat could help Muslims "put the act of worship back into the entire process of food production so as to ensure a lawful and wholesome meat product that will secure the blessings of God Most High in the lives and communities of people."[8] While other environmental organizations might promote sustainable food consumption based on environmental ethics or animal rights, Faith in Place discussed sustainable agricultural practices as acts of worship.

At the program's height approximately fifty families belonged to the cooperative, but it was always a failing business, supplemented by Faith in Place, and the board voted to close the operation in 2009.[9] However, because Faith in Place's goal for Taqwa was to serve as a recruiting device, not to make money, its leaders considered Taqwa a success. Butterfield told me in 2011 that Taqwa was "the only reason that we have relationships in the Muslim community at this point, because of all the doors that opened."[10] By starting with an issue that Muslims cared about—healthy, organic food that fulfilled Islamic dietary requirements—Faith in Place was able to educate mosque participants about other environmental issues, connecting those concerns to fundamental tenets of Islam and encouraging Muslims to integrate other environmental steps into their daily lives.

Rel. Env. through food

In the area of sustainable food Faith in Place ran two additional programs. The first, The Good Loaf, was designed specifically for Protestants. Originally conceived as a full bakery that would provide a source of income for Faith in Place, The Good Loaf developed into a small-scale operation, sustained through the volunteer efforts of a baker, offering locally sourced communion bread for use in Protestant churches.[11] This project offered a simple way to remind churchgoers about the work of Faith in Place. Churches that used the bread were invited to include this bulletin insert in that day's program: "All breads from The Good Loaf are made with ingredients grown without pesticides by farmers nearby. That means the breads aren't only healthier for us, they are healthier for the people who grew the grain and for our environment. As Christians called to love one another and to care for God's creation, buying from local sustainable farmers can be a great expression of faith, love and justice." By reminding Christians about the religious implications of sustainable food practices, The Good Loaf offered a symbolic way to bring earth stewardship into the central act of Christian worship.

Faith in Place promoted its third sustainable food program, winter farmers' markets, as a project that supported values related to religion, ecology, and justice. The markets, according to Faith in Place's promotional material, were designed to "link issues of food and faith, connect farmers to consumers, and help farming families in times of crisis."[12] Each fall, Faith in Place recruited approximately fifteen congregations to host a rotating series of farmers' markets between November and April. Markets drew shoppers from the host communities, in addition to a loyal following of Faith in Place supporters who traversed the city and suburbs to shop at the markets. Congregations gained no financial benefit by hosting, but they could host markets to advance a justice goal of supporting local farmers by providing them a place to sell their food in the off-season. Further contributing to the justice element and thus enhancing the project's religious mission, farmers did not pay to participate in the market. Instead they donated a small portion of their earnings (over a threshold amount) to an emergency fund for farmers in need.

In addition to its food projects, Faith in Place offered educational programming to promote urban sustainability. For the general population it hosted two annual community-wide workshops on Sunday afternoons at different partner congregations. Generally attended by fifty to one hundred people from numerous congregations, the workshops included keynote speakers and breakout sessions on various environmental topics. Every winter, the "Faithful Citizenship" workshop provided information

about the environmental policy agenda for the upcoming Illinois state legislative session and prepared individuals to participate in Environmental
Lobby Day later that spring. Each fall, "Best Practices" workshops educated participants on issues such as alternative energy, fair trade, sustainable use of water, local food, and building of environmental ministries.
Workshops often featured presentations from the staff of other environmental organizations, such as the Sierra Club, the Illinois Environmental
Council, and Chicago's Department of Environment, and green businesses
such as CSA programs and solar installation companies. They also featured presentations from participants who had instituted stewardship
projects at their own congregations.

Besides the workshops, Butterfield ran Clergy Café, a lunchtime discussion group for clergy leaders and seminarians to discuss earth-
focused books or particular environmental topics. The group also took
periodic field trips to organic farms and sites of mountaintop coal
removal. Approximately fifty clergy were involved with the group, with
ten to twenty attending any given meeting. Butterfield created the group
to provide clergy with the opportunity to discuss openly ideas with
which they grappled, outside the scrutiny of their parishioners. She also
ran the group to keep earth stewardship on the minds of its participants, fostering concern for the planet among local congregations.[13]

Faith in Place became increasingly involved in policy work as the
organization developed. Butterfield contended that while individual
environmental steps such as recycling or reducing energy consumption
were important, Faith in Place and its partners could make the biggest
impact in the area of policy. However, just as Faith in Place became
active in the policy arena only after focusing for several years on environmental steps in people's daily lives, it encouraged congregations to
focus on smaller steps and develop a "culture of environmental awareness" prior to working on environmental policy. Butterfield cautioned
that policy work tended to be tedious and came with few rewards, so
that people who jumped too quickly into political advocacy would lose
interest if there was not already a culture in place to support them.
Once congregations had established the necessary culture, Faith in Place
encouraged them to advocate for environmental policy by contacting
their state, local, and federal legislators, attending in-district meetings
to show their support for sound environmental policy, and participating in Faith in Place's annual Lobby Day.

While Faith in Place collaborated with other environmental groups
to advocate for environmental policies, Butterfield did not want her

organization's participants to understand themselves as just one voice among many in the coalition. Instead, Faith in Place leaders represented themselves as "the moral voice of the environmental community," leveraging their religious authority to make their voices heard. While Butterfield disapproved of secular organizations that attempted to appropriate religion for their own agendas, she did encourage Faith in Place participants to make their religious commitments visible while engaging in policy advocacy. In partnership with the Christian environmental group Restoring Eden, Faith in Place hosted a prayer breakfast for clergy in advance of an Environmental Protection Agency hearing on coal ash in September 2010. Following the breakfast, Butterfield wrote in an e-mail inviting clergy to participate, "Those who can join us will process down the street together (clerical shirts, etc. are encouraged for this—I might even dust mine off for the occasion) to attend the hearing for as long as possible. This is being co-sponsored by us and Restoring Eden (and I freely acknowledge that it was their idea—I think it a very good one)."[14] Butterfield defended such instrumental uses of religious identity, writing, "We have a new-found leverage in the halls of Congress and our state assemblies when we turn out in clerical collars, robes, stoles and other religious symbolism. We need to not be afraid to use it in defense of the Earth and our grandchildren."[15] As they performed their role as "the moral voice of the environmental community," Faith in Place participants contributed distinctively and intentionally religious symbolism to Chicago's political and urban environmental landscapes.

The one arena where Faith in Place's leaders expressly avoided religious talk, however, was in its youth program, From the Ground Up/De La Tierra Para Arriba.[16] An enrichment program designed to teach low-income elementary school students about urban sustainability, From the Ground Up was funded through federal grants that prohibited recipients from promoting religion. Faith in Place's youth director, the only staff member without strong ties to institutional religion, designed a curriculum to convey ecological ethics and values without talking specifically about religious teachings. Instead she instructed youth about their relationship to the natural world, especially in an urban setting, by studying subjects from ecosystems to waste management to food.

From the Ground Up was something of an outlier among Faith in Place's programs because it was not faith based. However, by serving low-income youth from minority urban communities the program advanced Faith in Place's goals of promoting social justice and bringing environmental awareness to an ethnically diverse constituency. It also

contributed to the organization's allure for its wealthier, white supporters. In the years when Faith in Place struggled to recruit minority communities to its urban environmental efforts, the youth program was its
primary venue for working with the communities that the organization
aspired to serve. As Faith in Place developed new measures to work in
African American communities, however, its resources shifted away
from the youth program, and From the Ground Up officially ended after
its coordinator left Faith in Place in 2013.

CULTIVATING RACIAL DIVERSITY

While the youth program provided Faith in Place's main source of
minority involvement in the organization's early years, its constituency
radically shifted after Veronica Kyle joined the staff to conduct African
American outreach in 2008. A charismatic leader with personal ties to
Chicago's south-side communities, Kyle rallied widespread support and
enthusiasm among African American churches. The focus of Faith in
Place's programming shifted as the organization devoted significant
resources to African American congregations. When Faith in Place's
deputy director left the organization for a new job in 2010, Faith in
Place further signaled its commitment to working in African American
communities by hiring a woman from a prominent African American
church to fill the position. This shift initiated significant growth in the
organization in terms of participation and funding, as racial diversity
came to define Faith in Place's network.

As coordinator for African American outreach, Kyle developed a
number of projects to address issues related to health and joblessness on
Chicago's south side, while also cultivating "environmental literacy" in
a community where traditional environmental topics were not widely
discussed. Aiming to improve community health while also cultivating
interest in environmental issues, Faith in Place helped African American
churches develop gardening projects and healthy food initiatives. They
offered gardening workshops, individual consultations, and fund-
raising assistance to help churches build raised-bed and container gardens on their properties. As part of a federally funded program aimed
at providing employment and career development training for low-
income youth, Faith in Place also offered paid summer internships to
train community gardeners in 2010 and 2011.

Aiming to address issues of chronic unemployment, Faith in Place
created temporary work for African Americans through involvement in

campaigns for "weatherization," processes intended to conserve resources and save money by keeping heated or cooled air inside buildings.[17] Capitalizing on resources and opportunities afforded by the Reinvestment and Recovery Act of 2009, Faith in Place recruited church members to participate in two weatherization campaigns. Both were designed to help residents reduce their energy use, educate them about earth stewardship, create employment opportunities, and offer participants job experience within the green economy. In the first project, a low-cost weatherization program cosponsored by the city of Chicago, Faith in Place recruited teenagers from partner congregations to install simple weatherization kits in homes around their neighborhoods. The project included stipends for adult supervisors at partner churches and payment to the youth for each kit they installed. The second program, in partnership with an environmental nonprofit dedicated to creating job opportunities in the green economy, involved using churches as recruitment sites for locating home owners eligible for free professional weatherization services.[18] In addition to hiring minority contractors to complete the services, the program provided employment for intake workers at four churches. Both of these weatherization programs involved partnerships with nonreligious environmental groups who collaborated with Faith in Place because they needed help recruiting minority participants into their causes. Faith in Place was able to recruit these people using the language of faith. The significance of Faith in Place's work in African American communities was reflected in the following statement from a minister at the closing celebration for a weatherization project at his church: "We love Sister Veronica because in her vision of impacting Chicago, she included the west side. We had a great time, and we thank the visionary, Sister Veronica, for including us."[19] As this comment indicates, African American congregations embraced Kyle's leadership and became involved with environmental projects through her work.

FORGING URBAN PATHWAYS

As Faith in Place offered guest sermons in affluent suburbs, gardening projects on Chicago's south side, and community celebrations downtown, it contributed to creating a distinctive set of urban pathways, constituting what Robert Orsi has called an "urban religious cartography."[20] Building on George Chauncey's concept of a "sexual topography," or a mental map that told gay men in early twentieth-century New York which spots were welcoming and which spots they should avoid, Orsi suggests that urban religious cartographies highlight particular religious sites in the city while minimizing the importance of others. A Santeria map can tell adepts where they might encounter spirits and where to find other people who understand space in that same way. Orsi points out that numerous maps shape practitioners' urban existence, as they sometimes follow a religious cartography and at other times traverse a financial or sexual cartography. Religious maps, he contends, "constitute as they disclose to practitioners particular ways of being in the world, of approaching the invisible beings who along with family members and neighbors make up practitioners' relevant social worlds, and of coordinating an individual's own story with an embracing cultural narrative."[21]

As they instigated a particular way of being across the spaces of the city and suburbs, Faith in Place leaders also contributed to the social organization of the city by pushing boundaries that often confined particular people to particular parts of town. Many of Chicago's neighborhoods and suburbs were racially segregated, yet Faith in Place sent staff members, volunteers, and participants to sites throughout the city and surrounding suburbs, including areas where those participants would not otherwise have reason to visit.[22] With congregational partners reaching out to the far suburbs of greater Chicago area, and within the city from Rogers Park to the north, Avalon Park to the south, the Gold Coast to the east, and Austin to the west, Faith in Place formed a religious map that included dozens of religious communities across the region.

Butterfield sometimes referred to the early days of Faith in Place when she spent all of her time in her car, as if that were a situation of the past. But by 2010 she and other staff members still routinely traveled great distances multiple times each week. Within a few days Butterfield might go out to Schaumberg to meet with a diocesan social justice committee, then over to Morton Grove to meet with a pastor, and then to Grayslake to preach on Sunday morning. She would even travel to numerous distant sites within a single day. Faith in Place sent other staff members and interns in all directions across the region as well, to meet with a pastor about starting a winter farmers' market, to talk to a green team about developing environmental initiatives, to attend a neighborhood meeting on public health, or to distribute free compact fluorescent lamps (CFLs) at a city church. Throughout my fieldwork, I also became familiar with these routines, traveling to both ends of the Red Line, riding the bus through Park Manor, journeying from downtown Chicago to Evanston in Butterfield's hybrid, or borrowing a car to fight busy

Highway 55 traffic to reach Bridgeview. By helping to "green" communities in all of these places, Faith in Place contributed to remaking urban environmental maps of the city and region, familiarizing people with parts of town far beyond the boundaries of their regular travel.

While distinctive urban pathways were most pronounced among the staff, Faith in Place provided opportunities for many of its participants to forge new ground as well. Workshops, meetings of the Clergy Café, and other Faith in Place events were hosted by different congregations across the region. Rotating locations was partially a matter of practicality: Faith in Place participants lived across the region, so organizers held events within a reasonable distance for as many people as possible. If one workshop was too far south for North Shore residents to reasonably attend, the next workshop would be more accessible. But more than that, Faith in Place organizers encouraged people to leave the boundaries of their familiar urban pathways, integrating into the larger religious-environmental community by visiting fellow congregations. Most workshops included tours of the host congregation's building, and Faith in Place's outreach staff members actively encouraged their constituents to travel to other areas of town to attend Faith in Place events.[23] Several participants reported that they attended a 2006 workshop specifically because they had never before visited a mosque, and Faith in Place organizers considered that feedback when deciding on future workshop locations.[24] In that way, they capitalized on the lure of urban curiosities.

In addition to religious congregations, Faith in Place's religious-environmental topography included environmental sites across the city. Kyle encouraged constituents to learn about urban environmentalism by visiting the Center for Green Technology, a city-owned resource center that provided practical support for urban sustainability efforts. She strategically hosted meetings at sites that she wanted people to be familiar with, such as the Rebuilding Exchange, a leading innovator in "deconstruction" technology.[25] She also took the Just Eating Bible study group to a farmers' market to reduce their apprehensions about visiting an unknown place. Faith in Place also offered field trips for participants to visit an urban farm in the south-side Englewood neighborhood, a Leadership in Energy and Environmental Design (LEED)-certified synagogue in Evanston, and a "toxic tour" led by community activists working to fight the negative impacts of pollution in the Little Village neighborhood.[26] Other sites on Faith in Place's urban environmental map included community gardens where partner congregations grew food; the beehives on City Hall's rooftop garden, where Faith in Place youth harvested honey; Garfield Park Conservatory, a beautiful city-owned property where Faith in Place twice held its annual fund-raiser; and Eden Place, a nature center in the south-side Fuller Park neighborhood, where Faith in Place held a weatherization seminar training.

Faith in Place leaders especially wanted participants to be familiar with and appreciate the rich offerings available to them right in the city. But they also talked about connections between city existence and the sources that supported urban lives. Field trips for youth, clergy, and the organization's general population included visits to organic CSA farms and ranches that supplied animals for the Taqwa meat cooperative. Thus Faith in Place not only established pathways to farmers' markets and resource centers where participants could return but also expanded the experienced landscape of environmental knowledge. More than helping people "go green" in their own neighborhoods, Faith in Place helped participants become familiar with sites across the region, adding these sites to their own urban maps.

The creation of urban religious-environmental maps was most pronounced among active Faith in Place participants who took part in many of the organization's programs, but it was not restricted to this group. The active participants who attended Faith in Place events represented a small percentage of the nearly five thousand households that received its monthly e-mails and quarterly newsletters.[27] But when those nearly five thousand people across the state read Faith in Place's communications and learned about solar panels on a mosque, a "bucket garden" workshop at a south-side church, or a new butterfly garden for urban youth, they became symbolically connected to activities in neighborhoods they might never have visited. By participating with Faith in Place to screen a film, collect signatures to support environmental legislation, or build a rain garden, congregations acted in solidarity with a much larger community. Through this wider network, they represented a particular way of being religious in the modern world.

REDEEM THE CITY TO SAVE THE WORLD

In addition to its influence on the city's social fabric, Faith in Place's work contributed to altered mental formations related to ideas about the city. Through its efforts within the urban landscape, the organization subverted a legacy of negative attitudes toward the city that has existed in the United States for the last two hundred years.[28] Orsi points out that while America officially became an urban nation in 1920, the first year when more than half of all Americans lived in cities, "Nostalgia and dissatisfaction with the qualities of urban life in an industrial and then postindustrial society have created a lasting myth of small towns and family farms as the bedrock of all that is characteristically American."[29] Among early twentieth-century urbanites, nostalgic attitudes toward the disappearing frontier, coupled with a romantic appreciation for wilderness, contributed to a full-fledged Arcadian myth.[30] Wilderness emerged as a place for purification and salvation, as cities became repugnant, confusing, crowded, and noisy. Nature lovers who contributed to the modern environmental movement—Henry David Thoreau, John Muir, Aldo Leopold—focused their efforts on wilderness environments, and environmentalists emerging from the 1960s counterculture left the city to go "back to the land." In literature and the popular imagination, environmentalism has to do with wild, unspoiled landscapes, untouched by human hands. American life and environmental thought were defined in opposition to cities.

Participating in efforts to "green" the city of Chicago, Faith in Place leaders acted as religious improvisers as they remade the city into a salvific landscape and a site of opportunity. They subverted long-held American attitudes toward the city as filthy, crowded, and chaotic. Chicago indeed was crowded and chaotic, and it could be filthy (although it was significantly less filthy in those parts of town where power and wealth were concentrated). But instead of despising those elements of urban life, Faith in Place leaders celebrated them, minus the filth, looking for the positive benefits and great resources that accompanied urban life.

In a discussion guide that Faith in Place leaders created for the sustainability circles in 2000, two sessions highlighted the importance of cities. One of the sessions, "Cities as Solutions," challenged ideas of cities as an ecological nightmare. "Cities may alienate from natural surroundings, or, at least hide them," the study guide acknowledged. Nevertheless, it encouraged citizens "to understand that high-density settlements are not an environmental 'problem' but in fact provide a solution to the increasing demands that growing populations place on limited resources." After making the case that cities could be good for the environment, the discussion guide proposed "opportunities for action" around this idea. Members of sustainability circles might participate in CSAs, find ways to conserve energy, purchase products locally, and travel using bicycles and public transit.[31] Another session, "The Sacred City," appealed to people not just to accept the city as necessary but to celebrate it for all it could offer. In this session, the "opportunities for action" focused not on preserving the natural environment but on finding opportunities to embrace and appreciate city life by building community, attending interreligious events, and "being attentive to the sacredness all around us."[32]

As green city advocates recast cities as good for the environment, they began to overcome negative legacies of the city. Green cities became sites of opportunity for underemployed urban populations, as green jobs training programs helped them engage in the "green" economy. Moreover, fresher air, urban gardens, expansive bike lanes, and abundant trees made the green city a more hospitable place to live. Some green city features offered symbolic improvements, whereas others had measurable physical effects. Physical markers of the green city—rooftop gardens, solar panels, recycling bins, rain barrels, CFLs, community gardens, bicycle racks, farmers' markets, native plant gardens and trees, and citizens traversing city streets and railways with their reusable coffee mugs, water bottles, and grocery bags—all designated a way of being on the part of earth-conscious city dwellers. They also improved city life in measurable ways. Rooftop gardens have been shown to reduce the urban heat island effect, lowering temperatures by up to ten degrees.[33] Urban gardens create a peaceful site for community building, even amid the buzz of city traffic. Dotting the urban landscape with these features served to mark the space in particular ways.

To be sure, Faith in Place leaders did not suggest that everyone should move to the city. Important activities take place in the countryside, and people must be there to do them. Faith in Place's expansion into central Illinois represented its dedicated effort to understanding these populations and the issues they faced. But Faith in Place leaders celebrated city living as a good option for most. During a presentation about the growing worldwide water crisis, Butterfield suggested that it might be necessary to make space for even more people to live in Chicago. Because water supplies can recharge themselves, but only if water remains in its bioregion, Butterfield said that "we can't ship water out of here, but we can welcome strangers who need water. It makes me nervous to think of even *more* people coming to live in this already crowded city, but this is where the water is."[34]

While people generally could be convinced that city living was better for the environment, the possibility that the city was a place to lead "the good life" was a tougher sell. This was a central topic of discussion during a 2008 retreat outside Goshen, Indiana, that I attended with Butterfield and ten other clergy. Surrounded by the retreat center's high grass, restored prairie, ponds, and wetlands—a sea of green with a few small buildings made of natural wood that fit seamlessly into the landscape—I felt as if we were in an entirely different universe from the skyscrapers, concrete, and busy traffic of Chicago. During a discussion of finding places to commune with nature in the city, one participant remarked: "Walking here, you can feel the good life. You can't feel it in the city on the sidewalk, looking at a tree in concrete with painted woodchips. But I can feel it here, on the soft ground, where you have contact with the earth."[35] Other participants agreed about the feeling of enchantment at the retreat center, but one person suggested that the retreat was like a Sabbath, which must be connected to the rest of creation. While we all enjoyed this time in rural nature, the experience had to be connected to the good life when we all returned to the city.

As that participant noted, an appreciation of rural nature does not have to imply a devaluation of the city. Even after the enchantment of a retreat into the wilderness, individuals could still appreciate the city for what it was and want to return to it. Nonetheless, this conversation revealed a tension. Intellectually, these clergy leaders wanted the city to be a site for the good life. They joined green city advocates in applauding the city as an ideal site for leading a sustainable life, and they joined Faith in Place efforts to promote urban environmentalism. But they still experienced a romantic urge that lured them toward vast expanses of nature that could be found only outside the city. Negotiations such as these revealed the widespread tensions and contradictions that emerged as Faith in Place participants worked on their urban religious worlds.

3

Paths Leading to Faith in Place

Evidence
Expertise

A statistical analysis of Faith in Place's database conducted in 2014 offers a bird's-eye view of the organization's network.[1] Of the 4,474 individuals who subscribed to Faith in Place's e-mail list, donated to the organization, or were otherwise involved, 67 percent were female, 67 percent were over age fifty, and 75 percent lived in the greater Chicago region. Of the 1,458 supporters who provided their religious affiliations, 81 percent were Protestant, with Unitarian Universalism, United Church of Christ, Lutheranism, and Methodism representing the largest denominations within that group.[2] Another 12.4 percent identified as Catholic, 4.5 percent identified as Jewish, and 1.4 percent identified as Muslim. The analysis also listed Baha'is and Buddhists, each representing less than 1 percent of Faith in Place's network.

This chapter considers some of the varied paths that led individuals and groups to work with Faith in Place. It builds on the previous two chapters' examination of Faith in Place's organizational priorities, strategic practices, and religious environmental messages by considering how participants negotiated the organization's work in the context of their own lives. While the women and men I encountered during my fieldwork generally supported the organization's values and messages, additional factors contributed to their religious environmental involvement. Religious environmentalists brought a diverse set of motivations to their work with Faith in Place, and those motivations often entailed

TABLE 3   FAITH IN PLACE SUPPORTERS BY AFFILIATION

Affiliation	#	%
Christian	227	15.57%
Unitarian	223	15.29%
Catholic	181	12.41%
UCC	171	11.73%
Lutheran	148	10.15%
Methodist	121	8.30%
Episcopal	106	7.27%
Presbyterian	98	6.72%
Jewish	66	4.53%
Baptist	47	3.22%
Mennonite	31	2.12%
Muslim	21	1.44%
Quaker	10	0.69%
Buddhist	7	0.48%
Baha'i	6	0.41%
TOTAL	1,458	100.33%

SOURCE: Data courtesy of the Voter Activation Network, "An In-Depth Analysis of Faith in Place Supporters," Faith in Place, internal document, 2014.

priorities, concerns, and urges that did not seem directly connected to religion or the environment.

A SNAPSHOT OF FAITH IN PLACE PARTICIPANTS

Faith in Place focused its efforts on recruiting participants who were "people of faith first, environmentalists second," but self-identified environmentalists found Faith in Place on their own when they were seeking to connect their environmental values with their religious lives. In particular, women and men who already cared about the environment found Faith in Place through their own regular networks. Seminary interns and volunteers who devoted hundreds of hours to their work with the organization invariably fit this model. Gavin and Kate, two white seminary students who interned at Faith in Place between 2008 and 2010, both learned about the nonprofit through the Beatitudes Society, a progressive Christian organization. Both had cultivated environmental values during college, and they selected Faith in Place as a year-long seminary internship site because that was the only option where they could integrate their religious and environmental values.[3] Lauren, a white recent college graduate who committed to two years of service at Faith in Place through the Lutheran Volunteer Corps (LVC), also came to Faith in Place because it supported environmental values she already embraced.[4] Although she had grown up in a politically conservative Western state where *environmentalist* was not a positive identifier, Lauren came to embrace environmentalism during college when she worked at her campus recycling plant and took courses in marine biology. When she was searching for a placement for her LVC service, she selected Faith in Place because it allowed her to deepen her environmental values while also aligning them with her lifelong Lutheran faith.[5]

Anita, an African American seminary graduate in her late twenties, found the organization through a related path. She did not consider herself radical enough to fit the label of "environmentalist," but she had studied eco-theology during a seminary class and was interested in the ways that theology could bridge her concerns about food access with principles of her faith. After learning about Faith in Place through a fellow seminarian, Anita contacted the organization and scheduled a meeting with Veronica Kyle. When Kyle asked Anita to help facilitate a Bible study on food and faith at an African American church, Anita enthusiastically accepted.[6] From there she became involved with other Faith in Place activities, including workshops and meetings of the Clergy Café. Anita told me she appreciated the ways Kyle attempted to align environmental principles with African American history and culture.[7]

While internships and volunteer opportunities provided an intense connection with Faith in Place, the vast majority of the organization's supporters found connections by signing up for the mailing list, contacting the organization for direct support with congregational programming, or participating in Faith in Place activities at their own congregations. Jessica, a white commercial account executive in her midthirties, found the nonprofit through an Internet search when she wanted to bring greater environmental awareness to her Presbyterian church. Having come to environmentalism through an "urban planning perspective"—she told me that her childhood in a walkable Chicago suburb had shaped her commitment to living a green urban lifestyle without the use of a car—Jessica sought out Faith in Place's support as part of her efforts to promote sustainable living among her fellow parishioners. Jessica helped her church develop green initiatives such as Earth Day Sunday and a cycling club, and she told me she appreciated Faith in Place because it promoted interfaith dialogue. When I asked her if she understood earth stewardship as a religious commitment, however, she said probably not, and she elaborated that she typically used secular language when advocating for environmental causes.[8] Jessica offered a perspective that many Faith in Place participants shared: she was actively involved with a religious community and was committed to bringing environmental activities to her church. She believed her faith and ecological principles were compatible, but her faith commitments did not really motivate her environmentalism.

Other participants perceived a more fundamental connection between their religious and ecological values, describing eco-friendly practices and activism as expressions of their faith. Danielle, a white college professor in her late thirties, represented that perspective. Like Jessica, Danielle already identified as a committed environmentalist when she discovered Faith in Place. She told me that since finishing graduate school she had developed a growing environmental and feminist consciousness, grounded in a rage against the culture of consumption that led to unsustainable habits and exploited women by treating them as objects. When Danielle moved to Chicago for work she wanted to find a church that upheld her ecological and feminist values. She found that in Resurrection Lutheran Church, the home congregation of Faith in Place's development director. Danielle discovered Resurrection when she was reading an article about Faith in Place in the *Lutheran,* a magazine of the Evangelical Lutheran Church of America.[9] Intrigued that the church had a female pastor, served organic communion bread, and had recently installed solar panels through a partnership with Faith in Place, Danielle decided to visit on the day of its solar panel dedication ceremony. "The prayers were focused on taking care of creation, and praying for wisdom and strength to do that," Danielle told me during an interview. "It was just so worshipful to me, because nature is the place where I tend to meet God." She immediately joined the church and had been attending ever since. Danielle told me she considered her growing environmental awareness as part of an "awakening of faith" because it enabled her to live out biblical ideas such as stewardship. At the time of our interview she had attended only one Faith in Place event, but she faithfully read the organization's monthly newsletter and enjoyed the environmental programming at her church that had resulted from its partnership with the religious environmental nonprofit.[10]

Paul, a white clinical psychologist in his midforties who was active in a suburban Methodist church, also understood environmentalism as deeply connected to his faith and had sought out Faith in Place on his own. Paul told me he had attended a meeting of the radical environmental organization Friends of the Earth during college but otherwise had never been particularly involved with environmental activities. In recent years, though, he had started to reflect on current society and the ways that current behaviors would affect his children's opportunities in the future, and he wanted to make some changes. Vaguely aware that some religious communities had begun to cultivate environmental ministries, Paul decided to attend a Faith in Place presentation that he saw advertised at a nearby church. He met with Butterfield after the presentation and decided to start volunteering in the office. Whereas Danielle was involved with Faith in Place indirectly, primarily because of its work at her church, Paul became more directly involved with the organization, seeming to rely on it for support that he did not find at church. Paul spoke disparagingly of his own congregation, indicating that people tended to be politically conservative and denied the reality of climate change. Faith in Place, by contrast, offered Paul "a community of people who are supportive and yet encourage what I'll call environmental growth, spiritual environmental growth."[11] He also explained that Faith in Place gave him the space and resources to reflect on his spiritual and environmental growth, as well as the opportunity to *do* something besides just thinking. Moreover, he elaborated, "It feels like the environmental issue in some ways is the driving factor in my spiritual growth, although I don't think it's always been that way."[12] Whereas Jessica sought out Faith in Place as a resource to help her promote her environmental values within her religious community, Paul and Danielle placed earth stewardship at the very heart of their personal spiritual journeys. Paul, moreover, found at Faith in Place a supportive environmental community that was unavailable at his own church.

Other people I met at Faith in Place had become involved with the organization, and had embraced its ecological principles, only after encountering it through their regular religious networks. Marcus, a white executive in his fifties, was a longtime member of Unity Temple Unitarian Universalist Congregation, Clare Butterfield's home church and Faith in Place's original partner. Marcus had always considered himself as an activist more on social justice causes than on environmental ones, and he had never really connected his activism to his Unitarian identity. Butterfield's leadership at his church, however, convinced Marcus that "it can be a spiritual path to do social justice or environmental work." Butterfield "had a huge influence on me," Marcus said when I asked how his environmental consciousness had developed, "kind of bringing in the spiritual aspect on how we're treating nature and how we're treating ourselves through the way we treat nature." As a result of this thinking, Marcus told me, he had switched to energy-efficient appliances at home, he tried to eat organic food as much as possible, and he had gradually introduced green innovations at work. He also joined his church's Green Sanctuary Committee and regularly attended Faith in Place workshops and lobby days. Marcus thought the Bible was full of good advice and teachings, and he saw his eco-friendly behaviors as "a way of living out my beliefs in my life, instead of just reciting your beliefs, the Ten Commandments or whatever your beliefs are on the Sabbath, and then going home to have brunch."[13] Much as Paul saw religious environmental activism as helping him actually *do* something besides just thinking, Marcus understood earth stewardship as a way to align his practices and personal beliefs.[14]

Jerry, a white man in his early seventies who was retired from a career in organizational development, also identified with environmentalism only after encountering Faith in Place. He became involved through a screening of *An Inconvenient Truth* that Faith in Place offered at his church in 2006. Jerry was one of two thousand people who saw the film at the 144 churches where Faith in Place screened it, and the religious environmental programming he developed in response was part of a new wave of growth for the organization.[15] Jerry told me that only three people had attended the film screening at his church. But they found the documentary inspiring, engaged in a really interesting conversation after the movie, and decided to host an environmental workshop at their church a few weeks later. That workshop attracted twelve other participants, and from there an environmentally concerned church community emerged. With Butterfield's guidance they developed an action plan and implemented initiatives ranging from study groups to infrastructural changes. Jerry had never particularly cared about the environment in the past, but since becoming involved with his church's environmental ministry he had undergone significant changes in his own life. After commissioning an energy audit at his house, Jerry took measures to reduce his consumption by 18 percent. He and his partner also gave up one of their two cars, planted a garden, and ate locally as much as possible. Jerry regularly attended Faith in Place workshops along with others from his church's green committee.

Interestingly, during our conversation Jerry signaled that his interest in religious environmental programming did not really stem from his concern about the earth or from his spirituality or religious principles. Instead, he said that environmental programming was "the most successful way to get more people involved" in church life. Capitalism and overconsumption were two of the key issues of the times, Jerry contended, and "hopefully the church will be speaking to these kinds of issues." At his church, he said, it was clear that "there was a lot of energy there that people could form community, give them some cohesion in their own experience of being at church. Theologically, I think it's pretty cool."[16] Much as Marcus wished to align his beliefs and practices through environmental activism, Jerry understood religious environmental programming as a way for the church to speak to pressing current issues and ultimately to help church participants feel more connected to each other and to their church.

Religious Environmental Involvement and Identity

Sociological literature on social movements suggests that considerations of identity can offer a key locus for understanding why individuals decide to join particular groups.[17] Before individuals become involved with a particular social movement, according to identity convergence theory, their individual identities must align with the collective identity of that movement.[18] Sociologists David Snow and Doug McAdam propose two main processes through which this alignment occurs. In the first, identity seeking, individuals who strongly identify with a particular set of values search for groups that can help them solidify and express their identity around those values.[19] In the case of religious environmentalism, the identity-seeking model would suggest that members of religious communities who strongly identify as environmentalists search for a group that allows them to express their religious and environmental values. The second process that Snow and McAdam discuss, identity appropriation, involves recruitment of individuals who might not otherwise identify with a particular movement by making use of their existing social networks.[20] Individuals who become involved with the movement then adjust their identities to correspond. In the case of religious environmentalism, identity appropriation would entail recruitment of individuals who do not identify as environmentalists through their faith-based solidarity networks.

Individuals came to Faith in Place through both of these processes. The interns Gavin, Kate, and Lauren, along with the church participants Jessica, Danielle, and Paul, became involved with Faith in Place and its religious environmental projects through the identity-seeking path. They sought out the religious environmental organization in part because that enabled them to express the identities they already held:

environmentalist and person of faith. Marcus and Jerry did not identify as environmentalists prior to becoming involved with Faith in Place. But the organization aligned with other aspects of their identities, social justice activist and community organizer, respectively, and both men developed identities as environmentalists through their involvement with the organization. These participants brought different understandings of how exactly their environmental commitments related to their religious lives—the connection was tangential for some and fundamental for others—but their involvement with Faith in Place in some ways related to their religious and environmental selves.

For women and men who might not have sought out a religious environmental group on their own, often members of minority groups who did not identify as environmentalists, Faith in Place leaders offered direct recruitment that relied on personal connections, employing the identity appropriation process. The organization intentionally hired outreach workers who had "deep roots" in the communities they sought to involve, so that outreach workers could make use of their existing networks when they began to recruit for Faith in Place. Butterfield told me that the first Muslim outreach worker was not a longtime member of the local Muslim community and did not bring her own contacts when she began working for Faith in Place. When Aisha Tehrani joined the staff, however, Muslim involvement soared in part because Tehrani successfully recruited her friends and family members and helped other staff members gain access to key leaders in her Muslim community. When Tehrani got married and left Chicago, her connections also disappeared.

African American Protestants similarly came to Faith in Place as the result of personal connections with Veronica Kyle, who grew up in Chicago, was married to a pastor, and was involved with a network of southside United Church of Christ (UCC) congregations. Mrs. Weldon, an African American retired social worker in her seventies who had known Kyle through her UCC network for decades, told me she had begun to attend Faith in Place events because Kyle was a "good salesman." Mrs. Weldon recruited Jayla, a younger member of her church, to attend a Faith in Place event as well, and after that Jayla became a regular participant at Faith in Place and other environmental organizations in Chicago.[21]

Snow and McAdam caution that structural factors such as race, ethnicity, and class are only one set of contributors to identity and that the relevance of those factors varies depending on the setting. Gender might be the most relevant feature of an individual's identity in one context, while her occupational identity might become primary in another.[22] My

fieldwork among participants at Faith in Place indicated that racial identities were salient in many religious environmental contexts. When Faith
in Place audiences were entirely white, people noticed. During a breakout
session of a workshop in 2008, one woman expressed disappointment
that the people around the table all were "well educated, liberal, knowledgeable about organic, and white." She indicated that diversifying Faith
in Place's constituency would enable them to address the environmental
crisis more equitably.[23] Board members similarly observed and lamented
that the organization drew primarily white, affluent audiences when they
reflected on their work in 2008. Describing images they associated with
the nonprofit, board members expressed that Faith in Place was the kind
of organization that cared about environmental justice and struggled
with white privilege.[24] A Catholic lay leader initiated a related conversation during a Clergy Café meeting when she asked the group, "What does
it say that we're all white?" "It's systemic and says something about life
in general," a Lutheran pastor responded with a tone of regret. "We're all
white and all of our friends are white." Butterfield added that Faith in
Place's work grew out an environmental project and that it was predominately white, just like the larger environmental movement. She said the
staff members tried to address that disparity but they wanted to do so in
a sensitive manner because "it's not appropriate to tell people that they
have the wrong priorities."[25]

In these contexts white participants exhibited what sociologist Ruth
Frankenberg calls race cognizance, acknowledging that race made a difference in their lives and that racism was a continuing force in contemporary life.[26] They expressed remorse that Faith in Place attracted primarily white people, suggested that its limited audience detracted from
its work, and wanted to find ways to responsibly involve other people
in environmental conversations. In some cases they experienced their
racial identities in the context of guilt or shame, as in the board members' remark about their struggle with white privilege.[27] Kate, the seminary intern, expressed those emotions to me most clearly during an
interview. Describing a research project she had conducted on environmental racism, she recalled visiting Altgeld Gardens, a housing project
on Chicago's southeast side. Altgeld Gardens was surrounded by munic-
ipal and hazardous waste landfills, toxic waste incinerators, and other
polluting industries.[28] Kate told me that she was assaulted by terrible
smells when she visited the housing project and was horrified as she
thought, "My God, people live here, and everyone is a person of color."
She said the experience made her feel "terrible, because as a white

person I don't have to deal with that unless I want to. It was another piece of evidence that we still live in a racist society, that racism continues to go on."[29] The white participants I met at Faith in Place tended to recognize that they had privileges that were often unavailable in communities of color, and they wanted to overcome racial disparities in their religious environmental work.

Faith in Place's African American participants also commented on the whiteness of environmental events, indicating that African American identities represented barriers to environmental involvement. Anita told me it could feel uncomfortable to be an African American environmentalist. "When I see black people in environmental movements, it's kind of anomalous. It's like, hi! And then we go back to our particular groups," she explained.[30] Tom, an African American seminarian who participated in a Faith in Place training session, declared that prior to seeing *An Inconvenient Truth* he had not been interested in environmentalism because he considered it "a white man's problem." The film convinced Tom that he should care about the earth too, and he wanted to convey that message in a way that would be relevant and accessible to fellow African Americans.[31] Kyle frequently commented on the dearth of people of color at the environmental events she attended, prompting Butterfield to remark after one conference that it was the last "white event" Kyle would have to attend for the foreseeable future.[32]

These observations and comments indicated that participants associated the environmental movement with white, affluent communities even as they acknowledged that environmental problems were relevant to everyone. The white participants I encountered were much more likely to answer affirmatively when I asked if they identified as environmentalists. Gavin, Kate, Lauren, Jessica, Danielle, and Paul all sought out Faith in Place precisely because it aligned with their environmental identities, while Marcus and Jerry embraced that identity after spending time with the organization. By contrast, Mrs. Weldon, the retired social worker, did not consider herself an environmentalist, even though she served on her church's green team ministry, attended Environmental Lobby Day, ate locally whenever possible, and took other conservation measures. "A *real* environmentalist wouldn't call me one," she responded when I asked about her environmental identity. Mrs. Weldon suggested that real environmentalists "eat, breathe, and sleep" environmentalism, whereas she was merely "aware and concerned."[33] Jayla and Anita also rejected the environmentalist label because they did not consider themselves adequately radical.

To be sure, racial and ethnic identities were not of primary importance for all Faith in Place participants. Mrs. Kinkaid, an African American church deacon in her early sixties, told me she "gave the environmental movement no color" and readily identified as an environmentalist.[34] Nazneen, a Zoroastrian survey scientist who grew up in Pakistan, also became involved with Faith in Place on her own after learning about it from a fellow Zoroastrian. Nazneen told me she had come to identify strongly as an environmental activist in the previous five years, and she concluded that her religious views supported her environmental values without her needing any convincing from Faith in Place.[35] As the examples of Nazneen and Mrs. Kinkaid indicate, there is no simple dichotomy to suggest who will or will not align with environmentalism. Environmental identity, furthermore, was just one factor among many that contributed to decisions to participate in religious environmentalism. Nevertheless, white participants often more readily identified with Faith in Place's programming on their own, while the organization relied on additional methods to recruit minority participants. In particular, the organization relied on direct recruitment through personal connections as they sought to cross the eco-divide.

Faith in Place leaders most often described their work as a way of putting faith teachings into practice, an understanding expressed by participants such as Marcus. Identity convergence theory offers an additional tool for understanding the path to involvement with Faith in Place. But as my conversation with Jerry indicated, a variety of additional factors also motivated participants to become involved with religious environmental work. Jerry understood partnership with Faith in Place as a way to make the church more relevant and get more people involved, a motivation that I heard in other venues.[36] Just as social movement research indicates that motivations for involvement are always multifaceted, my research at Faith in Place evinced a wide array of drives that supported religious environmental involvement.[37]

RELIGION AND ENVIRONMENT IN A COMMUNITY GARDEN

Faith in Place offered internships, volunteer opportunities, workshops, and other projects that engaged faith communities in religious environmentalism directly through the organization. But they also sought to create "cultures of environmental awareness" at partner congregations so that communities would develop their own projects without the support of Faith in Place. By 2010 Unity Temple Unitarian Universalist Congregation, Faith in Place's original partner, had developed extensive programming on its own, so many of its participants were engaged with religious environmental practices that were not directly tied to the nonprofit. The Purple Radish Community Garden, established by six white women associated with Unity Temple, provides an example of an independent religious environmental project that developed after Faith in Place had helped cultivate environmental values across an entire church community.[38]

As members of a Unitarian Universalist congregation, the Purple Radishes participated in a religious culture that promoted environmental awareness. Unitarian Universalism offers explicit language for connecting religion and environmental concern: one of the seven principles that Unitarian Universalist congregations affirm is "respect for the interdependent web of existence of which we all are a part."[39] Unity Temple constantly reinforced the seventh principle, placing environmental concern as a primary community value. The congregation's mission statement set the intention to nurture individuals' search for meaning while demonstrating "our shared values of compassion, peace, justice and respect for the earth," and they expressed their respect for the earth in their worship practices and in the physical features of the church. Unity Temple's senior pastor told me that he and his associates periodically included themes about nature during their services. The congregation's Green Sanctuary Committee ensured that the church adhered to environmental principles in its daily practices.[40] Many Unity Temple members were individual donors to Faith in Place, and the congregation consistently sent large groups to the nonprofit's events, workshops, and lobby days.

Since the Purple Radishes were members of a community that offered explicit language for connecting religion and environmental values, supported those values in daily practice, and maintained a close partnership with Faith in Place, their decision to initiate a religious environmental project comes as no surprise. As I interviewed the women and spent time with them in the garden, however, I observed an intricate web of motivations—related to religion, environment, and other factors—that combined to support their religious environmental work.

Roots: How the Purple Radishes Began

The Purple Radishes developed out of Menu for the Future, a discussion class on sustainable food that Unity Temple's Green Sanctuary Committee offered in 2009.[41] Having learned about the negative effects of modern industrial agriculture on communities, health, and the environment, six white women from the class decided to create their own source of local, sustainable food by starting a community garden.[42] They worked out an arrangement with the owners of a local restaurant to use the backyard space behind the restaurant and began meeting to work together in the garden on Wednesday evenings. Throughout the rest of the week the women took turns coming to the garden to water, harvest, or take care of any other time-sensitive matters, and some liked to come to the garden just to hang out. After meeting two of the Purple Radishes through my research at Unity Temple and Faith in Place, I inquired about conducting fieldwork in their garden. They invited me to join their weekly gardening rituals in the spring and summer of 2010. I also conducted formal interviews with five of the women.

The Purple Radishes' garden fulfilled a practical need for the women: it offered a source of local, organic food. Along with sustainable food, the women also found a source of community, identity, and meaning through the garden. Unlike the format of many community gardens, which are divided into separate, individually managed plots, the Purple Radishes worked collaboratively, planting together and sharing the work and the harvest.

When I asked the Purple Radishes about their reasons for starting the garden, they all pointed to food concerns they had discussed during Menu for the Future classes. Two of the women, Doris and Andrea, wanted to grow their own food because it was overwhelming to get all the information they sought before purchasing commercially produced food. Teresa, a mother of four, joined the garden because it was related to her passion for providing healthy, fresh food for her family, and Jean participated in the garden because she did not want to support corporate food production.

Although the ostensible purpose of the garden had to do with reclaiming control of their own food supply, the gardeners talked as much about creating community as they did about growing food. Both Marilyn and Teresa signed up for the Menu class not really to gain new insights about food, they revealed, but to make connections with people. Marilyn had already taken the course two times, but she was relatively new to the Chicago area. Even though she already knew a lot of the content, she said, "I really wanted to meet other people who would be attracted to such a course. So it was the course, but knowing that it would attract like-minded people."[43] Similarly, Teresa already had extensive knowledge about sustainable food and even had run a small organic grocery store before her children were born. Rather than seeking new knowledge, she took the course to find people as concerned as she was about food quality. Doris expressed great joy for the community that unexpectedly grew out of the garden, telling me that the garden offered "an amazing sense of camaraderie and purpose, and sort of a joy of life. Everyone is so different, and everyone brings such different personality and skills, and I'm constantly learning, constantly laughing, with a common purpose."[44]

Comments about the search for like-minded community and the joy of engaging in shared tasks with a common purpose support the identity-seeking model of social movements research. The women had clear identities as environmentally concerned citizens, which they communicated primarily through their concerns about food, and their involvement with the group helped them express and solidify those identities. I never heard the women comment on the racial or ethnic composition of the group, and their racial and ethnic identities did not seem salient to them in the context of the garden. Yet certain comments indicated that they were cognizant of their privileged social locations. Marilyn had been an activist in the feminist, civil rights, and urban renewal movements in the 1960s and 1970s, and she hoped the garden could become an extension of those social justice–oriented endeavors. Andrea remarked that the challenges of making informed food choices must be especially burdensome for the poor and the working class. Jean told me that the Purple Radishes hoped to donate some of that year's harvest to a local food bank. Aware of their good fortune and wanting to share the garden's bounty with others, the Purple Radishes included education as part of their mission. In 2010 they offered a free gardening class at the YMCA, set up an information booth at a local street festival, and sought to reach others through a garden blog that Andrea ran. The Purple Radishes recognized that they had privileges that were unavailable to those who were less fortunate, and part of their experience in the garden involved a desire to share its benefits.

The women's relative affluence shaped their garden experiences in other ways too. Their quest to build a like-minded community to support their environmental values was structured by the geography of where they lived, worked, and worshipped, a geography also structured by race and class. As residents of the same relatively affluent suburb, all six Purple Radishes were middle to upper middle class, college educated, and white. These characteristics contributed to their identity convergence with the mainstream environmental movement, and the five Purple Radishes whom I interviewed all answered affirmatively when I asked if they identified as environmentalists.

The Purple Radish women also held positive symbolic associations with agriculture that were shaped by their social status. Marilyn told me that all of the Purple Radishes had roots on a farm somewhere. When I asked about these roots during interviews, the women shared fond childhood memories about time spent outdoors and visiting family members' farms. Marilyn told me that as a child she had maintained a flower garden in her own suburban backyard and that she had always looked forward to visiting her grandparents' Georgia farm during summer vacations. "We'd go out and pick the food," she recounted, "eating tomatoes right off the vine, picking corn, digging up potatoes, and literally going from the ground to the kitchen."[45] Her grandmother prepared meals that Marilyn recalled as "unbelievable," serving mounds of food to the family on a "typical southern long table." In the evenings the family would gravitate to the front lawn, sitting around a fire pit and gazing at the stars.

For Jean, who grew up down the road from her uncle's Illinois farm in the 1950s, memories of farm life also revolved around recollections of bountiful food. After describing freezers and food cellars stocked with abundant produce canned straight from family members' giant gardens, Jean told me, "I was well into high school before we really ate anything that we didn't put up ourselves. . . . We just never had to really go to a store, because we had the milk cows too, so we had fresh milk." Meat was plentiful as well, because her uncle went to auction each year and purchased several calves for the family to raise. "So I remember in high school coming in and saying, 'Oh, man. We're having steak for dinner again.'" Jean recalled with amusement. "It was just like, you know, uuu-ugh!"[46] Jean hoped that the Purple Radish garden could help her restore her childhood diet of local, fresh foods, and a picture a much-leaner Jean that I saw a few years after our interview suggested that her diet had undergone a significant change.

Doris was the only Purple Radish who had actually ever lived on a farm, but when I asked about her agricultural memories she offered sparse details and said she did not remember much. The daughter of an agricultural engineer, Doris grew up on an experimental farm that her father managed for a large international corporation. Doris's father held a management position in which he oversaw agricultural laborers, and there was no expectation that Doris would contribute to the farm's daily operations. Thus, while she did not connect her experiences in the garden to idyllic memories of life on the farm, neither did she have to overcome memories of toil, drudgery, or poor working conditions. As a child she indicated that she had no interest in working on the family's farm, and that was a decision that her parents accepted. From idyllic family dinners and summer vacations to the "burden" of eating steak for dinner every night, or at least an agricultural childhood free from drudgery and toil, the Purple Radishes held positive agricultural memories, made possible in part by their relative affluence, that contributed to their experiences in the garden.

Remaking Religion in the Garden

Through their time in the garden the women found a source of sustainable food and a community of like-minded women. They also found a source of identity and meaning, and some of the women expressed that meaning in religious terms. Only two of the Purple Radishes regularly attended Faith in Place events, but all five of the Unitarian gardeners were familiar with the organization and its religious environmental principles because of its long-standing partnership with their church. Their familiarity was evident in their descriptions of religion in the garden. Jean told me that the garden was related to her religion because it expressed Unitarian principles: "It's about respecting the earth and dignity for all, and that we are all entitled to the goodness of everything, the goodness of the earth, the goodness of the experience that we get, with no judgment about what that is for people."[47] Marilyn invoked the seventh principle in her description of an improved world. The benefit of being in the garden, she explained to me, "is in that little seed. So if we nurture the place for that little seed to grow, it grows in us as well. That, to me, is the seventh principle of Unitarianism, that we're completely connected to this. You sever that tie, I think that's the source of dysfunction, loneliness, mental illness, cancer, et cetera."[48]

The other Unitarians also tied the garden to the seventh principle of Unitarianism, but they spoke more in terms of a spiritual experience that developed in the garden, related to making things right in the world and being a better person. In an overview of the garden that she wrote for a community newsletter, Andrea explained that the group was "not officially linked to any religion or organization." But the women did meet at a class at Unity Temple, she conveyed, "and we do consider gardening a nondenominational spiritual experience."[49] Just as Andrea hesitated to align gardening with any particular religion but associated it with a spiritual experience, the other Purple Radishes described some sort of spiritual gardening experience that connected with their religions to varying degrees. The women associated religion with institutions, rituals, and teachings of the formal church and indicated that spirituality involved a direct experience of something greater to be found outside themselves, separate from any institutional form.[50] For the Unitarian gardeners, a shared religious identity and the group's origins in a church setting contributed to their experience of the garden as a religious space.[51] Employing popular rhetoric differentiating "religion" from "spirituality," however, they more often described the garden as a spiritual space and engaged the garden as they constructed spiritual experiences that overcame many of the problems they associated with traditional religions.

The spiritual experience the Purple Radishes shared stemmed from an understanding of nature in general, and the garden in particular, as something greater, an expression of what's "really real."[52] As Doris explained it succinctly, the garden "transcends the silliness of human struggles, whatever they might be."[53] Marilyn talked about the garden in almost animistic terms, describing it as representative of something greater. She related the Purple Radish garden to a farm where she had spent time back east. At that farm, Marilyn told me,

> It was as though the land was alive and in its own spirit. And I relate to the land like that. There's this need to connect to something that's greater. Watching a little weed grow through a crack in a sidewalk is to me, the earth trying to speak, even in a very built-up environment such as a city. Just look everywhere and there's life, the essence of life. But on that farm, it just seemed so special. It's almost as if the land floated. It was just deeply imbued with spirit. It was spiritual. It's like something is coming alive, beyond who we are. To me it's sacred. It's a spiritual experience, and that's sacred.[54]

Andrea expressed a similar sentiment about the Purple Radish garden. Nature, she explained, "is a pure representation of, a manifestation of the mysticism of the universe. I feel like it's a connection to the bigger thing, and that the more that we lose touch with it, the more we're getting away from our own community and divinity and all that kind of stuff. I feel like nature *is* spirituality. And the closer we are to it, the closer we are to our best selves."[55]

A sense of the garden as really real also became manifest in some of the gardeners' belief that pure nature—both in the garden and within the human spirit—was a source of greater truth. Marilyn espoused what she called "intuitive gardening," or drawing on the wisdom of nature devas in tending the garden, and she preferred simply listening to the garden and experimenting with various techniques rather than a more scientific, studied approach.[56] More than offering wisdom about how to tend nature, Andrea believed the garden gave her wisdom for becoming a better person. She explained that gardening was a way for her "to express my better self. It's a good way for me to spend my time. It has a purpose; it connects me to others that I care about very much." Andrea elaborated that spending time in the garden gave her the opportunity to reflect on her values and that when she came home from being in the garden she felt restored.[57] Jean likewise expressed that there was something "good" about being in the garden. Semiretired, Jean spent the whole day in the garden several times a week, both working and just hanging out. The garden, she explained, "is where I feel the most comfortable. . . . I go home and I don't know what to do, because [the garden] is where I want to be." For Jean the garden offered a space for meditative practice because she enjoyed "just sitting here and paying attention to all of the stuff that's going on around here."[58] Understanding the garden as a source of truth, wisdom, and goodness, the women differentiated their time in the garden from the mundane tasks of daily life, marking the garden as a sacred space.

If the garden offered the Purple Radishes a place to create and maintain their spiritual selves, they ensured that their garden spirituality did not include the aspects of traditional religion they rejected. The five Unitarian Purple Radishes all had found Unity Temple as adults, after rejecting their cradle religions and engaging a process of religious seeking. The spirituality they created in the garden was shaped by their negative memories of the religions they rejected. Jean, a devout Lutheran as a child and young adult, found her way to Unitarianism after dabbling in Wicca and "back to the earth" spirituality.[59] When she told me that the principles of the garden were "very Unitarian," she qualified her statement by saying, "But we're not out to recruit. We don't really say. We're just the Purple Radishes."[60] Implicit in this statement is her association of "bad religion" with evangelizing. Doris told me that she rejected the Congregationalist faith of her childhood because she did not believe in the miracle stories. She embraced Unitarian Universalism because it was "the only religion that acknowledges that we're only part of existence, that humans are just part of animals in the world, and that it's very important that it all be integrated."[61] Her time in the garden enabled her to experience her role as only one part of existence.

Perhaps the Purple Radish who most strongly rejected the religion and culture of her youth, Andrea brought negative associations with conservative Christianity to her experiences in the garden. Andrea's most vehement criticism of Christianity had to do with people who purported to be religious but whose Christianity was superficial, and she wanted to ensure that she did not replicate that hypocrisy in the garden. She aspired to align her entire life with the values that she and the other women expressed in the garden. Prior to joining the Purple Radishes, Andrea told me, she used to be obsessed with her hair and makeup, had a closet full of aerosol cans and harsh chemicals, and smoked cigarettes. Since joining the garden she had begun to reduce her reliance on beauty products and had quit smoking because those aspects of her life did not align with her new sense of self. "I thought that if anyone ever saw me smoke then I'd be the biggest hypocrite on the face of the planet. And worse than what people think of me, I'm living with a conflict in my values," she explained.[62] Understanding the garden as an expression of her spiritual self, Andrea strove to align her daily practices with the values she expressed in the garden. She and the other Unitarian gardeners combined their Unitarian principles with both positive and negative memories from the past as they experienced the garden as a space of enacting their spirituality.

The Purple Radish gardeners shaped their religious environmental project to meet their own particular needs. The five Unitarians in the group embraced religious language to explain their gardening rituals as extensions of their religious lives, referring to the seventh principle and also employing language about spirituality and creating better selves. Their time in the garden represented a response to a pressing environmental concern—their desire to participate in a sustainable food system—but the Purple Radishes came to see the garden as offering much more. They returned to their Wednesday night gardening ritual week after week not only to maintain a source of sustainable food but also to find an intimate community of friends that could help them express their best religious and environmental selves.

CONNECTING ENVIRONMENTALISM AND CIVIC IDENTITY

The Purple Radishes' religious environmental project related to their perceptions of themselves, as they indicated through comments about wanting to express better selves and align their practices and values. Another community involved with Faith in Place, the Bridgeview Mosque Foundation, worked on the ways that other people perceived them through their religious environmental work.[63] Located in the village of Bridgeview, thirteen miles southwest of Chicago's Loop, the Mosque Foundation served more than fifty thousand Muslims, predominately second- and third-generation Americans. Mosque leaders developed a set of environmental initiatives in close partnership with Faith in Place beginning in 2007. Prior to that year, Faith in Place had tried to cultivate a relationship through the Taqwa meat cooperative, but that relationship did not flourish until Aisha Tehrani took over the Muslim outreach position. Tehrani offered educational events at the mosque to inculcate concern about the environment, and she helped other Faith in Place staff members gain access to Mosque Foundation leaders. The mosque installed a solar water heating system in 2008, and Faith in Place declared it the first solar-powered mosque in the United States. Building on community enthusiasm around the solar panels, the mosque developed additional green initiatives in the following years, establishing a "green team," developing environmental programming for youth, introducing practices for a "green Ramadan," and incorporating eco-friendly measures in their renovations. The mosque's greening initiative received significant coverage in the local media, including stories on public radio and in the *Chicago Tribune,* and garnered the attention of then-lieutenant governor Patrick Quinn, who honored the mosque with an "environmental hero" award in 2008.[64]

The mosque's positive press for the solar panels stood in sharp contrast to negative media attention it had received regarding alleged ties to terrorism. The mosque's solar panels figured prominently into the community's response. In 2008, the *Wall Street Journal* published an article that characterized the Mosque Foundation as "fundamentalist-controlled."[65] Rany Jazayerli, a physician and journalist active in Chicago's Muslim community, drew on the mosque's environmental commitments to counter those accusations in a post on the political blog *FiveThirtyEight.* He wrote: "The consensus of the vast majority of Muslims in Chicago is that the mosque is not a fundamentalist anything, which is why it has such a large membership. Some of the mosque's more recent projects include donating a riverfront garden to the city of Chicago and becoming the first mosque in the country to run on solar power."[66] Jazayerli offered the mosque's greening projects as evidence in the informal cultural court. While the *Wall Street Journal* projected an image of the mosque as engaged in political activity that promoted violence, Jazayerli believed that the mosque's participation in environmentalism offered self-evident proof that its leaders could not be fundamentalists.

In a similar rhetorical move, Ibrahim Abdul-Matin, author of *Green Deen: What Islam Teaches about Protecting the Environment,* offered a related piece of advice at an event for Muslim youth that Faith in Place cosponsored in 2011: "When people talk about terrorism, change the subject to water."[67] Rather than allowing fears of terrorism to dominate discussions about Islam, Abdul-Matin advised, the youth should demonstrate they are just like other Americans and should share their concerns about major environmental issues that affect every human. Like Jazayerli, Abdul-Matin proposed that Muslims embrace environmental identities as a way to challenge discourse that linked Islam and terrorism. He instructed the Muslim youth to let people know they cared about major issues that affect every human—energy, food, water, and waste. Doing so would give them a positive way of relating to those who continued to perceive Muslims as un-American.[68]

The mosque leaders I interviewed also discussed the solar panels in the context of a positive civic identity, but that was not their primary explanation. When I asked about the mosque's environmental programming, the leaders first told me about passages from the Quran and Hadith. Dr. Tahir Haddad, the mosque's board president, explained that numerous Islamic sources supported caring for the earth. On the basis of the Quran, he told me, "We believe that we are the descendants of Adam and Eve, and one of our main responsibilities on earth is to protect earth, protect creation, and not to shed blood or to ruin the earth."[69] Haddad went on to offer numerous examples from Hadith that emphasized protecting trees, conserving water, and avoiding overconsumption.[70] Sheikh Eshaal Karimi, an imam at the mosque, also told me that environmental concern was central to his faith. "I just need to go and bring out the references in the Holy Quran and the tradition of the Prophet, and compare it with what is happening around us," he explained. "And you see it's matching in all aspects."[71] Aligning their viewpoints with constructive scholarship in the area of Islam and ecology, mosque leaders indicated that environmental values lay at the heart of Islam.[72] A desire to live out what they considered basic religious teachings offered one motivation for these men's religious environmental involvement.

When I asked about the origins of the mosque's greening initiative, however, conversations revealed an additional set of motivations. It is no surprise that Jazayerli offered the mosque's solar panels and lakefront garden as evidence to counter accusations of fundamentalism, because the mosque's leadership developed its green projects with their community's public image in mind. When I asked Haddad about the origins of the mosque greening initiative, he immediately spoke of the 9/11 terrorist attacks. Before 9/11, he told me, the mosque had prioritized issues typical of immigrant communities such as maintaining certain values and taking care of their youth. As they experienced prejudice in the aftermath of 9/11, however, they sought ways to expand their focus and demonstrate that they were "good neighbors" who cared about Muslims and non-Muslims alike. To that end, the mosque opened a food pantry to serve both Muslim and non-Muslim families in need, joined an Illinois coalition to work on comprehensive immigration reform, and developed an interfaith relationship with the Chicago archdiocese. In addition, the board discussed taking steps to protect the environment as another way for the Muslim community to "be more relevant, and take more of a leadership role in general affairs of the community at large, not only focused on what's happening within the congregation, but also focused on issues that touch every American."[73] Karimi offered a similar explanation for the origins of their green initiative as an effort to participate in projects important to many Americans: "When Dr. Haddad started as president, this idea came in reference to the movement that was taking place nationwide."[74] Both of these men talked about environmentalism in terms of participating in a movement that was important to a broader American community.

Complicating "Pure" Intentions

Toward the end of my interview with Haddad, he asked me what I planned to write about Muslims. I told him that I wanted to convey the complex motivations that different people brought to their environmental practices, so I found it interesting that he had immediately talked about 9/11 when I asked about the origins of the mosque's green programming. Having encountered a wide variety of motivations that contributed to green behavior in other settings, I was not surprised that he offered reasons that extended beyond concern for the earth. But Haddad wanted to assure me that his community's greening initiative was motivated by pure intentions. He paused for a moment as he thought about a way to clarify his remarks. "Maybe it started with that [being a good neighbor]," he finally responded, "but it's not like that anymore. I'm against showing people that we are 'good Americans,' and because of that we are taking care of the environment. This is not something that I believe in. I believe that unless you are genuine and you believe that this is your role in society, then it will not be successful."[75] Haddad explained to me that intentions are of utmost importance in Islam, and good deeds are nullified if not undertaken with positive intentions. If you give charity to the poor because you want people to say you are generous, or if you pray to God just to look pious, those actions do not count. Actions with impure intentions, Haddad told me, "may succeed for a certain period of time, but eventually you will not be successful. People will discover that you are not genuine, you are a hypocrite, if your intention is not right. And secondly, God will not accept your work, and that's the most important thing."[76]

Haddad wanted to assure me of his community's environmental authenticity: they were not simply using environmentalism for the instrumental purpose of generating a positive civic identity. But members of the Mosque Foundation engaged with religious environmentalism in particular ways that had to do with the interests and needs of their own community, as did every other community that engaged with the movement. From Jessica's desire to inculcate her environmental principles among her religious community and Jerry's embrace of environmentalism as a way to make the church more relevant, to Mrs. Weldon's initial involvement with Faith in Place as a result of a social connection and the mosque leaders' strategies for linking environmental activism with a positive civic identity, motivations for participating with Faith in Place were varied and complex. While concern for the planet or living out religious principles surely contributed to religious environmental commitments, these priorities intermingled with a host of other factors that varied among individuals and communities. Greater understanding of these various factors contributes greater depth to our understanding of the messiness of religious environmentalism on the ground.

4

Food and Environment at an African American Church

"I'd like to offer a kudos to my nephew, who was just honored as student of the month at his high school," said Veronica Kyle during a Faith in Place staff meeting. Since there are so many negative accounts of black teens in the news, she explained, she always enjoyed sharing positive stories. "My nephew was going down a bad path, but they put him in a high school with no girls, and now he's doing a lot better."[1]

Although Kyle's announcement had no clear connection to religion, the environment, or Faith in Place, it was indicative of an underlying motivation that she brought to her environmental work. For Kyle environmentalism certainly had to do with protecting the planet for current and future generations. But just as importantly she envisioned environmentalism as a movement that could bring respectability and opportunities to African Americans, and it was that vision that she transmitted at Faith in Place. Just as Kyle wanted to share positive news about her nephew at the staff meeting, she hoped that African American involvement with environmental projects could lead to more positive stories and could counter negative stereotypes associated with her community. Throughout my fieldwork I saw other Faith in Place leaders endeavor to diversify their coalition by distancing their environmental work from associations with elitism, but it was precisely those associations of environmentalism with middle-class status that Kyle emphasized in her work among African Americans.

In the previous chapter I discussed various pathways that led individuals to Faith in Place and analyzed the complex factors that motivated some of its supporters. I presented two processes that influence social movements research, identity seeking and identity appropriation, and discussed the Purple Radish gardeners in the context of the identity-seeking model. While the Unitarian women understood the garden in relation to their own self-perceptions, I demonstrated, leaders of the Bridgeview Mosque Foundation highlighted their environmental projects as they sought to improve the ways they were perceived by others.

This chapter builds on those themes as I examine Veronica Kyle's efforts to involve African Americans in her work at Faith in Place. Kyle employed the identity appropriation model, making use of her United Church of Christ (UCC) social network to attract individuals who might not otherwise relate to environmentalism.[2] In addition to helping African Americans adapt their identities to align with the environmental movement, however, Kyle sought to adapt images of environmentalism to better accord with African Americans' identities. In the process she offered a set of motivations she thought would inspire African Americans to become involved with environmental projects.

In the present chapter a Bible study on food and faith that Kyle facilitated on Chicago's south side places in sharp relief the process by which Faith in Place convinced African Americans to "go green." Taking place just over a year after Kyle joined the staff, the Bible study was one of her first sustained recruitment efforts, and through the group she developed her approach for attracting others. Religious environmentalism would suggest that the Bible and Christian tradition offer sufficient support for an ethic of earth stewardship—all religions inherently are green, so environmental concern ought to develop naturally from a correct reading of the Bible and understanding of tradition. The women in this chapter did encounter environmentalism in a Christian setting. Yet rather than conforming to the norms of religious environmental ideology that developed primarily through the work of white scholars and activists, Kyle helped the women cultivate an awareness of and language about the environment through a distinctive focus on the history and current circumstances of African Americans. At the same time she relied on a monolithic image of the white people one might expect to find in environmental circles—affluent, liberal "tree huggers" who shopped at Whole Foods—as a totalizing representation of whiteness and the environmental movement. Directly responding to that image of mainstream environmentalism, Kyle helped the women cultivate a self-consciously black environmentalism that was shaped by essentialized visions of both blackness and whiteness.

CROSSING THE "ECO-DIVIDE" WITH FOOD

Until the early twenty-first century, African Americans were not widely involved in the environmental movement, for a number of reasons. One of these was a sense of alienation from what one environmental leader has described as the "John Muir mythology" that separates nature from human activity.[3] Environmental historian Mark Stoll points out that environmental and African American leaders have discussed this problem for decades, yet "American environmental activism [has] narrowed the gap between environmentalist and African American concerns very little, if at all."[4] This gap is all the more ironic, Stoll suggests, because "environmentalists in general tend to be among the most broadminded, well-meaning, politically progressive white people. The lack of people of color in the environmental movement has been a point of embarrassment to them since the 1960s."[5] The one place minority communities have received widespread attention is in the context of environmental racism and justice. While the leaders and most participants at mainstream environmental organizations are white, environmental justice campaigns focus on minorities, and especially African American communities, as the most immediate victims of environmental problems.[6]

Faith in Place shared other organizations' challenges of racial diversification for years, but with the addition of Kyle's position in 2008, Faith in Place's coalition shifted dramatically. Staff members and interns had previously tried to recruit south-side congregations by talking to ministers about environmental issues and distributing free energy-efficient lightbulbs, but that approach proved ineffective. When Kyle joined the staff she thought about cultural barriers that might prevent her community from becoming involved with Faith in Place and determined she would have to develop a different approach. As she later explained it, "When I first arrived at Faith in Place I told Clare [Butterfield], I can't talk about solar panels. I needed to talk about something more relevant, like health and green jobs. But now we're talking about solar panels."[7]

Kyle implemented Faith in Place's method of starting with an issue the targeted community cared about and then addressing that issue in a way that also aligned with Faith in Place's environmental goals. She wanted to avoid the tendency of talking about African Americans only as victims of environmental devastation and instead strove to develop active environmental advocates within her community. She often pointed out that African Americans were middle class too and emphasized that they needed to think about their unsustainable habits just as much as white people.

To inculcate change she decided to begin with a focus on food and health, issues of great concern among African Americans she encountered, by organizing a Bible study on food, faith, and the environment. Following a curriculum titled *Just Eating? Practicing Our Faith at the Table,* the group would discuss units on health, hunger, the environment, and creating community.[8] The curriculum's central theme, based on the wordplay of the title, was that meals do not *just* involve eating. Instead, every meal contributes to or detracts from justice in the world. Participants were encouraged to eat more justly because eating entails not *just* a meal but a central expression of one's values. According to the book's introduction, the curriculum "use[s] the Christian practice of the Eucharist as [a] starting point [to] explore what it means to eat well in relationship to our own bodies, other people, and the earth."[9] Starting with a focus on one's own health, the curriculum gradually guides participants to expand their concerns to include the people who produce their food and the environmental implications of their decisions about what to eat. Each unit includes Bible passages and commentary, healthy eating tips, contemporary examples of people embodying the Bible study's ideals, and "faith in action" steps that help participants enact each week's values.

While Kyle appreciated the Bible study's approach of introducing environmental concerns through conversations about food and faith, she thought the book's images, stories, and cuisines privileged white experiences and would not be appealing to African Americans. For that reason she established the Bible study as a focus group and editorial team that would develop an "Afrocentric" version of the curriculum.[10] As a philosophical concept Afrocentrism refers to a 1980s intellectual movement to analyze information from a "black perspective," but Kyle employed the term in the much broader sense described by historian Wilson Jeremiah Moses, simply as "the belief that the African ancestry of black peoples, regardless of where they live, is an inescapable element of their various identities—imposed both from within and from without their own communities."[11] Throughout the Bible study Kyle encouraged the women to connect environmental practices to their own racial identities, offering examples of how sustainable behaviors grow directly from African culture and African American history. Her efforts were supported by Anita Walters, a recent seminary graduate in her late twenties who was interested in the environment and organic farming.

Faith in Place hired Walters to help Kyle lead the Bible study and rewrite the curriculum to reflect the input of the group.

The Bible study was organized at a UCC church on Chicago's south side and drew participants from a consortium of African American UCC congregations. Eight women from three churches participated regularly, while two of their husbands, the church's male pastor, and a few other women attended periodically. All participants and leaders were African Americans. All but one were college graduates, and several held advanced degrees.[12] The timing of the group, which met at 1:00 p.m. on Thursdays, catered mainly to retirees, although a couple of younger women had flexible schedules and managed to attend most of the meetings. I attended five of the seven sessions and conducted follow-up interviews with half of the participants one year later. I also joined meetings between Kyle and Walters as they developed an Afrocentric edition of the curriculum, and I reviewed a draft of their manuscript.

Although the *Just Eating* curriculum was designed to connect eating with Christian tradition, practices, and rituals, during the Bible study sessions that I attended we spent very little time discussing the Bible or even Christianity. Weekly sessions began with a *lectio divina* during which we read a Bible passage several times, then commented on what the passage meant in our own lives. But after those first few minutes, conversations rarely returned to ideas about the Bible or Christianity, and in the final few weeks we skipped the *lectio divina* entirely. We followed the book's instructions on eating shared meals, including a healthy food makeover meal, a comfort food potluck, and a hearty communion meal, but rarely discussed any of the other Bible passages referenced in the book. Instead, we diverged from the curriculum in order to discuss specific issues as they related to African American history and culture.

CULTIVATING BLACK ENVIRONMENTALISM

During the first meeting the women shared their reasons for participating in the group. One woman mentioned that she saw this Bible study as an extension of a diabetes and obesity workshop she had attended at church, while another expressed concern that a black-owned grocery store in her neighborhood was moving to the more affluent area of Hyde Park. Other reasons that came up included diabetes prevention, feeding the Third World, and eating biblically. In follow-up interviews two women indicated they had joined the group largely because of personal invitations from Kyle, whom one described as "a good salesman."[13] Aside from the mention of the black-owned grocery store, which points to concerns about food access, none of their reasons directly pertained to standard environmental issues such as climate change, conservation, or pollution. *or what get attn*

While comments during the opening session indicated that the women brought a diverse set of motivations to their involvement with the group, Kyle quickly shaped the conversation to prioritize the concerns that drove her work at Faith in Place: a distinct racial consciousness focusing on the overwhelming absence of African Americans from the environmental movement. "We're here because Faith in Place has been part of the *Just Eating* program for years," Kyle professed to the group, "but do the words and images speak to the African American community? No!"[14] Kyle asked participants to help her revise the curriculum so it would reflect "who we are as a people" through considerations of "ideal meals" such as collard greens, macaroni, and grits; issues that pertain to justice in African American neighborhoods; and cultural traditions such as "mother care" that might contribute to an ethic of protecting the earth. Most importantly, she expressed, the women would make history as the *time* first exclusively African American group to participate in this Bible study. By becoming experts in environmental issues, she promised, participants would become "mini-environmental celebrities" and would receive invitations to speak to audiences across the city.

Having spent years feeling like the lone black woman in an overwhelmingly white environmental movement, Kyle's sense of urgency for diversifying American environmentalism weighed heavily on her mind. Bible study participants, on the other hand, had not been involved in the mainstream environmental movement and did not share Kyle's sense of isolation. One participant told me privately that she "gave the movement no color, because environmentalism has always been around," and none of the other participants expressed any particular sense that environmentalism was connected to their racial identities.[15] As the weeks progressed, however, they increasingly followed Kyle's lead and replicated her language about the significance of African American involvement in the environmental movement. Jayla, one of the group's most enthusiastic participants, had previously learned about environmental issues through a college course but had never considered the disproportionate availability of that information in minority communities. Motivated by Kyle's approach during the Bible study, she told me, she "channeled Veronica" as she helped develop a green team ministry at her own church, frequently pointing out "the historic lack of information about environmentalism in the black community."[16]

As Kyle encouraged the Bible study women to become "mini-environmental celebrities" by embracing a movement that had not attracted many African Americans, she intended to overcome twenty-first-century stereotypes among liberal white communities that assumed most African Americans were impoverished, plagued by violence, poorly educated, and too overwhelmed with everyday problems to care about the environment.[17] She simultaneously offered a challenge to mainstream environmentalists to interrogate cultural practices that made their movement unwelcoming to minorities. Kyle's work with the Bible study, and more broadly her work at Faith in Place, was driven by a sense of racial pride and duty as she strove to bring African Americans the opportunities and resources she suggested were widely available to white people. She was very explicit about that goal, having expressed to Faith in Place's board of directors that she was committed to "building a generation of foot soldiers. I'm not apologetic about the fact that I'm doing this for my community. I work for my community."[18]

Following Kyle's lead, other participants expressed desires to work on behalf of all African Americans as well. The group discussed the importance of bringing both health and positive opportunities to their community, supporting black entrepreneurial efforts, and speaking out on behalf of all African Americans. Reverend Jones, a UCC minister who occasionally participated in the group, presented the issue in stark terms: "How can we stop contributing to the murder of our own people by the way we feed them?" he asked during the first session. Jones also brought up the issue of outsiders' negative perspectives of the black community as a whole. Describing his church's involvement in a city program to provide meals for senior citizens, he told the group, "I learned that the meals' nutrients were terrible. They had way too much salt and sugar. One single meal had the suggested daily intake of salt for two days, all within one serving." But when he called the city to complain, Jones recalled, "They said *your people* wouldn't eat it if we didn't put all that in there."[19]

Even as Kyle embraced environmentalism as a means to defy white stereotypes of African Americans as impoverished and in need of their help, ideas about aiding the black underclass motivated the Bible study women's work. The women themselves had achieved middle-class status, but many came from working-class backgrounds, lived in close proximity to poor neighbors, and had family members who were not middle class.[20] As a homework assignment Kyle asked participants to drive through different neighborhoods and examine the various food options available for different communities. That assignment proved to be quite meaningful for Jayla, who reflected, "I've always been accustomed to the areas we've lived in, where we've always had full-service grocery stores or something that provides fresh produce that's reasonably priced." After reading the *Just Eating* book and having conversations about food deserts, however, she began to recognize the issues that other people faced. "It's not until someone presents the information to you that you're really aware. It's like, you lived in that world, but you never really saw it."[21] By focusing conversations on issues of access to food and information, Kyle led the women to understand themselves as working on behalf of the entire race, most often discussing the problems of African Americans as the problems of the poor. Even though the women already maintained relatively healthy diets, they expressed concern about their neighbors who did not. None of the women were eligible for food assistance programs, but they were thrilled to learn about local efforts making it possible for farmers' markets to accept Link cards (food stamps) and planned to share this information with their neighbors.

Despite the women's connections with and concerns about African Americans across boundaries of class, the way they framed their community's problems and the best approach for addressing them inevitably was shaped by their own middle-class experiences. The women acknowledged that purchasing food at farmers' markets was more expensive than relying on conventional or discount grocery stores, but they believed that "just" eating practices were available to everyone. One participant suggested that poor people could shop at farmers' markets if they were conscientious about how they used their food. "It costs more," she explained, "but because it costs more, we buy, eat, and waste less."[22] In their excitement about informing their neighbors that the local farmers' market accepted Link cards the women did not discuss other potential barriers such as the market's limited hours (open only on Thursday mornings) and the time, knowledge, and skills required to prepare fresh, local produce.

DISHING OUT HEALTH AND SOUL

The Bible study participants' path to "environmental conversion" began with a discussion of food and health in their communities. As the weeks progressed, Kyle and Walters would direct the group's attention to environmental topics, but they began by talking about an issue that participants had already considered: the challenges of introducing healthy eating habits in their community. Expanding on Rev. Jones's concerns about the poor nutritional content of city-provided meals, the women anticipated enormous challenges in trying to convince fellow parishioners to change what they ate and served to each other, pointing to complex connections between dietary preferences (especially for soul food) and African American identity. Walters talked about ways that church mothers used soul food to nurture their community, such as "the cultural practice of cooking foods like fried chicken, or gumbo with a million pounds of butter, or fried green tomatoes."[23] She sighed longingly as she imagined the taste of those foods on her tongue, then continued:

> So there's that cultural practice of food is the way I say I love you, and if I don't love you I'll give you bad food, and if I do love you I'll give you good, filling comforty type foods, like macaroni and cheese. You have these women who come to church and bring food, and it's their way of saying I care, and I'm part of this community, and also that's their identity in this community, as someone who brings good food. And how do you go to them and say, you know, your food is kind of killing the congregation?[24]

The concept of soul food developed along with soul music as part of Black Power ideology in the early 1960s, but it described a type of "down-home" cooking, traditionally food for the poor, that featured foods traditionally grown in Africa and had already been associated with African Americans for generations. In the early twentieth century members of the black bourgeoisie rejected the cuisine as they sought to counter primitivist portrayals of their culture, and soul food's significance remained contentious throughout the Black Power era.[25] While some Black Power leaders rejected soul food for generating complacency and representing "Massa's leftovers," others upheld down-home cooking as central to their heritage, celebrating hopping John, hush puppies, and hoecake as characteristically black cuisine.[26] Father Divine, a charismatic preacher who attracted a large following of poor and middle-class African Americans in the first half of the twentieth century, was known for feeding bountiful meals of down-home cooking to his followers. The meals resulted in significant weight gain for many of his formerly impoverished disciples, and for them it symbolized, according to R. Marie Griffith, "victory over poverty" and "the sheer wealth and multiplicity of nutriment available to them everyday."[27] Although this topic did not come up during Bible study sessions, Kyle and Walters pointed to similar issues as they worked on editing the Afrocentric version of *Just Eating*. Recognizing that being slender is not necessarily a goal for African American women, they proposed that the Afrocentric edition should talk simply about health, not weight.[28]

Despite soul food's contentious history among different groups of African Americans, Griffith concludes, "The mainstream black Christian denominations [have] settled themselves squarely on the side of soul food, an expression of black pride."[29] That conclusion seemed to play out during the Bible study, as participants discussed the importance of maintaining a tradition of soul food even though that cuisine tended to be fattening and contributed to poor community health. One response to this challenge was to rethink what was meant by "soul." "When I first came into the curriculum I thought, man, no more black food!" Walters told me,

> But it's actually been identifying and reclaiming certain foods in my tradition, like okra and greens. There's more soul in the seasonings and the beans and the cornbread and the vegetarian stuff. And there's more celebratory soul in the chicken, and the hams, and the neck bones. I mean neck bones; you burn more calories trying to get the freaking meat off! So just recognizing that there's tons of good soul in vegetables, and trying to regain that part of my tradition has been a little difficult.[30]

Some of the women followed Walters's conciliatory approach, arguing that dishes can be made healthier by tweaking the recipes and that a lot of traditional food already is nutritious. Mrs. Harris pointed out that healthy food "is part of our culture too. Not just fried chicken and ham. Healthy stuff from the garden."[31]

Kyle tended to discuss soul food as an expression of black pride, defending the traditional cuisine and suggesting that numerous factors besides diet have contributed to poor health in the African American community. "I had an eighty-year-old great aunt tell me once, Honey, it's not the fried chicken. It's the television," Kyle recounted. "The lifestyle we've adopted doesn't fit this kind of food, and there's the conflict. Fried corn opposed to boiled corn, fried chicken opposed to baked or grilled, but then we sit down, where they worked very, very hard. I mean the slaves worked from sunup to sundown and all in between. And the portions were incredibly smaller."[32] Mrs. Kinkaid agreed, saying, "Our ancestors may have eaten fried tomatoes, but they didn't eat all the other junk."[33]

While the women could have avoided the issue entirely by following the healthy recipes suggested in the *Just Eating* book, they expressed concern that those recipes were part of a cuisine that African Americans did not typically eat. After following the book's instructions for a

Healthy Foods Banquet that included items such as couscous and spinach salad, participants proposed that the Afrocentric version should instead suggest a "Soul Food Makeover Meal," in which participants would "change a favorite/traditional soul food dish into a more nutritious, and thus more soulful, food."

Conversations during the Bible study suggested that soul food was quite important for the women, but during follow-up interviews several of the women revealed to me that they did not personally care for the cuisine. Mrs. Weldon, a retired social worker in her late seventies, explained:

> My mother was born and raised in the South, but the South wasn't in her. So we didn't eat a lot of fried food. And I think that because she did a lot of cooking for other people, white people, who didn't eat a lot of fried food, she learned to cook it. We ate soul food, we ate beans and greens and all that kind of stuff, but she didn't fry it. So that wasn't new to me.[34]

Jayla, who at age thirty-seven was one of the youngest members of the group, similarly told me that she rarely ate food associated with "soul." She explained that her husband had been learning healthy cooking techniques from the Food Channel for several years and that her family's dietary practices diverged significantly from the way she had eaten as a child. Other women said they already ate quite healthily and rarely consumed soul food because they either had diabetes themselves or lived with someone who did.

The women's ambivalence when it came to soul food underscores the many important functions of food beyond simply providing nutrition. Etta Madden and Martha Finch suggest that food can function "*symbolically,* as a means for representing and communicating group values; [and] *functionally,* as a primary factor in the construction of bonds within and boundaries around a community and as a means of material and ideological negotiations with the outside world."[35] Even though several of the Bible study women did not personally care about soul food, it was clear that soul food held symbolic value, contributing an important part of their racial consciousness as a symbolic representation of African Americans as a group. Preparing, serving, and even discussing soul food were expressions of caring and love and functioned to unite the women with fellow African Americans.

Conversely, the women discussed, mainstream environmentalism embeds a different type of ideal cuisine that functions to exclude African Americans: vegetarianism. Reduced meat consumption often is associated with a more sustainable diet, and the *Just Eating* book encourages participants to replace some meat with alternative sources of protein. Some of the women were open to this idea, and one often brought up the example of her vegan daughter. Yet Kyle tended to steer conversations away from this possibility, tacitly equating vegetarianism with characteristically "white" cuisine, as though reducing meat consumption were a simple task for white families. Most participants agreed that vegetarian meals would not go over well in their homes. Kyle had been vegan for several years when her children were young, but her extended family had a difficult time accepting her choices. She recounted, "Ultimately, you don't win with grandmothers and culture. Because you just have so many people, and also, let's just face it, it just tastes good. There's nothing like good ol' potato salad and fried chicken at a picnic. So if you wanna eat your tofu burger, they're like, 'Go ahead! We're eating this!'"[36]

Although vegetarianism is not a dominant strain in African American culture and history, there are historical precedents for it among African Americans. Some within the Black Power movement embraced Elijah Muhammad's insistence on purity and restraint in dietary practices to the point of becoming vegetarian, and members of the Black Hebrews embrace a vegan diet.[37] Participants in the Philadelphia-based black liberation movement MOVE also maintain diets that are mostly raw and vegetarian.[38] But instead of drawing from those particular examples, Kyle relied on idealized images of "the previous generations" and their agricultural past as models for living sustainably in the present. When Walters introduced the concept of community-supported agriculture (CSA), in which individuals purchase a share in a farm, Kyle likened the system to her own childhood memories: "We used to have a truck farmer come by the house. He had a wagon pulled by a mule, and he sold stuff by the bushel. Our parents would get so excited about green tomatoes; they'd fry and eat them right away—fried green tomatoes and shuck beans."[39] Whether or not soul food was important to different individuals, continuity with their ancestors and African American history certainly was. As participants became more familiar with present-day environmental practices, Kyle helped them connect those practices to the lives of their ancestors, or how things were done "back in the day."

Bible study conversations about food and health, issues that long had concerned the women, initiated a process of thinking about the health of the environment, an issue that had not previously commanded their attention. The *Just Eating* curriculum offered a type of healthy, sustainable "environmental" cuisine that its white authors did not likely recognize as conveying any particular cultural symbolism, but when it was presented to a black audience the food's cultural markers became clear. Environmentalism might bring to mind crunchy-granola types who eat tofu and shop at Whole Foods, but for the Bible study women this vision would not work. It was important to them that black environmentalism reflect black culture and that sustainable food retain a place for "soul."

SUSTAINABILITY IN AFRICAN AMERICAN HISTORY

As the Bible study progressed, conversations shifted from health to broader discussions about food and sustainability. The *Just Eating* unit on food and the environment asks participants to think about the Christian virtues of hope, humility, loving your neighbor, and intercession as they relate to the planet. It encourages practicing hope by caring for the planet, humility by recognizing that humans are utterly dependent on a "web of relationships" including animals and ecosystems, and loving one's neighbor by purchasing fair trade items. The discussion of intercession asks participants to think of the planet as they would a sick friend and to offer "prayerful attention" to muddy rivers, monocultures, and missing farms.[40]

Just as the Bible study women thought about the importance of inflecting sustainable eating habits with elements of African American culture, they discussed the challenges of conveying standard ideas about sustainability and the importance of establishing environmentalism's relevance within their own communities. First and foremost, participants discussed the history of slavery in the United States. Whereas educated young white people were drawn to the resurgent organic farming movement, the group discussed, this was not an appealing goal among African American communities because farming immediately brought slavery to mind. As Walters recounted, "I was looking through pictures of black farmers, and [my friend] said, 'Are these pictures of slaves?' And I said, 'No, these are farmers, in the twenty-first century!' So that association of black people out in the sun working fields, those are obviously pictures of slaves."[41] For some of the elders in the group, the disdain was even more intimate because they had experienced sharecropping themselves as children. Like many children of farmers, they wanted to escape from the farm to the city as quickly as possible. Mrs. Scott shared her visceral childhood memories of the farm and said, "I don't often eat blueberries because I had to pick them. I have a bad association with them."[42] Likewise, Mrs. Kinkaid, a church deacon in her early sixties, shared memories of backbreaking summers spent on her grand-parents' farm in northeast Texas. One summer, she recalled,

> I promised myself that if I never saw a pea again I wouldn't care. Because you picked your food you were going to eat every day. And not only did you pick it, you sat there shucking those peas. And my sister and I made up a song. "I'm sick of peas, peas, peas, I'm sick of peas. I don't care if ever again in life I see a pea, I'm sick of peas."[43]

Conversations about the ambivalence of African Americans toward the land developed into discussions about their ambivalence toward environmentalism more broadly. The women pointed out that the most publicized environmental campaigns had focused on issues that did not immediately concern African American communities. Walters recalled, "I grew up in the nineties, when they were all about saving the whales, and raising all this money to save the whales. And I'm sitting here like, there's people who are hungry, we can't go to the doctor. So there's that kind of like, 'rrrrr' around all this energy and care being given for whales and not for babies."[44] She suggested that environmental issues were relatively new to most of the Bible study participants as well, explaining,

> I feel like there is a strong narrative about food and health in the black community, but not about food and the environment. Not environmental practice, period. I don't feel like, in the communities I've been in, that's a story that's been told, or a story that's been held up. When I see black people in environmental movements, it's kind of anomalous. It's like, "Hi!" And then we go back to our particular groups.[45]

Yet Kyle changed the discourse to help the participants understand how environmental concerns can develop organically from black culture. Having thought not only about their own health but also about the relationship between their eating habits and the health of other people, participants were prepared to expand their concern and think about the effect of their food choices on the earth. They had language to think about these issues in relation to health, justice, and the African American community as well. For example, Kyle encouraged participants to purchase fair trade coffee, which is better for farmers and for the environment, because "we've been exploited and we don't want to exploit others."[46]

Through these discussions the women came to realize that they actually had positive memories of working the land, but these were not the types of stories often shared in their communities. Despite her negative memories of peas, Mrs. Kinkaid affectionately recalled other experiences on her grandparents' farm: "Our favorite thing was when Big Mama would take us into her personal garden where she grew watermelons and peas and all kinds of stuff. And you'd get a watermelon and just sit there and break it open on the ground and stick your face in it. We enjoyed that."[47] Mrs. Scott, a retired nurse, fondly recollected her childhood growing up on a farm. "I have memories of my family. We used to miss school to pick. But we were never hungry. We canned everything, even meat."[48] Walters was removed from her family's farming history by two generations—her great-grandfather was a sharecropper and her grandmother loved to garden—but she remembered that her grandmother "had this real love affair with the soil, and just growing things and watching things grow. She had this bathtub in her backyard, and she'd grow roses in it. They were the best roses on the block."[49] The women seemed to enjoy sharing their stories with each other. Smiling at Mrs. Kinkaid's recollections about her grandmother's farm, Mrs. Scott exclaimed, "I knew there was a reason I liked you, farm girl!"[50]

While discussing their positive memories of working the land, participants considered reasons why these types of stories were not held up in their families and communities. Their grueling memories of farming life offered potent reminders that farming can be arduous and boring work, giving the lie to romanticism about organic farming and back-to-the-land movements. The elders in the group understood why their children and grandchildren would not want to embrace a farming life and generally agreed that parents in their community wanted to see their children progress to careers away from the land. As the youngest member of the group, Walters had inherited those expectations from her own parents. "I didn't know that my grandmother grew all their food until my dad told me recently," she realized. "We just never talked about it. It was just something that wasn't that valuable. It was more like, wanting to hear about an uncle who went to college. They wanted to give us a picture of what they wanted us to do, like you can go do these things."[51] Others talked about an implicit hierarchy that privileges office work and education over agriculture, not to mention the unspoken understanding that Walters pointed out: "You don't want to spend too much time in the sun because you don't want to get too dark."[52]

To counter these narratives, Walters emphasized the importance of "addressing the value of working the land, and also lifting up those metanarratives of black people in the soil who enjoyed it."[53] Other women explained how they were already trying to do that, passing on their memories through experiences for their children and grandchildren. Mrs. Kinkaid said that she had enjoyed planting flowers when she was growing up at an apartment complex in New Orleans and that when she moved to Chicago and had children she had also gardened with them and taken them to visit nearby farms. She explained:

> I like to play in the dirt in the summer. My skills at gardening are limited, but it was enough that we could make a little garden and get a lot of food all summer. We had a tomato plant at either end, maybe about four poles of green beans, mustard greens, and some celery. And when the baby saw the carrots come out of the ground, it was like we'd found gold. . . . That was a good experience for us, so we did it several summers in a row.[54]

These negotiations held up in their discussions of other environmental activities as well. Through the Bible study some participants came to identify activities they had always done as "environmental" even though they had never seen them that way and certainly had never though of themselves as environmentalists. Mrs. Weldon had recycled ever since curbside pickup had become available in her neighborhood, and Jayla had done vermicomposting in her house as part of a women's empowerment project. But in their minds they were just taking out the trash and earning money, not protecting the earth. Through conversations in the Bible study these women began to see their activities in a new light.

The women's environmental identities became much more concrete when they took a field trip to the Englewood Farmers' Market, a short drive from the church. Although several of the women were aware that this weekly market took place on the south side, none had ever considered attending. After attending the market as a group, however, the women discussed plans to return every week. Especially impressed by the presence of so many black farmers and entrepreneurs, Mrs. Weldon declared after the field trip, "To go and support one of our own, that felt *good!* It's not as easy as it is to go to the closest store, but it felt good."[55] For Mrs. Scott the experience was reminiscent of her childhood when she spent summers picking and canning tubs of green beans. Kyle built on Mrs. Scott's recollection. "Yeah, I remember you used to go into people's pantries, with beautiful jars marked with the date. Beets, green beans, peaches. We ate local all the time."[56]

As the women continued to reflect on the experience, Kyle steered the conversation to focus on connections between sustainable practices and supporting the black community. She told them about one of the vendors at the market, Growing Home, whose south-side urban farms

offered job training and transitional employment programs for individuals with histories of incarceration, substance abuse, and homeless-
ness. Marking the power of supporting such a program, Kyle recounted
that when she had purchased her vegetables from Growing Home's
stand that morning the saleswoman, a former incarceree, had not provided her with enough change. After an initial reaction of anger, Kyle
said, she took a moment to reflect and decided it was an honest mistake.
"I went to the market today to look at the face of Christ," she declared.
"What I realized looking at the face of that woman, I kept thinking
about all the faces of women being abused. . . . But even the beater is
someone's child. What happened to him?" Without directly bringing up
the issue of class status, Kyle's story connected a sustainable practice, in
this case shopping at the farmers' market, to a sacred opportunity to
empower the black underclass. Walters added that Growing Home
offered a CSA program and that the women in the group could support
it by becoming shareholders. "This is a consciousness issue for African
Americans in our community," Kyle piped in. "Some people go in it
together and buy a basket. It's like the truck farmer we used to have
come by the house, when they sold stuff by the bushel."

The following week Kyle asked the women to reflect on how the class
had affected them so far and how they might inspire similar changes for
future *Just Eating* participants. "Now I appreciate my friend in Calumet
City who grows her own vegetables and cooks them," Mrs. Harris
offered. Mrs. Kinkaid built on that response: "I've become aware of
where my food comes from, and problems that people have with food
issues. Food is connected to everyone else in the world. With the circumstances of being born here [in the United States] we have all this stuff, but
that's not the case for everyone." To convey their experiences to others,
the women discussed how the Afrocentric edition could help African
Americans reconnect with the land in positive ways. Many offered their
own family photographs of farming ancestors for use in the new book,
although these artifacts were hard to find because most portraits por-
trayed families in their Sunday best and not with their farming tools. By
sharing their photographs, participants wanted to express that farming
is something to celebrate. The women recognized that growing food was
an attractive possibility only to a few, but they wanted to encourage
community members to take advantage of emerging opportunities in
organic farming and the emerging green economy. In contrast to the
widespread idea that it is progress to get away from the land, the women
in the Bible study discussed ways that it could be empowering and joyful

for African Americans to grow their own food. A "faith in action" step they proposed for the Afrocentric edition encouraged participants to "take time this week to think about how the reality of slavery for our ancestors influences your relationship with and ideas about agriculture. . . . Reflect on stories from family, friends, and community about Black people enjoying the soil and agricultural work."[57]

GREEN IS WHERE IT'S AT

As she worked to help the women embrace environmental identities, Kyle drew upon a discourse of respectability and opportunity as she emphasized the vast resources available for those with environmental knowledge and skills. "Green is where it's at!" she frequently exclaimed, speaking about the "eco-divide" akin to the digital divide that had left African Americans behind in the last decade.[58] Describing this issue, Kyle recalled her lack of understanding back in the nineties when people had talked about sending e-mails and conducting research on the Internet. Participants recalled similar experiences of their own and agreed that when it came to the environment their community must not make the same mistake of missing out on knowledge essential for competing in the new economy. "We know why we got away from farming, like we didn't want to pick blueberries," Kyle said. "But with the new generation we have a chance to be farmers and great entrepreneurs. We know why the land became hostile to us, but we can't let people steal that from us." When Jayla's teenage son joined the group for a potluck, Kyle preached to him, "Green is the new IBM, the new Silicon Valley. If it doesn't have green in front of it, it's not good. Our young people can't afford not to be connected."[59]

As Kyle encouraged participants to become conversant with environmental concepts such as carbon footprints, climate change, and soil erosion—knowledge sets that she suggested were ingrained in white kids from an early age—she was encouraging them to become conversant in a language and way of being that signified membership in the middle class. In terms of quantifiable factors of success, environmental literacy provides a form of cultural capital, offering a set of soft skills that can affect success on the job market.[60] Acculturated into the dominant class, white youth (and here she used a specific segment of affluent white youth as representatives of all white youth) are exposed to environmental culture throughout daily life, facilitating their access to educational, financial, and occupational opportunities that rely on a base knowledge, awareness, and understanding of environmental issues. Without a base understanding of climate change, the need for energy conservation, and other environmental issues, Kyle worried, black youth would be not be able to access future opportunities in the emerging green economy. With the support of Faith in Place, Kyle brought a set of financial resources and provided experiences that could help African Americans seek out these kinds of opportunities on their own.

Communicating Black Environmentalism

Changing the thoughts and behaviors of African Americans was one element of Kyle's project, but equally significant was her aspiration to convey to white audiences that those changes had taken place. As I accompanied Kyle to numerous different sites across Chicago, I observed the fluidity of her language as she adapted her message to convey different ideas to different audiences. On the south side Kyle worked to instill environmental literacy and values among black participants and hoped that they in turn would introduce these changes to the others in their community. Her goal was for the African American community to "go green" and become knowledgeable about environmental issues and practices. Even though most of the African Americans she worked with already were middle class, she wanted them to engage in classed behaviors such as organic gardening and shopping at farmers' markets that would signify that status to others.

Outside the Bible study Kyle frequently updated Faith in Place's white participants on the expansive environmental work that was taking place on the south side. As she strove to help African Americans to "go green," Kyle simultaneously explained to white audiences that African Americans had always been "green." By conveying a sense of African Americans' widespread activism surrounding the very issues that concerned environmentalists on Chicago's north side and in its suburbs, Kyle defied monolithic images of the south side as a marginalized community where residents were solely victims of environmental problems and had too many of their own difficulties to care about the long-term health of the environment.

But in the process of defying those images, Kyle addressed her community's problems from her own classed position. Sociologists and political scientists have identified ways that social class shapes how individuals interpret the world. African American studies scholars have found that rising social class affects the ideological positions through which the black middle class understand and address collective social problems, and many have identified Afrocentrism as a distinctively middle-class approach.[61] According to sociologist Algernon Austin, Afrocentrism's goal "was to have black Americans function as respectable, middle-class Americans who also had African cultural identities."[62] That seems to align with Kyle's approach to developing a self-consciously black environmentalism, as she understood environmental involvement as a means for overcoming white stereotypes of black people as poor and oppressed. If respectable white middle-class Americans cared about the environment, respectable black middle-class Americans cared about the environment too, but for reasons growing from African and African American culture such as traditions of "mother care," celebrations of "ideal meals" of collard greens and grits, and remembrances of the African American history of slavery, sharecropping, and community gatherings around food. Dissatisfied with the tendency of mainstream environmentalism to privilege the experiences of white people, Kyle positioned herself as an authoritative leader who could best understand and advance the interests of the black community.

In her role as both "green teacher" for black audiences and "black cheerleader" for white audiences, Kyle occupied a liminal position. Belonging fully neither among the white power structures at Faith in Place nor among the African American communities she served, Kyle fulfilled sociologist Mary Pattillo's description of the black middle-woman, who "speaks at least two languages in order to translate [and] has two sets of credentials for legitimacy" that enable her to move back and forth between two different worlds.[63] As a middle-class woman who worked for an organization that was primarily white (although striving to become less so), Kyle had the status and respectability necessary to speak authoritatively to white audiences. She voiced concerns on behalf of African Americans at Faith in Place's staff and board meetings and in the office, pointing out ways that Faith in Place needed to change in order to be more welcoming to her community. And her status as a Faith in Place staff member resulted in numerous invitations from white audiences wanting to understand how to involve African Americans in their efforts. Yet Kyle was not fully at home in the white world that she inhabited in her daily life. When Faith in Place's white assistant director accepted a new job at a predominately black organization, Kyle told her she would know her coworkers had accepted her when they started referring to her as "girl." I asked Kyle when she knew she had been accepted at Faith in Place, and she said that for her it was about getting *language*

a voice and knowing that people were listening to her. But a clear hesitation in her response indicated to me that in her third year of working at Faith in Place she did not yet consider herself to be fully accepted.

While Kyle's education, middle-class status, and association with Faith in Place contributed to her legitimacy and relatability among white audiences, among black audiences she drew upon a different set of experiences: her family's working-class roots. Kyle's voice shifted into a different cadence as she addressed black audiences, and she frequently referenced her ancestors' stories of slavery and oppression and her own childhood in Altgeld Gardens, one of Chicago's most notorious public housing projects. Through these cues Kyle marked herself as "authentically black."[64] Her legitimacy as authentically black made it possible for her to convince others of a different way of being authentically black. Kyle's insistence that south-side people should behave in particular (sustainable) ways, eat in particular (healthy) ways, and speak in particular (environmentally literate) ways enforced a particular way of being a middle-class African American. In her position as a black middlewoman, Kyle was able to shape fellow African Americans' behaviors in particular ways and effectively convey her particular view of blackness among both black and white audiences.

LIFE AFTER *JUST EATING*

The last day of the Bible study included a comfort food potluck where people brought their favorite foods. While enjoying chicken gumbo, spaghetti and meatballs, hopping John, and Caprese salad, participants reflected on what they had learned through the Bible study and committed to continuing a particular practice. The women talked about being more mindful when they ate, purchasing fair trade coffee, helping their communities eat more healthily, and shopping at the farmers' market. As individuals shared their commitments, the group responded by chanting, "May God bless your offering with a rich and bountiful harvest."[65] Kyle also spoke about other opportunities through various organizations to become more involved in the environmental movement. She again encouraged participants to become "mini-environmental celebrities," underscoring the importance of African American presence at environmental events in order to demonstrate that this was their issue too.

For approximately half of the women, the end of the Bible study seemed to culminate any nascent environmental involvement, and they never

diversity in participation

again showed up at Faith in Place events. But for a solid core of the group the Bible study functioned as an important springboard that led to participation in other environmental activities, both with Faith in Place and through participants' own initiatives. As individuals, some of the women began to see themselves and their activities in a new light. For Mrs. Kinkaid

self-image

and Mrs. Weldon, conversations about pesticides and soil erosion had lasting influence. A year after the Bible study ended Mrs. Weldon told me about her preference for eating organic produce. She still qualified that her concerns were primarily related to her own health, but she recognized it was also related to the health of the planet. She explained, "I think about the stuff I'm putting in my body first, but the pesticides that go into the ground, that affects the planet. So it all rolls over into one."[66] Mrs. Kinkaid told me the Bible study helped her gain a respect for the land and a concern about soil erosion. "When you discover that the soil only has about one-third of the nutrients that it did even when I was a girl, I say, okay this isn't going to work," she explained. "So what can I do differently to help get at least something a little better for my family? I've got to nourish the soil that we have at home."[67] While Mrs. Kinkaid had always enjoyed playing in the dirt, appreciated trees and flowers, and even taught her children to pick up trash on the streets, she had not thought of those things as being within the realm of environmentalism until the Bible study helped her gain a broadened understanding of environmentalism that need not entail cultural associations with the white middle class.

wow

Jayla also began to see herself as an environmentalist. Prior to the Bible study, she said, "At one time I had recycled, and then I stopped. I still used a lot of paper and threw it in the regular garbage."[68] She had also recently taken a college environmental science course that had taught her a great deal about environmental problems plaguing the world, but it was not until the Bible study that she began to act. Jayla explained that the college course "didn't make me want to join any environmental groups or do anything hands on. By contrast, she said, the Bible study "showed me how to become involved and enabled with what I have right now, that I can change some of the things I'm doing, and it's immediately beneficial to others."[69]

These women tried to initiate changes at their churches as well. Jayla and Mrs. Weldon returned to their church and established a green team ministry. In the following year the green team set up a recycling center at their church, switched to CFLs, helped their church participate in a weatherization program, and started a community garden. They helped their entire congregation "go green" by including monthly bulletin inserts about environmental issues and encouraging members to participate in the church's recycling and gardening programs. Jayla took great initiative in advancing her own knowledge, participating in several city programs to educate environmental leaders. Mrs. Weldon traveled to Springfield with a group from Faith in Place to lobby for environmental legislation. Mrs. Kinkaid attended numerous Faith in Place workshops, worked to implement more "just" eating practices at her church, and helped her congregation start a garden as an outreach project to other community members.

Mrs. Kinkaid, Jayla, and Walters each expressed independently the importance of the Bible study for changing how they thought about their own relationships to environmentalism. All three gave concrete examples of changes in their lifestyles that had resulted from conversations during the Bible study, but they also explained how participating in the group provided a new context for understanding things they had always done. After describing her lifelong enjoyment of gardening, collecting cans to recycle, and "playing in the dirt," Mrs. Kinkaid told me that "the conversation [about the environment] has always been there, but we just didn't use those words."[70] Jayla told me that *Just Eating* "was like a jumping point. It made me more aware and made me look at faith and environmentalism in a new way, and how they're interrelated."[71] Although previously she had done vermicomposting in her kitchen, had purchased organic foods, and at different stages in her life had made an effort to recycle, "I never really thought about it as environmentalism. That's the strange thing."[72] From my conversations with Walters I learned that this shift in thinking was precisely her goal for the group, as she saw the Bible study as "kind of giving people a space to think about these things and to spend some time getting language around it. . . . That was definitely one our goals, to address that dichotomy that we put ourselves in, and to give permission to say, 'I like getting dirty, I like getting in the sun, I like being black in the summertime. That's one of my favorite things to do.'"[73] While the Bible study might not have resulted in significant changes in behavior or political consciousness, it did help participants learn to frame their concerns and their identities in ways that cohered with contemporary environmental thought.

For Kyle, the dedicated Bible study alumni also served as successful models that she could hold up for others. She invited the group to attend the next Faith in Place workshop as a *Just Eating* reunion, and she made sure to introduce these honored guests to the otherwise white audience at the beginning of the program. In subsequent years Kyle developed additional programming for African Americans, including summer gardening internships for youth, weatherization projects, and Monarchs, Migration, Birds and Me, a program designed to help African Americans understand their own life stories as connected to a broader ecological whole. Through these and related efforts, by 2014 African Americans accounted for 19 percent of Faith in Place's supporters.

Following her success with the Bible study women, Kyle continued her role as an environmental black middlewoman at Faith in Place and beyond. Although she had the power to make significant changes at Faith in Place, she faced greater challenges in her efforts to change the culture of the environmental movement more broadly. This became abundantly clear in a conflict over food at a national conference for religious environmental leaders that I attended with Kyle and Clare Butterfield in 2010. During the conference I watched as Kyle grew increasingly uncomfortable as one of only two African Americans among one hundred conference participants. She finally expressed her concerns when she sat down to a third day of meatless meals. "See, this is part of the problem," she lamented:

> If we're going to try to make this [environmental] movement more diverse, if we want to invite more people in, we need to think about things like this. Because if you had more black folks here to begin with, they wouldn't be here by now. They would have left the conference and gone out to look for some meat.[74]

Even though Kyle had been vegetarian herself at several points throughout her life, she saw the absence of meat at this conference as a significant cultural barrier that would exclude other African Americans. While the conference's vegetarian menu may have conveyed alignment with environmental values to most of the diners, to Kyle it represented something else: the exclusivity and cultural insensitivity embedded in a cuisine that catered to the preferences of the conference's affluent white participants.

Kyle's point seemed to be lost by the other people sitting at our table, but that moment exemplified her role at Faith in Place. Hired to conduct congregational outreach especially among African American communities, Kyle functioned as a cultural mediator, a black middlewoman working to bridge the divide between Faith in Place's black and white audiences. At Faith in Place she pointed out cultural barriers, such as food choices, that she saw as obstacles preventing African Americans

from developing a sense of full membership in the environmental movement. Through Kyle's influence Faith in Place shifted its major fund-
raising event, the Harvest Celebration, from a formal affair featuring
gourmet food prepared by locally renowned chefs to "a fried-chicken
and macaroni and cheese kind of night . . . with plenty of comfort food
and cheer to go around."[75] Kyle also endeavored to cultivate an image
of African Americans as respectable middle-class citizens, not as victims
in desperate need of white people's help. But even as she worked to challenge white stereotypes about her community, Kyle offered an essentialized blackness of her own, illustrated at the conference by her suggestion that black people would feel alienated without meat. She enforced
a normative view of blackness to the Bible study women as well, silencing any possibility of a black vegetarianism and privileging an idealized
agricultural past in which African Americans grew their own food and
built community solidarity by harvesting, canning, and purchasing vegetables from the truck farmer. Even as she worked to defy white stereotypes about African Americans as poor and oppressed, she rallied
members of the black middle class to advance environmental efforts in
order to improve the situations of the black working poor. In her leadership role at Faith in Place, Kyle's use of racial language was fluid as she
approached different situations and different audiences. While embracing environmental activism as part of a display of middle-class respectability, she also emphasized the past errors of the environmental movement as evidenced by the persistence of an "eco-divide."

Kyle's complexities

5

Finding Racial Diversity with Religious Pluralism

On a Sunday afternoon in October 2009, 150 friends and supporters of Faith in Place traveled from across the city and suburbs to arrive at Garfield Park Conservatory on the city's near-west side. Dressed for a party, Zen Buddhists, Hindus, Zoroastrians, Catholics, Protestants, and Jews arrived at a spacious banquet hall, filled with elegantly decorated tables amid the conservatory's green foliage. There, they checked in for Faith in Place's tenth annual Harvest Celebration benefit dinner, the organization's primary fund-raising event of the year. Many guests had paid the suggested donation of one hundred dollars, while some had paid significantly more. Others filled seats at tables purchased by their congregations or came at no cost as guests of Faith in Place.

As guests arrived, they sipped wine and mingled. Some perused the offerings at the silent auction—baskets of freshly baked cookies and breads; tickets to the theater, symphony, and opera; memberships to Chicago museums; gift certificates for bike tours, organic restaurants, massages, and yoga classes. The silent auction included an interfaith section that offered a stay at a Catholic retreat center, a meditation cushion, a membership to Chicago's Spertus Institute of Jewish Studies, a gift certificate to a Muslim bookstore, and an interfaith calendar that listed religious observances for fourteen religions.[1] Other guests found their assigned tables and waited for the festivities to begin.

In addition to the devoted supporters who attended the fund-raiser every fall, the crowd reflected new partnerships that Faith in Place had cultivated over the previous year. African American Protestants who were new to the organization filled two tables, providing visual representation of Veronica Kyle's successful outreach in their communities during her first full year at Faith in Place. Latino Catholic schoolchildren who had participated in the youth program shared another table with their teacher as honored guests, prepared to receive a Faith in Place "green award." Near them sat several members of a suburban Jewish Reform congregation who attended the event to support their rabbi as he also received a "green award." While Muslims had been a visible presence in previous years, in 2009 none attended, as Faith in Place no longer employed a Muslim-outreach coordinator to recruit them directly.

The Harvest Celebration was structured to create a welcoming environment for people of every faith. While benefit dinners often take place on Friday or Saturday nights, the Harvest Celebration was always scheduled on a Sunday to accommodate observant Jews who would be unable to travel during the Sabbath. The menu included vegetarian and meat options, prepared using local, sustainable ingredients, and featuring meat from the Taqwa Eco-Foods cooperative. Because Muslims avoid alcohol, past Harvest Celebrations had been alcohol-free. In 2009 the event's organizers decided to serve wine for the first time, persuaded by a consultant's fund-raising advice.

Just after 6:00 p.m., the evening's emcee announced the beginning of the program. After a brief welcome from Clare Butterfield, religious leaders and board members who represented several different religions— Reform Jewish, Lutheran, Hindu, African American Protestant, and Zoroastrian—gathered at the microphone. One by one, each offered a blessing from his or her faith tradition. Following that display of interfaith celebration, the meal was served and the party began.

The Harvest Celebration offered a public display of interfaith commitment to the earth. Staff members worked diligently to recruit a religiously diverse population for the annual event, offering personal invitations and bestowing "green awards" to attract constituencies that would not otherwise choose to attend. Yet this public image of interfaith cooperation contradicted the realities of Faith in Place's religious environmentalism in daily life. In contrast to the concerted efforts to display religious diversity at the Harvest Celebration, staff members spent most of their time the rest of the year working in single-faith settings such as congregations or denominational governing bodies. Most other Faith in Place events were attended primarily by Protestants.[2]

FIGURE 1. This image was on Faith in Place's website, with the caption "Dancing to Sikh Bhangra music at our annual Harvest Celebration." Photo courtesy of Faith in Place.

image

Why did Faith in Place organizers work so hard to display their interfaith constituency at the annual fund-raising event? What did they gain from being interfaith? In this chapter, I argue that Faith in Place's use of *thesis* "interfaith" discourse helped the organization build a racially and ethnically diverse coalition, while at the same time limiting the kinds of people willing to associate with the Faith in Place. By using the discourse of "interfaith," Faith in Place tapped into a resonant trope in American life—the valuing of religious diversity and religious differences—to talk about a subject with a much more difficult set of associations: race. In turn Faith in Place gained strategic benefits from the racial diversity within the organization.

*Race
+
Religion*

PLURALIST COMMITMENTS AT FAITH IN PLACE

Faith in Place's interfaith relationships were fundamental to the organization's image, a central feature observers would notice when they encountered the nonprofit. Written materials such as brochures, fund-raising appeals, and grant applications always began with a statement of the organization's wide-ranging partnerships: "Since 1999, Faith in Place has partnered with over 900 congregations in Illinois—Baha'i, Buddhist, Christian, Hindu, Jewish, Muslim, Sikh, Unitarian, and Zoroastrian." In sermons Butterfield said she worked "with hundreds of congregations *of all faiths* to connect the teachings of faith to sustainable environmental practices."[3] Faith in Place's website immediately conveyed its interfaith identity as well. Photographs of Latino youth digging in a garden, turban-wearing Sikhs dancing at the Harvest Celebration, and a veiled Muslim woman riding a tractor indicated the array of participants that one might encounter at Faith in Place. A selection of "stories from our partner congregations" featured the environmental work of Protestant, Jewish, and Muslim congregations who had partnered with Faith in Place, and the website included earth-themed passages from the scriptures of different world religions.[4] The composition of Faith in Place's board of directors especially suggested the organization's religious diversity, in 2011 including a Reform Jew, a Zen Buddhist priest, a member of the United Church of Christ, an Episcopalian, a Presbyterian, a Hindu, and a Zoroastrian. These seven board members' faith traditions were listed on the website along with their photographs and short biographies that highlighted their involvement in congregational life and environmental issues.

In contrast to Faith in Place's religiously diverse public image, however, the daily life of the organization offered a different story. In 2011 the staff included five Protestants—a Unitarian, a Mennonite, a Lutheran, and two UCC. One other staff member had been raised Catholic but identified with a more spiritual disposition. Staff members put great effort into recruiting a religiously diverse set of guests for the Harvest Celebration, but when I attended other Faith in Place events such as workshops, presentations, or policy meetings, the vast majority of participants were Protestant. Other attendees might include a couple of Catholics and Jews, and occasionally a Zen Buddhist, the Hindu board member, or Nazneen, the one Zoroastrian woman who was actively involved with Faith in Place. Meetings of the clergy group drew a similar array, including mostly liberal Protestants and especially Unitarians, some Catholic lay leaders, and very occasionally a Jew or Zen Buddhist. Seminary interns always were Christian—usually Protestant and occasionally Catholic.[5]

In terms of congregational partnerships, Faith in Place was overwhelmingly Protestant as well. Butterfield offered the pragmatic view that "we'll go anywhere there's energy," suggesting Faith in Place's resources were better spent supporting those already concerned about the environment rather than convincing skeptics that there was an environmental crisis. Yet the places where there was "energy," perhaps unsurprisingly, were among liberal Protestants. During the years I spent with Faith in Place, staff members led Bible studies, initiated gardening programs, held workshops, and offered individual consultations almost entirely at Protestant churches. A 2009 community workshop took place at a Jewish synagogue, but the rabbi was the only person from that congregation who attended the event. Congregational involvement often was initiated by individuals who had personal contact with representatives of Faith in Place, and the Protestant-heavy staff attracted a Protestant-heavy following. Staff members offered guest sermons at partner congregations, but again, because the staff members all were Protestant, these invitations came almost entirely from Protestant churches. By delivering their outreach efforts to places where they found "energy," Faith in Place leaders catered to audiences that were like themselves.

Staff members did not deny the organization's Protestant imbalance, but neither did they apologize for it. When a Clergy Café participant observed that the group was excessively Christian, Butterfield brushed off the concern and replied, "Yes, that represents the Chicago area, which is 94 percent Christian."[6] Butterfield frequently returned to that idea of building a "representative" population, suggesting Faith in Place's coalition should mirror the population of the region. Hanging in her office was an Illinois map that depicted religious affiliation by county. She would point to the map and suggest that since Illinois was overwhelmingly Protestant, it was reasonable for Faith in Place to be mostly Protestant as well. But actual measures of representativeness were obscure. At times Faith in Place leaders spoke about representation in terms of religion but then referred to racial and ethnic categories, as if those were all measures of the same thing. In terms of religious affiliation, staff members used "representation" to excuse the Protestant imbalance and sometimes to jokingly celebrate their religious diversity, pointing out that the two Zoroastrians involved with Faith in Place represented a significant proportion of the tiny Zoroastrian population in

Illinois. But they did not seem concerned that their interreligious coalition included little Catholic involvement in a metro region that was home to more than two million Catholics or that it featured no significant involvement among evangelical Christians. Butterfield considered the organization to have active Jewish involvement, and there was always a Jew on the board. Yet throughout my fieldwork I struggled to find Jews who identified with Faith in Place.

Butterfield's explanation that Faith in Place "will go anywhere there's energy" also overlooked the fact that Faith in Place strategically cultivated energy in particular communities where they wanted to forge partnerships, while paying little attention to communities that did not so readily advance the organization's strategic aims. Outreach staff members were hired and organizational programming was designed to recruit particular groups to Faith in Place. Muslim communities in Chicago were not especially interested in the environment until Faith in Place devised strategies to draw them in. African American congregations joined the organization only after Faith in Place hired Veronica Kyle to recruit them. As a small nonprofit with limited resources, Faith in Place leaders had to make choices about where to dedicate their time. Yet even as they suggested their coalition was influenced by many external factors beyond their control, the organization's religious culture, hiring practices, and strategic decisions strongly shaped the contours of their coalition.

ENFORCING NORMATIVE RELIGION

Among the major factors that attracted some participants to Faith in Place while repelling others was the organization's commitment to religious pluralism. That general value played a central role regardless of the extent of its actual implementation. For Paul, a white clinical psychologist in his midforties and a member of a suburban Methodist church, Faith in Place's commitment to religious diversity was "a huge draw." Paul volunteered extensively for Faith in Place in 2009, rearranging his work schedule to make room for a full day of volunteer work each week. He told me that he enjoyed spending time at Faith in Place because he disliked the narrow-minded outlook he perceived among fellow members of his church; as he explained, "It's important to be open to learning from other people's faiths and their experiences, which I won't get at my church." Furthermore, Paul elaborated, "It's easy to get caught up in believing your faith is the only faith and it's the right faith. And we can spend a lot of time and energy worrying about that . . . when there are bigger issues, such as the environment."[7]

Paul spoke passionately about the importance of Faith in Place's broad commitment to interfaith partnerships, but when I asked him to describe Faith in Place's pluralism in practice his responses became more vague. Having extolled the opportunity to learn from other people's faiths and experiences, he was hard-pressed to describe how that opportunity actually materialized at Faith in Place. Trying to recall an interreligious encounter, he finally offered an example of an interracial one: "I guess the little time I have spent with Veronica [Kyle], and understanding how African American churches may differ from the white church I'm in has been helpful." I asked Paul to elaborate on those differences and his response moved away from the church and instead conjured differing experiences of the environment based on race and class: "I think it's easier for white middle-class folks to think about polar bears than it is to think about underprivileged, underserved poor kids who often happen to be of color or another minority."[8]

Other Faith in Place participants expressed similarly positive yet vague ideas about Faith in Place's commitment to religious pluralism. Throughout interviews my interlocutors overwhelmingly affirmed that Faith in Place's many interfaith partnerships made the organization attractive, but few could recall any actual experiences of interfaith encounters. Instead they described learning about different religions from Faith in Place staff members and newsletters or by watching documentaries that Faith in Place recommended. One participant told me she knew that all religions support earth stewardship "because Clare [Butterfield] has done the research for me and she says it's true."[9]

In a national study of interfaith groups in the United States, Kate McCarthy suggests that community-based interfaith groups offer two basic rationales for their work: either they come together to achieve a common goal such as alleviating poverty or improving public education, or else coming together itself is the goal.[10] While Faith in Place ostensibly would support both of those rationales, their work was generally missing an essential element of each: the actual act of coming together. Instead participants seemed to rely on Faith in Place staff members to engage in interfaith encounters on their behalf, and they readily accepted the staff members' authoritative interpretations of every religion. When I asked interview subjects to describe what they had learned about other religions through Faith in Place, they invariably offered wide-ranging affirmations of the unity of all religions, such as "It has solidified my belief that we have more in common than we have at odds," and "It has raised my consciousness that this is an issue others have focused on." Anita Walters, who helped Kyle lead the *Just Eating* Bible study, recognized that Faith in Place's commitment to interreligious partnerships did not always materialize in practice, but she still indicated that its commitment to that value was significant:

> I'm a little suspicious of people who are like, the Jesus way. So yeah, [Faith in Place's commitment to religious pluralism] actually helped. I was like, okay, this is good. And it's not just like they say they're interfaith. They *are*. When you read their stuff and go to their events, even if it's predominately Christians there, there's an obvious invitation. Not just lip service, but people are invited and talked to, and there's follow-through.[11]

But in practice the "obvious invitation" that Anita perceived was distributed unevenly at Faith in Place. In some cases, Faith in Place avoided certain religious groups for strategic reasons, and in others its leaders unknowingly enacted subtle mechanisms of exclusion. At one point I asked Butterfield why Faith in Place had never hired a Jewish staff member or developed projects specifically targeting the Jewish community.[12] She responded that some communities did not need outreach projects specifically tailored to their needs because Chicago's "mainline" religious communities—"which consist of Catholics, mainline Protestants, and the liberal Jewish branches"—were easy allies for Faith in Place so that people from those groups began participating with the organization without requiring targeted outreach. Butterfield pointed out that Faith in Place had not directly targeted Unitarians or mainline Protestants either, explaining, "I speak those languages, so I've been the organizer for those communities."[13]

Equipped with her scholarly knowledge of Jewish customs and a Jewish text (although trained to interpret it through a Unitarian lens), Butterfield worked to welcome Jews, most notably by enforcing a restriction against holding Faith in Place events on Saturdays out of respect for the Jewish Sabbath. This was a measure that struck me as more symbolic than practical because I never found observant Jews at Faith in Place who strictly followed the Sabbath laws and would be unable to attend Saturday events. Yet Butterfield insisted on upholding the rule even when it presented challenges for those who actually were involved with Faith in Place. At one staff meeting Kyle discussed her plan to organize a gardening workshop at an African American church on a Saturday afternoon. Butterfield reminded her that Faith in Place did not host community-wide events on Saturdays and encouraged her to host the workshop on a Sunday instead. Kyle countered that Sundays were often quite busy at African American churches because services lasted for several hours, yet Butterfield held her ground, reminding Kyle of the importance of creating a welcoming environment for Jews. She suggested that instead of holding the workshop on a Saturday, Faith in Place could still schedule it for a Sunday afternoon but they would provide sandwiches to accommodate participants who would not have time to go home for lunch.

The weight Butterfield gave to perceived Jewish concerns even at the cost of creating an obstacle for African American church members was especially curious given the lack of significant Jewish involvement within the organization. Despite Faith in Place's efforts to include Jews through symbolic measures such as banning Saturday events, the organization embedded an underlying Protestant culture that was invisible to Faith in Place's Protestant leaders but patently evident to people who were not Protestant. One rabbi, whom Butterfield described to me as a "good friend" of Faith in Place, referred to the organization as "a nice Unitarian group." Appearing skeptical when I corrected him to say that Faith in Place was interfaith, the rabbi suggested that differences in cultural ethos separated Faith in Place from the Jewish community. He expressed an admiration for Faith in Place's environmental work and said, "I haven't heard any negatives about working with them or anything, but it's just a bit of difference culturally, nothing more than that."[14] As the conflict over scheduling the gardening workshop demonstrates, Faith in Place leaders engaged in a careful dance as they strove to create a welcoming environment for people of every faith. Commitment to a culture of pluralism mandated "respect" for observant Jews, so enacting measures that acknowledged their interests was important for Faith in Place's symbolic identity. It demonstrated to liberal Protestants such as Anita that Faith in Place offered an "obvious invitation" to communities of every faith, regardless of the extent to which the invitation was actually received.

Advancing its liberal Protestant ethos, Faith in Place's theology of religious pluralism was a second factor undermining its "obvious invitation," in this case creating a significant theological barrier that repelled those with exclusionary religious views. This was a barrier that Faith in Place had no intention of overcoming. Butterfield told me that she had approached conservative Christian groups in the early days of Faith in Place but that most of them had ignored her calls. Occasionally, people would ask her not to contact them for religious reasons. "I got one from a Missouri Synod congregation," she told me. "They were very polite, really kind, and in one case they were praying for me because they thought my religious view was mistaken because of the interfaith nature of the work."[15] Over the years, Faith in Place developed strong partnerships in some communities that did not initially respond to Butterfield's efforts, but conservative Christians generally remained uninvolved.

Faith in Place's success in communities that initially were underrepresented in the organization resulted from concerted efforts at appealing to those communities, but conservative Christians were never a targeted group. Faith in Place took no active measures to exclude them, and one summer Butterfield overlooked her preference for avoiding college-age interns in order to welcome an evangelical volunteer because "she could bring an interesting lens" to Faith in Place.[16] Nevertheless, Faith in Place's underlying pluralist theology was one of many factors that shaped the organization's liberal Protestant ethos, and that theological commitment led most conservative Christians to self-select out of Faith in Place.[17] While Faith in Place leaders adapted their message to meet the needs of different faith communities, the emphasis on interfaith cooperation was a core organizational value that was non-negotiable. Conservative Christians were welcome to join in Faith in Place's work, but they had to do so at the cost of muting their own theological differences.

Neopagans were another group that remained underrepresented at Faith in Place, but in their case Faith in Place's exclusionary practices were more direct. In the first year of my fieldwork I was surprised to observe Faith in Place's careful avoidance of Neopagans and other earth-based religious groups given that those groups seemed like natural allies because of their religiously grounded understandings of environmental issues. Neopaganism emerged along with the New Age religion from the counterculture of the 1960s, shaped by social movements such as feminism, environmentalism, and the sexual revolution. It has roots in a history of alternative American religious practices.[18] A loose network of individuals and groups drawn together through books and websites, Neopagans vary in their beliefs and practices but tend to share an egalitarian, antiauthoritarian spirit and to worship individually or in small communities. Some find their religious homes in Unitarian Universalist congregations, whose governing association specifically welcomes "Pagans, Wiccans, and people who follow other earth-based spiritual traditions."[19] Neopagans understand their spiritualties as reinventions of ancient pre-Christian nature religions. Their worship practices, which include celebrations of new moons, solstices and equinoxes, and other seasonal festivals, focus on relationships between humans and nature, and often revolve around cycles of nature.[20]

During my first summer of fieldwork I told Butterfield about a local church that offered women's new moon celebrations, thinking that their inclusion of earth-based traditions in congregational practices would make them an easy ally for Faith in Place. I was surprised that Butterfield expressed no interest in reaching out to that church. Later that summer, when I was soliciting donations for the upcoming silent auction, I found an additional clue to the type of participants Faith in Place wanted to attract. I asked Faith in Place's deputy director, Emily Eckels, if I should accept a donation of a wheatgrass juicer that one company offered instead of the fruit juicer she had asked me to request. Chuckling, Eckels exclaimed, "Yeah right! Faith in Place selling a wheatgrass juicer?!" In my field notes, I wondered whether this item was too "hippy-dippy."[21] I surmised that Eckels associated wheatgrass with a kind of countercultural image that she did not want to project at Faith in Place.

Though that exchange with Eckels may be open to varying interpretations, in another exchange, while I was helping Eckels with a database project, I encountered a definitive boundary marking the kinds of people Faith in Place wanted to attract. Eckels asked me to sort through the list of Faith in Place's partner communities and create a category called "faith communities in Illinois," distinguishing religious congregations from other groups like green businesses or secular environmental groups. For the most part this was an easy assignment. Unity Temple, Jewish Reconstructionist Congregation, and Old St. Patrick's Church were all "faith communities in Illinois." Solar Panel Experts and the Sierra Club were not. However, I did not know whether Eckels would like to include a group identified as "pagan earthers" as a faith community. When I asked her, she instructed me to leave them off the list.[22] With the click of a mouse, Eckels had me draw a hard boundary for the religious communities who were invited to collaborate with Faith in Place. The nine traditions listed as partners on Faith in Place publications—Baha'i, Buddhist, Christian, Hindu, Jewish, Muslim, Sikh, Unitarian, and Zoroastrian— were officially religions. All other groups were not.

Unsure of whether Eckels's decision was indicative of a general attitude at Faith in Place or was an abnormally harsh declaration, I followed up on the issue with Butterfield during an interview. Initially Butterfield apologized for creating arbitrary boundaries between groups but said that, though regrettable, it was a strategic decision. "We'll work with any place where there is energy," she said, "but at the extreme end of the spectrum, first at the extreme conservative end of any religious group they won't work with us because we're interfaith. And at the other end, you have folks who may tend to drive others away."[23] Then Butterfield said that Faith in Place would welcome anyone but that they did not actively recruit Neopagans. She explained that the very introduction of environmental issues into religious worldviews evoked suspicion of New Age or Neopagan religions, an affiliation that she worried would repel many other communities.[24] The potential for such negative responses was amplified for Butterfield because of her leadership in the Unitarian Universalist community, where Neopagans were explicitly welcomed. Because Butterfield worried that people were already suspicious because of her Unitarian affiliation, she explained, she was especially careful about associating with Neopagans.

Worries about alienating more "preferable" faith communities was one reason for Faith in Place to avoid Neopagans. But its leaders' understanding of what counted as religion was another. After assuring me that she did not have anything against Neopagans, Butterfield added, "But you know, the [Neopagan] movement is very small anyway, and to a certain extent, ahistorical. You could ask some fair questions about that as a religious community, but that's not my issue. My issue is just that we wanted to be careful not to present a [Neopagan] image that would be disinviting to the overwhelming majority of the folks who work with us."[25] While offering a pragmatic rationale for suppressing the presence of certain religious groups—concerns about creating an image that might repel Faith in Place's primary supporters—Butterfield also enforced a subtle moral code for what actually counted as "real" religion.

Even as Faith in Place avoided those who expressly identified with Neopaganism or other earth-based traditions, the influence of those and other metaphysical traditions lurked unacknowledged just beneath the surface of Faith in Place's work. Staff members and participants may have dabbled in other religious streams, but Faith in Place recognized only individuals' involvement with fixed categories of "authentic" religion. Eckels, a deacon at her Lutheran church, provided a fascinating case study. Over lunch one afternoon, she mentioned that she had recently had her astral charts read to give her insight into her life. She said she had shared the information with her dad, a Lutheran pastor, even though she thought he would find the enterprise ridiculous. She was surprised when he told her the reading was "spot-on."[26] The two other people eating with us, a staff member and a volunteer, also had requisitioned their own astral chart readings in the past. During my interviews with other Faith in

Place participants, I encountered a churchgoing Lutheran who described herself as a "closet nature mystic"; a Zoroastrian who was certified as a Reiki master; a Methodist who described his daughter as "very spiritual" because she had a tattoo of a Hindu goddess on her arm; and a staff member drawn to "earth-based" and "Eastern" spiritualities. Faith in Place participants may have dabbled in multiple religious streams, but these varied influences never received official sanction at Faith in Place. Reiki masters, nature mystics, and yogis came to Faith in Place as Zoroastrians, Lutherans, and Catholics.[27]

From its subtle tactics that suppressed undesirable religious affiliations and expressions to its overarching theological viewpoints in line with a particular liberal view of religion, Faith in Place's daily work defied its public image as a universalistic organization that welcomed the diverse viewpoints of every faith. Perhaps wide-ranging religious diversity was not actually the ideal Faith in Place wanted to achieve after all. My interviews and observations revealed rather shallow engagement with ideals of understanding religious difference, but participants seemed much more interested in differing experiences of the environment shaped by race and class, as Paul's immediate jump from religious to racial difference suggested. Hence, one can surmise that Faith in Place was not interested in hearing from representatives at the "extreme ends of the religious spectrum" because those representatives did not give Faith in Place the type of diversity that its leaders actually sought. If they were really concerned about interfaith dialogue and bringing together different religious voices, then including Neopagan and conservative Christian theological viewpoints would contribute to that goal. But even as Faith in Place leaders *talked* about religious diversity, they seemed much more invested in cultivating diversity of a different kind.

DIVERSITY IN DAILY OPERATIONS

While downplaying the influence of alternative religious traditions within the organization, Faith in Place leaders accentuated the presence of religious groups who advanced the type of interfaith image they wished to convey. When I concluded my fieldwork in 2011, Faith in Place continued to boast of its partnerships with nine different religious groups—Baha'i, Buddhist, Christian, Hindu, Jewish, Muslim, Sikh, Unitarian, and Zoroastrian—yet in more than five years of sustained involvement with the organization I had never encountered a single Sikh or Baha'i and had met precisely one Hindu and two Zoroastrians.

Muslim involvement peaked in 2008 when Faith in Place helped a mosque obtain a solar hot water heating system but quickly dissipated when Faith in Place's Muslim outreach worker resigned in 2009. Nevertheless, Faith in Place continued to highlight Muslim involvement and the mosque's solar panels in the 2011 annual report.

Meanwhile, Faith in Place's daily operations suggested a much greater commitment to achieving diversity in terms of race and ethnicity, a type of diversity its leaders seemed hesitant to discuss. While almost entirely Protestant, the staff in 2011 included two African Americans, one Latina, and three Caucasians. Diversity in terms of race and ethnicity among the staff translated into similar diversity among the membership, an outcome achieved with great intentionality. Yet staff members found ways to circumvent language that directly identified their shifting goal. When I first began spending time at Faith in Place, staff members talked about expanding their reach "south of Madison," the street dividing Chicago's predominately white north side from the predominately black south side. While clearly conveying their intention to recruit African Americans, they employed a geographic designation to avoid actually mentioning race. After Kyle joined the staff, people continued to avoid discussing race even in the intimate settings of the office, talking about strategies to better involve "Veronica's people."

While using the discourse of religious pluralism, Faith in Place leaders actually categorized participants on the basis of race and ethnicity. Kyle was focused on outreach to the African American community, so her job was to mobilize African Americans, regardless of their religion. In practice, she was most successful in UCC congregations because that was where she had the most connections. Other Faith in Place leaders were quite impressed by her work, which supposedly increased Faith in Place's diversity but actually added more Protestants to an already predominantly Protestant group.

When I asked Butterfield how Faith in Place had chosen the African American community as a target for their outreach efforts in recent years, she replied:

Well, in that case it was just looking around the room and seeing who wasn't here that needed to be here. When you've got a large, significant part of the demographic community that exists in your area and that isn't present in your work, then you're not representative and you'd better do something about that. That's why we deliberately went after that community, and we're going to try to take that same approach with the Latino community, which to date has largely been present in our youth program but not otherwise.

I view that as a problem that needs to be fixed. We have to have someone organizing who is from that community and who speaks Spanish.[28]

Butterfield's comment about *looking* around the room to *see* who was missing was revealing. Religious diversity within a group may not be visible to an outside observer, but racial and ethnic diversity are. Cultivating such visible forms of diversity seemed to be a priority at Faith in Place. Accordingly, the 2009 strategic plan included a goal to hire an outreach worker to pursue Chicago's Latino community.[29] While there was no presumption of a religious requirement for the new staff member, the plan stated that he or she must be fluent in Spanish "to permit more successful outreach to the Latino community in the same model as outreach to the African-American community. . . . Increased resources [should] be devoted here to insure that Faith in Place participation resembles the area as a whole demographically, although outreach to non-Christian communities will also continue to be a priority."[30] Here, Faith in Place leaders prioritized ethnic over religious diversity, wanting to increase involvement among Latinos—regardless of their religious identity—even though that would likely result in even more Christians (albeit Catholics) involved with Faith in Place. The strategic plan suggested that recruiting non-Christian communities was important, yet it allocated no resources for achieving that goal. While Faith in Place spread its environmental message using the discourse of religious pluralism, its leaders strove to make the organization representative of the region's racial and ethnic diversity.

Without employing language identifying racial categories Butterfield often used coded language to reveal her actual diversity goals. She told a group of environmental educators, "If the messenger looks like the group, [outreach efforts] work better." Kyle was much more effective at recruiting congregations on the south side than Butterfield ever had been, she explained, because "it's not about the religion; it's about the ability to say 'we.'"[31] In that remark Butterfield elided any direct mention of race while conveying a tacit understanding that African Americans would join Faith in Place only when recruited by a fellow African American. Butterfield transgressed Faith in Place's unwritten rule against directly discussing race during the interview when I asked her why Faith in Place had never hired a Jewish outreach worker. Elaborating on her point that she herself "speaks the language" of Jews, she also hesitantly added, "In some cases, I have been the organizer for the white community, just to overstate the case."[32] Faith in Place had one outreach worker dedicated to African Americans congregations and hoped to hire another for Latinos, while Butterfield saw herself as the outreach worker for white people of all faiths. Even as Faith in Place used the discourse of religious pluralism, its outreach efforts were based upon racial and ethnic categories.

Celebrating Racial Diversity

The hesitance of Faith in Place leaders to use language directly identifying their goals reveals anxieties about differences of race, ethnicity, and class that were alleviated by talking instead about religion. While conversations about class, racial, and ethnic differences tend to be fraught with difficulties, as sociologist Stephen Warner points out, "In the United States, religious difference is the most legitimate cultural difference."[33] In the twenty-first century there are hundreds of interfaith organizations in America dedicated to finding unity amid diversity, but self-identified interracial or interethnic groups are significantly less common. Americans tend to be much more comfortable talking about religious diversity—a difference that is celebrated—than racial diversity, a difference that brings to mind struggles for equality and significant discrepancies in power. Those kinds of anxieties and longings were negotiated through everyday work at Faith in Place.

Using the language of religious pluralism to achieve the goal of racial and ethnic diversity, Faith in Place achieved a constituency unique among environmental groups in Chicago, and its leaders were quick to point that out. Butterfield mentioned to me that Faith in Place always brought the most racially diverse group of all the organizations that participated in Environmental Lobby Day, a distinction that partnering environmental organizations had noted and applauded. At Faith in Place events Kyle often found an indirect way to ask all the African Americans to stand up and be recognized, acknowledging variously the participants of the "Just Eating" Bible study or the leaders of a summer gardening program, distinguished groups that comprised the only African Americans in the room. With all eyes on these participants, Kyle would ask everyone to applaud and welcome these environmental heroes. "A lot of times I've been at events like this and I was the only one from my community there," Kyle asserted at a Harvest Celebration, "so we should thank these people for being here."[34]

Faith in Place leaders conceived of their coalition's diversity as inherently good, but they also recognized its instrumental value. I asked

Butterfield whether she found it important for Faith in Place participants to meet each other or if she saw Faith in Place primarily as a resource for different communities to utilize within their own congregations. "Oh, we want them to meet," she replied. "And these days we want them to meet in Springfield."[35] As this declaration indicated, Faith in Place leveraged its connections with congregations of "all faiths" to exert moral authority and to express the universality of the small organization's concerns. In written materials and public presentations Faith in Place leaders claimed, "We have the moral authority, based on our faith statements, to encourage society to make the necessary changes." A 2004 brochure encouraged faith communities to join Faith in Place because it offered "a movement of moral voices that can no longer be ignored," helping to change the future by "working to leverage the moral authority of the congregation." Along with other Interfaith Power and Light (IPL) chapters they developed the viewpoint that faith communities "don't have to be afraid to push the envelope" when it came to advocating for sweeping environmental policy goals because "we have moral authority behind us."[36] While individual religious environmentalists might claim moral authority based on the teachings of their own particular faiths, under the umbrella of Faith in Place their claim became much more powerful because the organization claimed to represent not just Christians but the entire faith community. By highlighting partnerships with representatives from nine different faiths—even if many of those partnerships were fleeting, involved engagement with only one or two representatives of a given faith, or had taken place years in the past—a few Protestant environmental leaders and their overwhelmingly Protestant coalition gained the capacity to express moral concerns on behalf of all.[37]

Faith in Place gained further strategic benefits from the racial diversity within the organization. At one staff meeting Butterfield announced that a representative from a potential donor foundation had called her to ask why there were no African Americans on Faith in Place's board, given the organization's stated commitment to serving that community. Butterfield responded that the addition of Kyle's position in African American outreach demonstrated Faith in Place's real intentions and that they were working to cultivate African American representation on the board.[38] From looking around the room at many environmental events, or looking at the staff of many environmental organizations, it is clear that the environmental movement continues its legacy as a predominately white movement.[39] There is a growing number of African American environmental groups, such as Blacks in Green, a

Chicago-based nonprofit organization dedicated to addressing environmental issues that affect the African American community.[40] However, Faith in Place was distinctive for the racial diversity it cultivated within a single organization, and this distinction was not lost on potential partnering organizations or donors.

The religious, racial, and ethnic diversity of Faith in Place's constituency had a strong appeal for many of Faith in Place's participants as well. For liberal cosmopolitans longing for contact with people from different cultural backgrounds, religious pluralism could ground interactions between people who were different without dealing with messy subjects such as power differentials related to race and class. Comments I heard from Faith in Place participants revealed a fascination with differing experiences based on race and class and, simultaneously a clear discomfort with directly discussing them. Rather than talking about African Americans, Faith in Place's white participants could more comfortably talk about the African American church, and in doing so they often confused categories of race and class as they assumed that all minorities were poor while all white people were wealthy. Margaret, a white, longtime participant at Faith in Place who worked at an environmental organization, provided a typical response when I asked how her whether and how her involvement with Faith in Place had changed her understanding of other religious traditions. First she said that Faith in Place had increased her understanding of different religious traditions and that she loved seeing all of the diverse people at the annual Harvest Celebration. But then Margaret abandoned her focus on religious difference as she shifted the conversation to the importance of Faith in Place's relationships with African Americans. "It's interesting. I have long discussions with [my colleague] down the hall about poor people and environmentalism," she said, "and I'm at my own extreme. It's like, listen, there are a lot of poor people on this planet. If we don't save this planet, then the poor people are screwed."[41] Similar to Paul, Margaret's response quickly slipped from religion to race to class, equating religious difference with racial difference and racial difference with class difference. When I asked people about the role of race in the environmental movement they were hesitant to discuss these kinds of issues, but by starting with differences of religion they seemed much more comfortable expressing their thoughts.

Faith in Place leaders emphasized their commitment to uniting diverse religious communities even as their actual engagement with members of diverse faiths was limited and as they tended to suppress the visibility of differing religious viewpoints within the organization. In practice they seemed not to promote opportunities for interfaith dialogue and instead sought to create opportunities for encounters of a different kind. Neopagans and conservative Christians could have amplified the diversity of theological viewpoints represented at Faith in Place, but in Chicago they would likely have contributed to organization's white, middle-class majority, creating opportunities for contact among people who already lived in the same neighborhoods, shopped at the same stores, and sent their children to the same schools. These were not the kinds of interreligious encounters desired by participants at Faith in Place. The hundreds of informal conversations and dozens of formal interviews I conducted involved very few recollections of actual interfaith contact or dialogue among Faith in Place participants, and I rarely witnessed such encounters in five years of fieldwork. But participants did frequently talk about the differing experiences of white people in the suburbs and black people on the south side, and they seemed continually fascinated by Faith in Place's partnerships with the immigrant populations one might encounter on account of Faith in Place's partnerships with Muslims, Hindus, Sikhs, and Baha'is.

Faith in Place's commitment to religious diversity functioned primarily to achieve diversity in terms of race, ethnicity, and class. Although Faith in Place took on the identity of an interfaith organization committed to finding common religious ground, at the end of the day there was no need to find common religious ground because a basic premise of religious environmentalism was that all religions taught the same thing on this matter. Hence, rather than prioritizing interreligious encounters, Faith in Place leaders used religious differences to point to differences based on other factors. Contact with people from different backgrounds offered a strong allure for both participants and supporters of Faith in Place, and this contact seemed to fulfill their desires for interreligious encounters.

6

Faith in Place's Religious Message

The obstacles I encountered as I tried to schedule an interview with Teresa offered great insight into the complexities of engaging religious environmentalism in diverse religious communities. Teresa, an Italian Catholic woman in her forties, belonged to the Purple Radishes, a community gardening group that had developed from a class on sustainable food systems at a Faith in Place partner church.[1] She initially agreed to participate in a formal interview about her experiences in the garden, but she called me to cancel after she read a line in my consent form that described my research as an attempt to understand how environmental concern is influencing the practice of religion in America. "I'm a practicing Catholic!" Teresa exclaimed to me over the phone. "The garden has *nothing* to do with my religion."[2] I assured Teresa that her viewpoints would offer rich insight into my research, and she agreed to participate in the interview as planned.

When we met I asked Teresa to elaborate on her strong reaction to the line on my consent form. "I just wouldn't correlate the two [the garden and her religion]," she told me. "Now, that's not to say it's not spiritual for me, because it really is. But as far as my religious background and the garden, no. No. No. I'm Catholic, my children are Catholic. . . . And the environment doesn't really fit into Catholicism for me."[3] For Teresa, being Catholic entailed dogma, scripture, obligations, and acts such as praying the rosary and attending church with her children. Despite this, she told me that she felt a strong commitment to the earth and the environment and that her time in the garden was an expression of her spirituality because it served her individual needs and purposes in life. Yet that spirituality, she insisted, was completely distinct from her Catholicism. Teresa explained that "the message of Catholicism is serving the Lord and serving others" and that it had nothing to do with the individual spiritual needs that she fulfilled in the garden. In direct conflict with Faith in Place's insistence that "all religions share a common responsibility to care for the earth," Teresa clearly delineated her "garden spirituality" as a category entirely separate from her formal religious life.[4] Teresa's opinions certainly did not represent the official viewpoint of the Catholic Church or the attitude of all Catholics. Nevertheless, her hesitance to identify the garden or environment as part of her religion—in sharp contrast to the five Unitarian Purple Radishes—is one example that challenges the purported universality of Faith in Place's religious message.

In chapter 5 I argued that Faith in Place used the discourse of religious pluralism to achieve racial diversity, while demonstrating significantly less concern for building connections across differing theological perspectives. Interfaith dialogue turned out to be unimportant at Faith in Place, I argued, because religious environmentalism's universalistic underpinnings suggested that all religions shared a common concern for the earth. In this chapter I build on that contention as I examine Faith in Place's religious message and ask, "What is the *faith* in Faith in Place?" Although Faith in Place leaders took pride in offering common ground for people of every faith, in practice it enforced a secularized variety of liberal Protestantism, supported by Butterfield's particular theology. Faith in Place leaders took for granted that this particular theology could be translated to fit with the teachings of every religion. While presenting earth stewardship as an ethic *within* all religions, they actually placed stewardship *above* all religions, demanding that religions bend and adapt to the earth's needs. Conflicts that emerged through encounters with people who were not liberal Protestants underscore the limitations of this process of translation. By examining the theological assumptions that supported Faith in Place's daily work and conflicts that arose in response to them, I show how ostensibly universal constructions of religious environmentalism are always marked by the attitudes and assumptions of a particular religious viewpoint.

MESSAGE OF SOCIAL JUSTICE

Faith in Place was intended as a meeting ground for people from diverse religious traditions, but the central ethical message it offered for everyone was the same: people of faith have a responsibility to be good stewards of the earth because environmental degradation is a social justice issue. Its mission statement placed social justice at the center of the organization's work:

> Our mission is to help people of faith understand that issues of ecology and economy—of care for Creation—are at the forefront of social justice. At Faith in Place we believe in housing the homeless, feeding the hungry and clothing the naked. But even if we do all those things, and love our brothers and sisters with our whole heart, it will not matter if we neglect the ecological conditions of our beautiful and fragile planet.[5]

Faith communities might object to explicitly environmental messages by indicating that environmental concerns were a passing fad, expressions of partisan politics, or closely connected to nature worship and not a central component of their religions. But an ethic of caring for the poor and vulnerable offered a more enduring and universal appeal, and Faith in Place leaders insisted that protecting the environment was a central component of caring for the poor. The mission statement brought attention, not to polar bears or melting ice caps, but to defenseless human populations without a place to live or food to eat. Protecting the earth's ecological conditions, the statement conveyed, contributed to justice for those vulnerable communities.[6]

The American environmental movement historically focused on issues of wilderness protection and endangered species, earning it a reputation as an elitist movement that did not adequately address the concerns of poor people struggling with matters of everyday life.[7] Faith in Place leaders made clear that their work prioritized social justice issues that affected fellow humans, going to great lengths to point out that they were not focused on saving animals in faraway places. In Faith in Place rhetoric, endangered species symbolized the type of environmentalism that the organization rejected. Discussing language that board members should use when describing Faith in Place, Butterfield declared, "We can't talk about polar bears on the south side where all their kids are getting shot."[8] Faith in Place's "Ten Tips" introductory talk emphasized the importance of discussing the environment in human terms, highlighting issues such as asthma, air pollution, and flooding.[9] Positioning Faith in Place's work against constructions of mainstream environmentalism as a movement for elites, Faith in Place offered its own version of earth stewardship in which concern for the earth was grounded in concern for the poor.

Rather than offering detailed scriptural references or complex theological formulations, then, Faith in Place leaders indicated that a universal religious requirement to advance social justice was the primary reason to support religious environmentalism. An introduction to the organization on the website established the universality of religious environmental teachings. According to the statement, "There are two great responsibilities common to all faiths: to love one another and to care for the creation that sustains all life. Faith in Place gives religious people tools to reflect deeply on these responsibilities, integrate the teachings of faith into practice, and work together for a just and sustainable future."[10] This construction of a universal set of religious teachings that transcend the boundaries of any individual religion, "the teachings of faith," established a common core central to all religions and suggested that the best way for people of faith to fulfill their religious environmental responsibilities was to work cooperatively with people of other faiths. Moreover, it sanctified Faith in Place as an authoritative religious leader that could help everyone more authentically live out their religions.

When Butterfield began organizing for Faith in Place in 1999, she told me, she encountered social justice–oriented religious communities that were hesitant to prioritize environmental causes because they wanted to focus on more basic problems affecting the daily lives of the poor. She tailored Faith in Place's message to appeal to those communities by indicating that the organization's work was related to, but even more fundamental than, day-to-day justice concerns. Building on their mantra that religious environmental work "is about people, not polar bears," Faith in Place leaders constantly reinforced the connection between environmental work and social justice, encouraging all people of faith to come together to address what religious environmental leaders described as "the most important moral issue of our time."[11] Butterfield upheld that theme at a workshop on reducing energy consumption, declaring, "All our faith traditions call us to care for the poor. And with global warming, the poor are hurt first and worst. . . . It is our moral responsibility to protect the most vulnerable communities as we transition to a clean energy future."[12] As these declarations indicate, Faith in Place leaders relied much more heavily on generalized religious prescriptions to advance social justice than on particular references to scriptures or religious ethics. Offering sparse details on how exactly environmental degradation disproportionately affected the poor, or how exactly every religion advanced social justice, they presented these central points as self-evident. Connecting religious environmental teachings to the Bible, the Vedas, or the Quran would indicate religious particularities. With their focus on social justice, the organization's leaders insisted that their priorities were applicable to all.

MAINLINE PROTESTANT UNIVERSALISM

Faith in Place leaders offered what they considered a core, universal religious message that could be "translated" into the language of different faiths. Different traditions might apply different concepts, according to this reasoning, but the underlying ethic was universal. Butterfield modeled this approach at one workshop as she discussed the relationship between humans and the earth according to Abrahamic religions.[13] Then she included participants of non-Abrahamic religions by saying, "If your faith tradition does not embrace the idea of creator and created, as if there are Buddhists among us, you can understand this language as simply a relationship of love and care, and perhaps of awe at the 'isness' of everything. *Translate as appropriate, please.*"[14] For people who did not know how to appropriately translate Faith in Place's environmental messages into the language of their own religious traditions, Faith in Place offered help. Butterfield's presentation notes for one workshop stated: "Every faith tradition has an ethic that calls us to care for creation. Don't know where to find your faith tradition's statement? Call Faith in Place."[15] Although Faith in Place's staff was composed entirely of Protestants, they claimed the authority to interpret the religious teachings of every faith.

A youth curriculum Faith in Place developed for congregations also relied on this understanding of a core religious message that could be translated by applying different religious idioms.[16] In 2009, Butterfield assigned a seminary intern the task of converting the youth director's lesson plans into a written curriculum that could be shared with different congregations. The youth program was funded primarily through foundations and government grants that prohibited grantees from promoting religious beliefs, so the lesson plans did not include any explicitly religious references. The seminary intern's task was to write down the lessons, then add relevant scriptural passages to connect each unit to different religions. The intern would use her knowledge of the Hebrew Bible and the New Testament to connect the environmental lessons to

Judaism and Christianity, and Butterfield hoped a Muslim volunteer could help insert appropriate references from the Quran and Hadith. Given general environmental themes, this approach suggested, different faith communities could insert appropriate scriptures into the curriculum's "general" religious template.[17]

During an interview, I asked Butterfield about her use of Christian, or at least monotheistic, language in her presentations for Faith in Place. She explained it was a matter of intelligibility and that non-Christians forgave her for using those particularities:

> Religious minorities in the US are very gracious about accepting the language of the majority as kind of a placeholder for the language they would use instead, because they know that no one would understand their language because we are a monolingual culture. . . . So we just refer to Creation, which implies the existence of a Creator, and again we had permission from the Buddhists who say, "Oh, go ahead and say it that way. We know what you mean."[18]

Butterfield apologized for using particularistic language, but she maintained that Faith in Place's underlying message was universal. Her point that Christian language was a "placeholder" for the language of Buddhism, Hinduism, or any other religion indicated an assumption that all religions taught the same thing. It implied that Christian language, concepts, and themes offered a generic template for all religions.

Nevertheless, Faith in Place offered a model of religiosity grounded in a liberal Protestant way of being religious, in contrast to the religious style and priorities of other American religious groups. As they insisted on the centrality of social justice, ethical living, and interreligious cooperation to any practice of faith, Faith in Place enforced a normative liberal white Protestant way of being religious, prioritizing tolerance and good deeds above specific requirements such as upholding religious law or saving souls. Their work embedded "a certain tolerant, practically oriented, Mainline theological style" that sociologist of religion Nancy Ammerman has called Golden Rule Christianity. Most prevalent among middle-class, white suburbanites, Golden Rule Christianity is defined more by practice than by belief as adherents characterize Christian life as seeking to do good, help the needy, and make the world a better place to live.[19] Affiliated mostly with mainline Protestant churches in the United States, Golden Rule Christians follow established patterns of interfaith activity, serving their communities (especially the needy), connecting their scriptures to actions in the world, and serving God through community service.[20] While other religious groups also participate in many of the same activities, these patterns are shaped and spearheaded by mainline Protestants and provide stark contrast to conservative Protestants and many sectarian groups who tend to emphasize a different set of priorities, such as serving the world by evangelizing or focusing on personal piety.[21]

Golden Rule Christianity's patterns of religiosity align closely with assumptions about religion at Faith in Place. As Faith in Place sought to unite participants with diverse religious viewpoints, religion became synonymous with advancing an ethical way of life. Theological and doctrinal distinctions could drop away because all that really mattered was how faith communities behaved toward each other and all inhabitants of planet earth. Yet ironically the position that behaviors trump theological viewpoints was itself the expression of a liberal theological viewpoint.

As they insisted on the centrality of social justice and environmental protection to every religion, universal ideals they constructed as the "teachings of faith," Faith in Place leaders were claiming the authority to interpret the very essence of every religion. Their strategic plan described faith as "a tool of social engagement" that could help people of faith "become the kinds of people who seek to change their societies," but Faith in Place clearly intended for people to change their societies only in certain ways.[22] Religious environmental leaders located their work in a history of religious advocacy for progressive change including movements for the abolition of slavery, women's suffrage, and civil rights, and they clearly did not align themselves with "the kinds of people who seek to change their societies" by restricting abortion rights or banning gay marriage.[23] Instead, Faith in Place leaders encouraged participants to become the kinds of people who "live gently and harmoniously with other living things," to "live in a manner that permits the flourishing of other life," and to "repair the world, care for Creation, and love your brothers and sisters," all as central faith requirements.[24] Butterfield has spoken of "our religious responsibility to use energy better and use better energy" and has described a duty to "eat meat that fits [your] values."[25] At an interfaith summit on food ethics she proclaimed, "God does not love the corruption of our soil and water through putting poison on vegetables . . . the corruption of confinement operations of animals . . . [or] the imbalance of mass production, but rather loves the balanced methods of raising animals and plant foods that respect the natural balances of the earth."[26] Advancing the universalistic ideology of religious environmentalism, Faith in Place made the case that the foundation for these particular ethics could be found at the heart of every religion. They offered highly specific instructions for enacting the "teachings of faith" and suggested their universal religious teachings could be transmitted through the particular forms of every religion.

MODERN RELIGION

In keeping with the organization's mainline Protestant thrust, Butterfield's theological outlook and, by extension, Faith in Place's work relied on particular theological assumptions characteristic of modern religion. In *Christian Moderns: Freedom and Fetish in the Mission Encounter,* anthropologist Webb Keane builds on the work of scholars such as Charles Taylor and Talal Asad to demonstrate how attitudes and assumptions of Protestant Christianity developed in close partnership with concepts characteristic of modernity. In particular, Keane defines modernity as centering on the idea that "modernity is, or ought to be, a story of human liberation from a host of false beliefs and fetishisms that undermine freedom."[28] According to Keane, the story of modernity involves familiar themes of progress in terms of technology, economic well-being, and health. But modernity is also a story about human emancipation and the emergence of progressively freer subjects.[29] "If in the past, humans were in thrall to illegitimate rulers, rigid traditions, and unreal fetishes," Keane writes, "as they become modern they realize the true character of human agency."[30] Modern religion, shaped by revolutionizing forces of the Protestant Reformation, involves recognizing the capacity of humans to think and act for themselves.

Keane suggests that modern subjects who improperly transfer their own agency to rulers, traditions, or fetishes seem to be out of step with the times. Such subjects also were out of step with Faith in Place, where Butterfield advanced a theological outlook expressly for modern liberals who had reached a point of "religious maturity" and could no longer accept traditional (premodern) views of God. When discussing her theological dispositions, Butterfield always clarified that she was offering her own idiosyncratic viewpoints and not the official viewpoint of Faith in Place. But she was the cofounder, first organizer, and executive director of a "strongly theological" organization that "believes in the transformation of religious people as a primary means by which society is transformed."[31] The "strong theology" underlying Faith in Place's work, and the personal and societal transformations that theology suggested, were inevitably informed by Butterfield's particular theological outlook.

Modern religion

Under Butterfield's leadership, Faith in Place's work embedded theological understandings characteristic of liberal, modern theology, including commitment to modern intellectual inquiry (especially modern science), belief in the authority of reason and experience, an understanding of Christianity primarily in ethical terms, and a priority on making religion believable and socially relevant in contemporary times.[32] Placing modern science at the core of her theological outlook, Butterfield described herself as "an ecologist who found [classical] ideas of God in conflict with the observable." She sought to offer Faith in Place participants an "ecological and religious sensibility" that was meaningful for "perfectly rational believing people."[33] She wanted that sensibility to be believable in contemporary times, describing her quest for a theology that was "intellectually consistent," "intellectually honest," and "credible." It had to be compatible with reason and natural science, while also being emotionally satisfying. Butterfield further understood religion primarily as a matter of ethics, insisting that ideas about God must compel people of faith to behave better. "Religion is a set of practices by which human beings become whole," Butterfield wrote in a discussion of her theological viewpoint, and religious ideas are worthwhile only to the extent that they can help people of faith live meaningful and righteous lives. At Faith in Place Butterfield sought to retain the positive contributions of religion—its ability to cultivate hopefulness, healthy-mindedness, and kindness—with the best insights of modern science. She located Faith in Place "at the intersection of the alarming scientific narrative of the Earth's condition and the religious narrative that tells us how to respond with hope and compassion."[34] Upholding ecological practices became acts of religious faith because such practices were essential for leading lives of integrity.

Butterfield's ecological and religious sensibility developed in response to what she considered one of the main limitations of classical Christian theology, a limitation she saw as a barrier to religious environmental work: the problem of suffering in the world. As a natural theologian who believed that something about God could be learned by using reason and empirical observation to examine God's creation, Butterfield wondered what kind of God was suggested by examining the natural world. Optimistic liberal Protestants tended to think of creation as inherently good, Butterfield observed, but in doing so they ignored the troubling parts of the world. "What kind of God does Darfur argue for?" she asked the students in "A Big Enough Box," a six-week course she had designed for lay audiences to explore ways that ideas about God and ideas about nature were related. "What kind of God is suggested by the desertification of sub-Saharan Africa? What kind of God, I ask you, would let the Polar Bears go extinct?"[35]

In posing these questions Butterfield was pointing out the problem of theodicy, a technical term describing efforts to explain the existence of evil and suffering in the word.[36] "The God who can stop the tsunami and doesn't is a God who actively punishes innocent people or a God who is curiously detached from the suffering of Creation. In neither case is that God the loving father described by Jesus in the Gospels," she elaborated. When people of faith acknowledged the problem of evil they reached a point of "religious maturity," insisted Butterfield, and this required the faithful to make some decisions. While some might choose to stop believing in God, a decision she indicated would be a rational response, others could choose to understand God in a new way. It was the second option that Butterfield chose, and the one she hoped to convey to the participants at Faith in Place.

Butterfield found an answer to the problem of theodicy through process theology, a twentieth-century liberal viewpoint that draws from the philosophy of Alfred North Whitehead. Process theology offers a radical reconstruction of classical Christian understandings of God as all-powerful, all-knowing, and all-loving. It addresses the problem of theodicy by giving up God's omniscience.[37] God is the ground of being, as Butterfield explained the process theological outlook, and God established "a set of rules by which Creation is governed."[38] Within creation, however, humans and other beings have the freedom to act within the laws of science, and that capacity for human freedom explains the presence of evil and suffering in the world. While understanding God's power as noncoercive, process theology retains a place for a God of great empathy who can support human sufferers through troubled times. God is "the great companion" and "the fellow-sufferer who understands," Butterfield explained to Faith in Place participants, borrowing Whitehead's language, and "Through the memory of God, nothing of value is ever lost."[39] Positing a God of great empathy who established the laws of science but cannot violate them, process theology offered Butterfield a viewpoint that met her requirements for intellectual honesty, emotional satisfaction, and recognition of human responsibility.

As she delved into her study of progressive Christian theologies, Butterfield joined a subset of process theologians who focus on theological possibilities that develop from the biological concept of emergence.[40] Within biology, emergence posits that complex systems in nature develop capacities that are more than the sum of the system's parts.

ants

Butterfield often explained this phenomenon using the example of ant colonies, which develop complex rules that every ant knows, even though individual ants live for only six months while colonies can last up to fifteen years. She also showed great delight when describing a similar process for slime mold, whereby a series of these single-celled creatures communicate using chemical signals during times of crisis.[41] There is great theological significance in the concept of emergence, Butterfield has written, because "the immediate and incarnate possibility of something more emerging from something less—of the collaboration of the parts producing more than any part could produce independently—strikes me as a resurrection capacity."[42] This theology worked for Butterfield in large part because it allowed her to hold a faith that did not conflict with reason. Describing herself as "scientific by nature," she told Faith in Place participants that "the lack of conflict between science and faith is essential, or I cannot be religious."[43] For Butterfield, the religious was always revisable, just as science was based on revisable data.

In describing her faith this way, Butterfield situated her theological outlook, and Faith in Place's work by extension, as thoroughly modern. The "faith" at Faith in Place was based, not on the "illegitimate rulers, rigid traditions, and unreal fetishes" of Keane's premodern religion, but on reason and empirical observations. The religious teachings that Butterfield offered for "perfectly rational believing people" assumed modern, scientific understandings of the world and works of purification ensuring that only the positive, helpful aspects of religion would be retained. Butterfield had little interest in accommodating those who held more traditional understandings of religion, rejecting "irrational" beliefs as harmful for a lived faith. Instead she sought to combine the positive contributions of religion with the best insights of modern science. The God of process theology was compatible with modern science because this God did not pull strings or intervene in daily life but rather acted as a cocreator with humans. The idea of humans as cocreators with God was useful for ecological work, Butterfield explained to Faith in Place participants, because "if we're in relationship with God and active creators with God, then the responsibility for getting us out of this mess, the responsibility to repair, lies with us."[44] In keeping with what Keane calls a "moral narrative of modernity," Butterfield's understanding of emergence theology encouraged participants to recognize their own agency in improving the world, throwing out fetishes and outdated theologies and progressing to a better future.[45]

FAITH HAS TO BE PRACTICED

For ethicist Gary Dorrien, "a concept of Christianity as an ethical way of life" is a hallmark of liberal theology, and this was precisely the understanding of religion advanced at Faith in Place.[46] Setting aside the particularities of religious belief to the realm of private faith, Faith in Place leaders sought to unite participants around the mantra that "faith has to be practiced," a slogan they established in a 2004 communications plan. Butterfield dismissed any possible symbolic, mystical, or legalistic orientations toward religious ideas when she declared at a workshop that religious ideas must be "grounded in practice—they must affect what we do or they lose their meaning."[47] This primary focus on practice, as opposed to faith, salvation, or any other mode of religiosity, underscored Faith in Place's liberal Protestant understanding of faith in primarily ethical terms.

The ethical practices Faith in Place required entailed a certain orientation to the world, as religious environmentalism directed adherents to orient themselves in the spaces of their daily lives—their homes, workplaces, and neighborhoods—as spaces of moral action in which they enacted particular environmental values as essential parts of living with integrity. By asking people to change their daily practices and their understandings of faith, religious environmentalism suggested a clear way of thinking and being in the world. At Faith in Place the central goal of behavioral change was clear. A strategic plan stated Faith in Place's ambition to facilitate changes in "the thoughts, hopes, and aspirations of religious people," hoping that "as people think differently about who they are and why they are here, they will change what they do."[48] Faith in Place leaders sought to create "the kinds of people" who "live gently and harmoniously with other living things, as our faiths require us to do," while cultivating a "shift in thinking" whereby faith communities "stop seeing ourselves as independent, autonomous beings, and start seeing ourselves as part of a larger system that supports our life and lives beyond our own, and that we impact."[49] Faith in Place leaders wanted participants to undergo a process of personal transformation in which they began to think, act, and behave in particular eco-friendly ways. By enforcing these principles, they told people not only what to do but how to think about what they were doing.

Religious environmentalism prescribed a way of being that included such practices as carrying reusable mugs, turning off lights, rinsing out bottles to recycle, taking the train even when it was easier to drive, and collecting rainwater in a barrel beside your house. It involved the sticky sensation of juice from a ripe peach cascading down your chin, because your fruit came from the farmers' market and was not genetically engineered to travel thousands of miles. It included the faint smell of vinegar lingering in your living room because you made nontoxic cleaning solution rather than using harsh chemicals that would contaminate the city's water supply. And it meant massaging your aching back after an afternoon of pulling weeds in your community garden. Through my time at Faith in Place I learned to pack a cloth napkin with my lunch, reuse old yogurt containers, prepare fresh foods that I purchased at farmers' markets, and abstain from supporting the "evil" Coca-Cola empire.[50] I was careful to use as little water as possible when I washed my dishes in the office, but I could never be as thrifty as the youth director, who actually *drank* the water she used to rinse residue from her jars of homemade smoothies. Faith in Place participants enforced these ways of being among each other. While I never saw Faith in Place staff members directly criticize anyone for wasteful behavior, participants used the authority of Faith in Place to police each other, saying things like "Don't let Sister Kyle see you wasting all that water!"[51]

As they increasingly embraced eco-friendly habits, the women and men I met at Faith in Place grew frustrated as they witnessed unsustainable habits in their communities and households. Several of my interlocutors said they became sad and annoyed when their spouses left the lights on, their classmates carried bottled water, or inconsiderate drivers raced down the road in SUVs and Hummers. Gavin and Lauren, who both interned at Faith in Place, said they loved shopping at the farmers' market during the summer. Both told me that they actually felt depressed when the farmers' markets ended and they were forced to get food from conventional grocery stores. Lauren recounted a time when she began to cry at the grocery store, overwhelmed as she weighed decisions about different foods' costs, origins, and organic labels. "I'm forced to make this moral choice every time I go grocery shopping," she said, and shopping at the farmers' market was the best way to ease her conscience.[52] When Gavin described his return to Jewel-Osco after a summer of local fare, he recalled, "It was just really depressing to feel so much less connected to our food, and to not even know where it's coming from. I mean, I could check the sticker, but I hate food with stickers! It seems so contrary to food." By contrast, Gavin said, preparing food he had purchased at the farmers' market felt sacred. Recalling a farmers' market eggplant he had roasted the previous summer, he said,

It was just so sweet, and juicy, we were roasting it left and right and putting it in all different dishes, and it was like, this is just how it's supposed to be. . . . I think there's really something to be said for the quality and the connection to the earth. And I really do believe that God is all things, so to that extent, sharing these kinds of meals with other people is sacred.[53]

Religious environmentalism entailed not only a set of practices but also certain feelings that emerged as participants tried, and sometimes failed, to enact their environmental values.

The women and men I met through the organization acknowledged that any individual's small steps would make no measurable difference in addressing the monumental environmental crisis, but they learned to see their small steps as essential to living with integrity. These symbolic interpretations of their religious environmental acts accorded with the Protestant thrust of Faith in Place, echoing early Protestant reformers' insistence that ritual acts were symbolic representations of individuals' faith and did not in themselves have any efficacy.[54] When Faith in Place participants embraced the organization's position that environmental degradation "affects poor people first and the worst," unplugging the toaster when it was not in use or buying locally grown tomatoes became matters of social justice. Butterfield was the first to admit that those kinds of individual changes might not be enough to reverse global warming, but she offered a liberal variety of premillennialism, guiding people to make those changes regardless of their efficacy because "the only choice we may turn out to have is what kind of human we want to be as the ship sinks. It's a gloomy but realistic possibility. I think it goes down more easily if you know that you did your best to stop it."[55] Along similar lines she wrote, "I don't know that this is going to be ok. It seems equally possible that it won't, if history is any guide. I do know that we are better off if we try to do something about it than if we don't—that our time here is passed more fruitfully in mindfulness of others and loving effort to preserve the good Creation."[56] Lauren told me that she practiced earth stewardship as a religious practice more than an environmental one, "because in a place like Chicago, when I recycle something and it probably gets thrown away, is there any practical reason for me to go the extra mile and take all my plastic bags to the recycling place? No, unless it helps me sleep at night. Unless it's something that I do because I believe in something."[57] Danielle offered a similar explanation, telling me that she engaged in eco-friendly practices "because it's right. At some point you have to be able to sleep at night."[58] Even concrete environmental acts were stripped of their material significance at Faith in Place, where conserving energy, reducing waste, and supporting local food economies became symbolic expressions of a religious environmental faith.

In addition to shaping bodily practices, religious environmentalism offered a certain aesthetic, encouraging adherents to appreciate processes and objects on the basis of their positive outcomes for the environment. Faith in Place leaders pointed out that many steps that were good for the earth also had positive outcomes in other areas. For instance, local, organic produce is better for the health of farmers, consumers, and the environment, *and* it tastes much better than conventional produce. Moreover, Butterfield has written, "Low VOC paints, energy efficient windows, good use of fresh air and daylighting are not only more efficient. They're more beautiful. The air inside the building feels better in the lungs. The light shines through the open window, not from an artificial source. The grey water that gets recaptured and fed to the native plants outside has a beautiful simplicity to it—a rounding of the circle."[59] Faith in Place leaders spread this environmental subjectivity, both a way of being and a way of thinking, to congregations across Chicago and across the state. Much more than simply teaching people to change their behaviors, they enforced a fundamental reorientation in what it meant to be a person of faith. Religion at Faith in Place involved such disciplines as taking shorter showers, eating with the seasons, and turning out the lights. These actions were meant, not to be austere, but to be undertaken with joy. And people of faith ought to follow them not because they were pleasing to God but because they were the right thing to do.

RELIGIOUS PARTICULARITIES

Faith in Place may not have seemed sectarian because it promoted goals of interreligious cooperation and social justice that aligned with the dictates of modernity. Comparison with differing viewpoints, however, can serve to highlight the organization's particularities. Teresa's refusal to situate her gardening spirituality within her Catholic religious world, in the example that opened this chapter, offered one case where religious environmentalism just did not *feel* right. Teresa did not propose complex theological formulations to explain why her concern for the environment and her religious world did not align. Instead, she offered clear explanations for her understanding of Catholicism and her understanding of spirituality in the garden and simply expressed a feeling that the two did not overlap.

Conflicting theological orientations, however, might contribute to the absence of other religious groups at Faith in Place. In *The Journey of Modern Theology*, evangelical theologian Roger Olson traces the ways that modern theologians have attempted to come to terms with a modern ethos, stemming from the Enlightenment, that has challenged traditional Christian understandings of the world. Olson suggests there are some cases where modern theologians, in their efforts to reinterpret traditional teachings to align with modern scientific knowledge, step over the line and construct theologies that cannot be considered authentically Christian. The primary criterion he proffers for this judgment has to do with belief in the supernatural.[60] From Olson's perspective, belief in the supernatural, defined as "reality of unseen powers and agencies, especially God's, that are involved in special ways in history beyond the ken of science," is a core component of orthodox Christianity.[61] Modern theologians have reinterpreted miracle stories as symbolic so they can make sense to the modern rational mind, but Olson considers certain traditional beliefs, such as Jesus's divinity and resurrection, as core components of authentic Christianity. "This is what all Christians of all churchly persuasions believed doctrinally for about a millennium and a half," he writes. "And, at least, conservative Christians of all denominational persuasions still hold these beliefs."[62]

Butterfield's pragmatic theological viewpoint represents a clear example of a modern theology that rejects belief in the supernatural in favor of a rational, scientific understanding of the world. When Christian doctrines conflicted with science, or the earth's well-being, Butterfield engaged in theological reflection to reinterpret, or even reject, those doctrines in maneuvers that failed to meet Olson's criteria for authentic Christianity. The point here is not to suggest that Olson provides the true meaning of Christianity while Faith in Place's work represents an inauthentic expression of Christian belief. Rather, Olson's criteria for judging authentic expressions of Christianity simply illustrate that Butterfield made theological assumptions that were not shared even by all Christians, much less by all people of faith. Butterfield told me that evangelicals were not involved with Faith in Place because they tended to dislike interfaith work. While that rationale may offer one factor impeding any potential alliances, Olson's insistence on belief in the supernatural reveals an additional and more fundamental theological assumption that undermines the organization's claims of universality.

Non-universality

Going Green at a Chicago Mosque

Teresa's rejection of religious environmentalism and Olson's defining characteristics of Christianity offer two viewpoints that destabilize religious environmentalism's claims to universality. A controversy that emerged at an interfaith conference on the environment provides a third example of the messiness of religious environmental practice in congregations that do not maintain progressive theological outlooks. Sheikh Eshaal Karimi, an imam at the Bridgeview Mosque Foundation, was one of fourteen invited speakers at "Shared Earth," a 2010 interfaith conference on the environment hosted by the Lutheran School of Theology at Chicago (LSTC). Butterfield was an invited speaker as well, and I attended the conference with her and two others from Faith in Place.

During the conference I attended Karimi's presentation, titled "Living Green at the Mosque Foundation." Karimi began his talk by offering basic theological approaches to explain why Muslims should care about the earth. A fundamental concept from the Quran, Karimi indicated, is that "I am the earth. Preserving the earth means preserving us, because we are not two separate entities."[63] Karimi also offered a series of Quranic references, including edicts to protect trees, preserve necessities, and conserve resources. Next he described the actions his mosque took as part of its greening initiative through a partnership with Faith in Place. In the previous three years they had installed solar panels, purchased recycled carpets, promoted the use of natural light, and offered seminars to increase environmental awareness among mosque participants.

Audience members listened to the presentation politely, but a controversy developed when Karimi discussed the ritual of animal sacrifice during Eid al-Adha, the Festival of Sacrifice, which takes place annually on the last day of the Hajj. To commemorate Abraham's willingness to follow God's order to sacrifice his own son, Muslims slaughter millions of sheep, camels, and goats. They consume some of the meat themselves and with their families, and also distribute a portion to the poor. Karimi brought up the issue during his presentation because some animal rights groups have criticized Muslims for participating in the annual sacrifice, and he believed their criticisms of Muslims were misguided.[64] Karimi distinguished between two types of environmental problems. There are some issues that individual communities can address, he suggested, and that was why the Mosque Foundation had installed solar panels, made eco-friendly infrastructural changes, and started a green committee. But Karimi maintained that some environmental issues were too big for individual communities to make any difference and that those must be addressed through policy. Critiques of animal sacrifice should be directed at government entities, which can regulate the production and distribution of the animals, he said, and not individual Muslims faithfully following the dictates of their religions.

Omar Ahmadi, a professor of environmental studies and another Muslim presenter at the conference, pressed Karimi on this issue. Interestingly, Ahmadi was the only one of the fourteen conference speakers who was not associated with a seminary or a religious organization by profession. Like Karimi, Ahmadi identified as both a Muslim and an environmentalist, but the differing weights the men placed on those two identifiers became evident through their disagreement about animal sacrifice. Disagreeing with Karimi's suggestion that governments alone are responsible for animal welfare, Ahmadi asked, "Would it not be possible to change this practice [animal sacrifice], given its negative impact on the environment?" Karimi shook his head no. He responded that instructions for the sacrifice come from "a clear text that cannot be multi-interpreted. The lamb slaughter is an instruction that is required, not optional, and not open to interpretation." Searching for a way to negotiate the requirement, Ahmadi suggested applying adaptations that are permitted under conditions of scarcity. "Even required instructions are negotiable in times of scarcity, such as some things are not required during a drought." Again Karimi shook his head, disagreeing that those conditions would apply. Unsatisfied, another audience member, an LSTC professor, piped in. "With the earth in such a dire state, and with animal waste responsible for such a large amount of carbon dioxide related to global warming, is this not a time of crisis?" he asked. Karimi maintained his firm position. "Comparing the five days of the Hajj to the slaughter worldwide, it is not that much. That is a shady way to legitimize change."[65]

For Ahmadi and the LSTC professor, animal sacrifice during Eid al-Adha represented an environmental problem. They believed that even the strictest Islamic requirements must be reinterpreted in the face of environmental crisis, and they suggested that Muslims should abandon a fundamental religious duty. As inhabitants of the type of modern, rational religious world that Keane described and Butterfield advanced at Faith in Place, these two men seemed to understand animal sacrifice as symbolic and an outdated fetish from which modern Muslims ought to free themselves. From Karimi's viewpoint, however, this critique amounted to an attack on Islamic practice. Ahmadi wanted to adapt an Islamic practice that Karimi insisted was not open to interpretation;

even worse, Karimi believed, the environmental improvement was merely symbolic. Karimi pointed out that animal slaughter during the festival amounted to a negligible proportion of annual animal slaughter worldwide, so there would be no significant environmental improvement even if Muslims entirely ended the ritual of animal sacrifice for Eid al-Adha. The sacrifice, on the other hand, could not be given up because it actually *did* something: God requires the sacrifice and rewards those who do it.

The opposing viewpoints Karimi and Ahmadi maintained were indicative of two differing Islamic environmentalist standpoints. Although Karimi considered himself an environmentalist to the extent that environmentalism was congruent with his faith, he was not willing to prioritize environmental concerns above religious ones. He inhabited precisely the type of otherworldly, ritualistic, seemingly irrational, and seemingly regressive religious world that is anathema to adherents of modern religion. Karimi embraced environmentalism to the extent that it did not interfere with his faith or challenge any important religious injunction. Ahmadi, on the other hand, considered himself Muslim but was unwilling to uphold Islamic practices that conflicted with his environmental values. Like Butterfield, Ahmadi valued religious teachings but believed it was necessary to adapt and update them when they conflicted with modern science and ways of knowing. Modern science indicated that climate change was an urgent issue, and Ahmadi insisted that religious practices should shift in deference to that reality. And it was Ahmadi, not Karimi, whose opinions converged with the other religious environmentalists at the conference.

The exchange between Karimi and Ahmadi epitomizes a fundamental issue in understandings of religious environmentalism and the religious message at Faith in Place. Religious environmental ideology has spread through liberal American religious cultures in tandem with another celebrated liberal religious ideal—pluralism—as a set of self-evident truth claims about what is inherently good. Upholding the norms of modern religion, religious environmental leaders such as those at Faith in Place claimed not to impose beliefs on anyone and followed conscious measures to respect religious diversity and religious difference. But religious environmentalism's explicit respect for outward differences overlooked an implicit lack of appreciation for differences in belief and ways of being religious. Embracing a progressive theological viewpoint that religion must adapt to be relevant in changing times, it did not have a place for the maintenance of religious practices that seemed to conflict with rational understandings of the world, or those might be read as antienvironmental.

Faith in Place's theological assumptions were not readily apparent as particularistic religious viewpoints precisely because its assumptions aligned with the dictates of modernity and were palatable even to non-believers. But they were particular theological assumptions nevertheless, and they had clear implications for the shape of Faith in Place's work. Cause-and-effect relationships and explanations of evil and suffering followed progressive theological understandings. In Faith in Place parlance, melting ice caps, polluted groundwater, destructive superstorms, and severe droughts were not understood as God's punishment for human sins. Neither could they could be explained away as part of God's mysterious plan. Instead, Faith in Place's programming assumed that environmental problems resulted directly from humans' environmentally damaging behaviors. Participants may have believed in a God who was a fellow sufferer and felt great empathy for their plight. By engaging with Faith in Place's particular programming, however, they at least tacitly agreed with Butterfield that it was the role of humans to "get us out of this mess." Such understandings might seem perfectly reasonable to those who embrace the dictates of modernity, believing that religious teachings must adapt to changing times because the role of religion is to advance progressive change in the world. But these assumptions clearly are not shared by all people of faith. Teresa maintained a static understanding in which religion entailed institutions, dogmas, and rituals that did not change in the face of contemporary problems. Olson and Karimi advanced a view that certain traditional theological assumptions were not open for reinterpretation even in the face of compelling, contrary evidence that resulted from modern thinking. Faith in Place, on the other hand, insisted that religious teachings must adapt to be relevant to modern times, and most women and men who joined the organization shared that viewpoint. Those who did not encountered significant barriers when they encountered the work of Faith in Place.

7

From Grassroots to Mainstream

An e-newsletter I received from Faith in Place in 2015 indicated how significantly the organization had changed since I had begun spending time there nearly a decade earlier. "Celebrate Earth Day and join us for a Nature Outing to Powderhorn Forest Preserve!" the notice urged. "Activities will include land restoration, pulling invasive plants, and building a bridge."[1] The newsletter also featured an upcoming workshop on activism and organizing that would prepare participants for the annual Environmental Lobby Day and urged readers to lobby their state legislators to support a clean energy bill. Accustomed to the "People, not polar bears" motto that had dominated rhetoric throughout the years I spent at Faith in Place, I was surprised to see the organization providing opportunities for conservation-focused activities and political lobbying characteristic of other traditional groups. Having established its unique niche in the Chicago environmental community by distancing itself from mainstream groups, Faith in Place seemed to be shifting back in the direction of a more traditional environmental agenda.

The Earth Day "Nature Outing" was part of a series of events that Faith in Place hosted to involve its participants in earth stewardship. While those events seemed to align with traditional forms of environmentalism, examination of the events' details indicated that Faith in Place had added its own distinctive characteristics. First, invitations to the "Nature Outings" emphasized that the events were free of charge and that free bus transportation could be provided to those who needed

148

Once upon a time, we hiked, biked, farmed, fished . . .

AND WE STILL DO.

Join us at Beaubien Woods Forest Preserves/I-94 & Doty Ave Chicago

It's Free and fun for all ages!

Saturday, June 13, 2015 **11am – 4pm**	Fishing, Hiking, Story Circles, Stewardship, ·Canoeing and Archery and More! ·Signed waivers needed.

Free bus transportation is available on a first-come, first-served basis. Under 17? Chaperone needed. Please register by June 10th.

For more info or to pre-register, contact Rev. Debbie Williams at 312-733-4640 Ext. 115 or revdebbie@faithinplace.org

faith in place

FIGURE 2. Faith in Place flier advertising an outing to Beaubien Woods Forestry Preserve. Photo courtesy of Faith in Place.

it. These details clearly were intended to remove barriers for participants who lacked the means to visit wilderness areas on their own. Even more striking, fliers advertising the events indicated the intended audience. In one, a photograph on the top left featured four African American women and men posing next to their bicycles and dressed in 1920s garb. African American girls wearing midcentury bathing suits filled the frame on the right. Beneath those photographs a collage depicted contemporary African Americans practicing yoga, posing with fishing gear, and contentedly gazing into the distance, all against a backdrop of bright green grass and trees. "Once upon a time, we hiked, biked, farmed, fished . . . ," the flier stated, "AND WE STILL DO." Advancing themes that Kyle had developed during the "Just Eating" Bible study, the flier sought to attract African Americans to environmental activities more often associated with white participants by reminding them that their histories involved enjoyment of nature.

This flier contrasted with the "People, not polar bears" message that Faith in Place had developed as it sought to distance its work from negative associations with mainstream environmentalism. While initially attracting a predominately white, middle-class audience, the organization concertedly projected an image of solidarity with low-income communities and working-class struggles. Through strategic hiring practices and programmatic decisions, it recruited an increasingly diverse membership as the organization grew and developed. With its effective diversification measures in place, Faith in Place then began to realign with the mainstream environmental groups against which it originally had defined its work, as the above newsletter conveys. But even as it shifted back in the direction of mainstream environmental programming, Faith in Place retained its commitment to racial and socioeconomic diversity that has largely eluded mainstream organizations.

In this chapter I examine Faith in Place's shifting identity as it developed from a tiny nonprofit with one paid staff member into a bustling downtown organization with two satellite offices and a staff of seventeen. Faith in Place's religious environmental message appealed to religious communities on the basis of its call for social justice, so it rested on the assumption that environmental protection would benefit the poor. In some instances Faith in Place leaders seemed to embrace that mandate, highlighting their work in minority communities to provide affluent white participants a symbolic connection with the urban poor. At other times they challenged the assumption that the minority communities they served were in need of social justice–oriented help, reminding Chicagoans that African Americans could be affluent, educated, and just as concerned about the environment as white people. This chapter shows how conflicting ideas about race, class, environmentalism, and urban life permeated the organization's religious environmental work in Chicago. While initially aligning its work with grassroots environmental causes relating to working-class struggles in the inner city, Faith in Place gradually shifted its image and message as it successfully attracted minority involvement and transitioned to an established and professionalized nonprofit.

TYPOLOGIES OF ENVIRONMENTALISM

Literature on environmental movements in the United States often divides activism into two main categories: grassroots and mainstream.[2]

Mainstream environmentalism, exemplified by national organizations such as the Sierra Club, is depicted as bureaucratic, professionalized, and centrist. Its leaders most often are white and male, and its constituencies are affluent and white. Inheriting the legacy of Progressive Era conservationism, mainstream environmental agendas focus on protecting wilderness, according to this literature, and their primary objectives entail litigation and lobbying for sound environmental policies.

Grassroots environmentalism, by contrast, seems to prioritize human health over wilderness protection. Its origin stories involve local citizens' struggles to combat pollution and health hazards in their urban or suburban neighborhoods, and it is more likely to involve leaders who lack formal organizing experience, especially women. Its human-focused agendas, moreover, tend to attract a broader cross section of American society.[3] These typologies construct mainstream environmentalism as elitist, out of touch, and closely tied to the very industry and government representatives who were responsible for environmental problems in the first place. Grassroots organizations fare much better in these accounts, because they seem to address the daily struggles of ordinary urban citizens.

If this dualistic characterization was problematic when the grassroots environmental movement developed in the 1980s and 1990s, it became even more so in the twenty-first century. The 2014 "Green Ceiling" report confirms that mainstream environmental groups continued to attract primarily white, affluent leaders and participants well into the twenty-first century.[4] But other distinctions between grassroots and mainstream environmentalism have dwindled. Since their origins in the 1980s and 1990s, some grassroots organizations have developed into sophisticated national networks, while so-called mainstream environmental groups have concertedly expanded their agendas to incorporate concerns about environmental racism and community health.[5] Nevertheless, such polarities illustrate ideas about environmentalism's elitist tinge in the popular imagination.[6] Faith in Place leaders employed these kinds of representations as they promoted their religious environmental work in Chicago, especially as they emphasized that they were concerned about "people, not polar bears" and as they highlighted their work in racially and economically diverse communities. While developing an agenda and a set of priorities that came to resemble the characteristics of mainstream environmental groups, Faith in Place leaders projected an image that aligned their work with the positive associations of grassroots environmentalism.

GRASSROOTS AUTHENTICITY

Faith in Place leaders aligned their work with grassroots, urban environmental efforts aimed at achieving justice for all. While attracting primarily white, affluent participants until Kyle joined the staff in 2008, Faith in Place issued promotional materials stating its intention to work among "low-income urban neighborhoods, diverse inner-ring communities, and affluent suburbs" that "reflected the religious, economic, and racial diversity of our region."[7] Prior to 2008, its vision of working with low-income neighborhoods was expressed primarily through the youth program, From the Ground Up/De La Tierra para Arriba. The youth program relied on federal funding, so it was not faith based and did not advance Faith in Place's strategic goal of inculcating earth stewardship in congregations. It did, however, contribute to the organization's unstated yet equally alluring social justice goals and helped amplify its image as authentically grassroots and urban. For years the main page of Faith in Place's website featured a photograph of Latino children planting a community garden. Butterfield wanted to retain symbolic associations between Faith in Place's work and Latino youth even when that program was struggling to recruit participants. In July 2006 Butterfield considered terminating the program because it had attracted only a handful of youth that summer, but she found a way to retain the program and make it more effective instead.[8] Beginning that fall, the organization restructured its youth program into a traveling curriculum that would serve children at schools and community centers, but only in impoverished areas. Faith in Place worked with hundreds of wealthy, predominately white congregations that offered religious education for their youth, but those were not the communities that the youth program served. Faith in Place's website directed those in search of stewardship resources and youth curricula from a faith-based perspective to visit two other websites: Web of Creation and Georgia Interfaith Power and Light's Green Vacation Bible School curriculum.[9] By contrast Faith in Place offered its own program to low-income children at schools and community centers in the city. During the years when the organization's participants were mostly middle class and white, the youth program offered a counterbalance that located its work in the heart of the inner city.

By highlighting its intention to work across the Chicago region, both in neighborhoods and suburbs dominated by affluent, white populations and in areas inhabited mostly by immigrant, minority, and working-class communities, Faith in Place positioned itself within an urban landscape that was the site of complex, sometimes conflicting, visions, uses, and needs. For some, a sense of the city's otherness turned certain urban places into sites of fantasy and desire and, conversely, anxiety and fear. In a discussion of urban religion, Robert Orsi writes that throughout American history, white middle-class people have turned to the city for "spiritually compelling and existentially real" experiences through contact with urban populations.[10] From early twentieth-century settlement house workers trying to protect urban youth from the dangers of life in the industrial city, to bourgeois pleasure seekers "going slumming" in Harlem in the 1920s, they have been "gripped by the particular desire aroused by and for the city as the space of the alien other, and for an encounter with the real or the primitive that the circumstances of their respectability occluded."[11] But for others, the city is a place of familiarity, the only home they have ever known. For these reasons, Orsi suggests, "Spaces on the urban landscape are both geographical sites where real people live and constructions of terror and desire among those who live elsewhere, including elsewhere in the city."[12]

A discussion guide that Faith in Place designed for its sustainability circles in 2000 reveals the organization's constructions of desire within the city. A session titled "The Sacred City" conveys two overarching points: urban environmentalism is important because the city is sacred, and the city is sacred because of its great diversity. Descriptions of that diversity support a particular imagination of the city. The discussion guide says:

> On any morning in our city rise people of every faith, color, ethnicity, language group, economic circumstance, and philosophy. They earn their livings in every conceivable way—educating children, caring for the sick, building buildings, cooking, cleaning, putting out fires. They do the work of the region. Each person is the repository of all the hopes of the preceding generations. Each has dreams for his or her children. They are here in densities and mixtures more complex and diverse than ever before in human history. Each one has a story. Each story is important, as the Rabbi Nachman put it, to the One to whom all belong. *If there are yet holy places on this Earth, the city is a holy place.*[13]

Notably, this account of the city includes a population of teachers, construction workers, firefighters, and maids, but not stockbrokers, attorneys, or corporate executives. It is the life experiences of a particular set of "real" city dwellers that make the city a sacred place.

With this urban population in mind, sustainability circle participants were next instructed to consider the kinds of behaviors that would support the city's holiness. The discussion guide asked them to contemplate the following questions: "How do we mark the holiness of this place? How do we conduct ourselves so that we do not tread on the hopes and dreams of our brothers and sisters? What are the circumstances of life, of a particular neighborhood, that can impede the sense of holiness? What can our circles do to remove these impediments, and allow the daily attentiveness to the sacred to flourish wherever people live?"[14] In essence, this session encouraged sustainability circle participants (a group that presumably would not include construction workers, firefighters, or maids) to consider ways they could improve daily life and help advance the dreams of an imagined urban population.

That idea of urban communities comprised the exact population that Faith in Place aspired to serve. The organization concentrated its efforts on tackling the circumstances of life that "impede a sense of holiness" in particular neighborhoods. While participants from liberal, white congregations could find their own way to Faith in Place, the organization dedicated significant resources to attracting new communities to environmentalism. In the years before Kyle joined the staff, Butterfield sent seminary interns out to visit south-side churches and deliver free compact fluorescent lightbulbs as part of an invitation to join Faith in Place. The aspiration of finding racial diversity flourished once Kyle took over the outreach efforts.

Resulting from its attention to particular urban areas, Faith in Place developed a reputation as a grassroots environmental organization in tune with the needs of the "inner city." Through that reputation, it secured a particular place within participants' "constructions of terror and desire" related to Chicago. As it developed programming for faith communities across the Chicago area, its leaders strove to involve participants from communities historically uninvolved in environmentalism. For suburban congregations Faith in Place provided resources to talk about consumption and voluntary simplicity, and their annual workshops educated participants about environmental best practices such as water-saving measures or green building. During my fieldwork, however, Faith in Place provided most of its direct programming on the south and west sides of Chicago, geographical areas widely considered violent, dangerous, and in need of help. To be sure, images of the south and west sides as dangerous were grounded in real social conditions. Between 2008 and 2011, over 530 youth were killed in Chicago, and almost 80 percent of those homicides took place on the city's south and west sides.[15] South-side parents certainly had to worry about their children's safety. But among Faith in Place's environmentalists, violence on the south side became a totalizing discourse as people assumed that since too many homicides occurred on the south side its residents could care about nothing else.

Todd, a Unitarian Universalist seminarian affiliated with a suburban congregation, exemplified that totalizing viewpoint during a clergy meeting in 2008. Discussing the challenge of advocating for environmentalism in the inner city, Todd said, "I've been trying to work on [environmental issues on] the south side, and I have good friends down there. But they say, 'We have other issues. You worry about environment. We have to worry about our kids being shot. We love what you're doing, but we're not there yet.'"[16] Todd's interpretation of his conversations on the south side set up a progressive environmental scheme in which environmental concern could develop only as other problems dropped away. He began with a real social condition—widespread violence—and extrapolated a set of assumptions about the kinds of concerns that were or were not available to the residents of particular neighborhoods.

Marcus, a white, middle-class executive who had participated with Faith in Place for a decade, made similar assumptions about residents of Chicago's south side. He explained the differences to me during an interview. "For those of us in the suburbs who are upper middle class, [environmentalism] is going to visit the national parks, and going out to the forest preserve, or having a green kitchen when we remodel our house. It's all the things that affluence can buy," he told me. By contrast,

For an inner-city person who's more working class and struggling, it's about breathing from the smokestack from the power plant on Western Ave. And it's about "I have cars driving by my house and lead paint in my apartment. And where I live is a food desert," you know? So there's a heck of a different meaning to environmentalism for them than for us in the suburbs, but it's still the same issue.[17]

These distinctions reveal a subtle moral topography of the city. Like Todd, Marcus imagined the south and west sides of Chicago (given that predominately white neighborhoods are not part of the "inner city") as inhabiting a less advanced position along a progressive scheme of environmental concern. For him, environmentalism was separate from the struggles in daily life, and affluent people had the privilege of actively advancing environmental agendas. Conversely, people living on the south side were victims who faced more pressing concerns. To the extent that they might care about the environment, it was to deal with problems that were imposed on them.

Through her activism at Faith in Place, Kyle wanted to challenge these kinds of images of the south side. Her efforts included measures to help African Americans become "environmentally literate" and lead more eco-friendly lives, but also to challenge charitable yet patronizing images of her community that other people held. She expressed frustration when people such as Marcus, although well meaning, held African Americans to lower environmental standards. At one point during my fieldwork Kyle asked me what I had heard people saying about African Americans. I recounted Todd's comments from the clergy meeting and Kyle became visibly aggravated. "You see, that's part of the problem!" she lamented. She reminded me that African Americans were middle class too and that they had to worry about their own consumerism and be responsible for their actions just as much as white environmentalists.[18]

A similar conversation took place during a staff meeting. Lauren, the intern who coordinated Faith in Place's winter farmers' markets, reported that one south-side church had sold mangoes and celery in plastic bags during their market the previous week. Although it was clear that these products were not local and thus defeated the purpose of holding a farmers' market, Lauren had not wanted to say anything to the churchwomen who ran the event, preferring to support their efforts rather than criticize. Again, Kyle spoke up. She insisted that someone needed to tell the women that they should be selling local produce rather than mangoes or celery imported from other places. Otherwise, they and their communities would not learn. "I watch what people tolerate in marginalized communities that they wouldn't tolerate in their own," Kyle said. "But people want to know!"[19]

Even as Kyle actively contested patronizing attitudes toward the south side, Faith in Place gained credibility precisely because it worked in risky geographical areas that outsiders deemed in need of help. Kyle did not want people to think that African Americans had so many other problems they couldn't worry about the environment. At the same time, that was the image of the south side that made Faith in Place's work so alluring to many of its white supporters. Comments I heard from affluent, white participants indicated they were drawn to Faith in Place's work because it had been so dedicated to activism in communities that other environmental groups had failed to reach.

OF, BUT NOT IN, CITY NEIGHBORHOODS

The physical structure and location of Faith in Place's offices initially contributed to its image as an authentic grassroots organization in tune with needs of certain urban communities, but that image became harder to maintain as the organization moved across city space. The original office visibly represented Faith in Place's unassuming status. When I first visited in 2006, the office was located in a small space inside St. Luke's Lutheran Church in the Logan Square neighborhood on Chicago's northwest side. Logan Square was a predominately Latino neighborhood with residential streets peppered with taquerias and fruit stands. Adjacent to the trendy neighborhoods of Bucktown and Wicker Park, Logan Square also had its share of eclectic dining spots and locally owned boutiques that sold handmade clothing and jewelry. When I walked the few blocks from my bus stop to the church, I routinely saw young men hanging out just through the dark entryway of a local corner store and children riding their bicycles along the neighborhood's wide, tree-lined boulevards. This neighborhood locale, so different from the downtown office of later years, gave a striking character to the budding organization when I first met Faith in Place.

St. Luke's Church was a one-hundred-year-old building in poor repair. The dimly lit cavernous sanctuary was much too large for the small congregation's dwindling numbers, but the space also housed other activities from a Boy Scout troop to a twice-weekly food pantry. Faith in Place's suite included two small rooms with two desks each and a crowded waiting area that doubled as the copy room. Staff, volunteers, and interns shared desks, and the development director took responsibility for vacuuming the suite. Staff members brought in personal touches such as plants, tapestries, and posters to make the space more intimate, but the air was musty and the carpeting was old. The rickety window-unit air conditioners were no match for Chicago's hot, sticky summers. Paint was chipped on most of the hallway's walls, and the ceiling leaked. Staff members kept old towels on hand to cover their computers when it rained.

By 2007 Faith in Place had enough funding to move. In its second location the offices were physically nicer but still projected an image of Faith in Place as a grassroots organization in close solidarity with working-class communities. The new offices were located on the near-west side in Garfield Park, a predominately African American neighborhood. The limited food options in the area included McDonald's, KFC, a greasy spoon diner, and a small grocery section at Walgreens. Whereas Logan Square had a mix of residents and I blended in with other people in the area, I often stuck out as the only white person as my bus approached Garfield Park.

The office space was in a two-story building on a quiet, treeless street. Faith in Place occupied two-thirds of the large, open space on the bottom floor. Each of the four regular staff members had her own desk against the long, west-facing wall. The space included computer stations for interns and volunteers and a long, wooden conference table for meetings. The tapestries, artwork, and plants brought from the old offices looked much more beautiful in the new, roomy space with direct sunlight and dark, hardwood floors. Some days three or four bicycles leaned against the room's large wooden pillars, as staff and interns frequently biked to work in the summer. The building offered central air conditioning, which made for a more pleasant environment in the summer, and the computers were in no danger of getting drenched, even in the worst downpour.

But by its ten-year anniversary, Faith in Place had sufficient funding to move downtown. Butterfield searched for a centrally located space where collaborators from other organizations could easily travel for meetings. She wanted a location that allowed staff to commute via public transit. Confident that the organization would survive into the foreseeable future, Faith in Place secured a seven-year lease for office space in the Loop on Lake Street, in the same building that housed the Sierra Club and the Council for a Parliament of World Religions. The staff looked forward to the new location with special relief after gunshots shattered the front windows of Faith in Place's offices one night a few months before the move. While police determined the bullets were likely directed at the rap producer upstairs, Butterfield happily noted that gunshots through the windows were unlikely to be an issue on the ninth floor of 70 E. Lake. With a new office space just three floors below the Sierra Club, a potent symbol of mainstream environmentalism, Faith in Place gained recognition as an important environmental player as well.

Ambivalence about Growth

Faith in Place leaders expressed conflicting attitudes when it came to the organization's growth. Describing the organization to others, they often embraced its grassroots identity. Promotional brochures explained that Faith in Place could help congregations conserve energy "primarily through grassroots organizing and education," and in a letter discussing a partnership with the city's Department of Environment Kyle wrote that Faith in Place cold help the city "shape an effective grassroots program."[20] A 2008 analysis conducted by a consulting group captured Faith in Place in that way, describing it as an organization "with roots in a grassroots model of transformation."[21]

At other times the organization concertedly moved away from the grassroots model. In a 2005 strategic plan, board members included the goal of developing "new congregational relationships with regional activities" in addition to its original "grassroots organizing model."[22] By 2009 the strategic plan abandoned the grassroots concept as it described its outreach methods, setting the intention to cultivate larger regional partnerships in faith-based organizations and their governing bodies.[23] Staff members also expressed appreciation of the organization's growing professionalism. The development director told me she was thrilled when they moved out of the Logan Square office because she did not think she could handle another summer in such a physically uncomfortable environment. Butterfield chuckled with amusement one afternoon in 2007 when three staff members were lined up to speak with her. Having spent so many hours working alone at Faith in Place, she indicated, she was delighted to have such a full office.[24] She remarked on the organization's growth again later that summer as she prepared to leave for a conference, observing that it was the first time the staff was big enough to keep Faith in Place running in her absence.[25] While embracing the positive aspects of grassroots environmentalism as a movement dedicated to the concerns of ordinary people, Faith in Place leaders also appreciated the benefits that accompanied their improving status.

As Faith in Place developed into a financially stable, professionalized organization, staff members wanted to ensure that its priorities and public persona remained the same. Butterfield was especially attuned to challenges that might accompany the organization's growth, worrying that people would think differently about Faith in Place when it moved downtown. She tried to minimize the symbolic significance of the new location when she announced it to supporters. "We love our little corner of the world on Warren Blvd., but as of mid-September we will be joining all the big shots in the Loop [Chicago's downtown] so as to be more central," she announced in a newsletter. Contrasting the organization with its new, "big shot" neighbors, she signaled that Faith in Place would retain its humble status even in its new location. The announcement further assured readers that the move would not cost the organization extra money because of low rent due to the recession.[26] Despite Butterfield's efforts to downplay the move, though, some people's attitudes toward Faith in Place did change. One gardening expert gave Faith in Place a deeply discounted price to conduct a workshop but later told me he wished he had charged more after learning about the new offices.[27] With the organization's growth and professionalization, Faith in Place leaders would have to work harder to emphasize their solidarity with the communities they served.

Choosing the Right Messenger

While its location in downtown Chicago might signal power, affluence, and distance from the experience of "real" urban dwellers, Faith in Place could still assert authenticity based on the life experiences of its staff. Butterfield told a group of students that Faith in Place tried to avoid being the kind of organization that says it targets a particular community but fails to hire staff members who come from that community. "If the messenger looks like the group," she told them, "it works better."[28] Indeed, Faith in Place drew its staff from the neighborhoods where it hoped to recruit participants. Aisha Tehrani, Faith in Place's second Muslim outreach coordinator, had grown up in the Muslim community of Bridgeview, south of Chicago's downtown. She understood the community and its inhabitants and had personally experienced prejudice in the aftermath of 9/11. Monica Barreto, the youth director, had grown up in the northwest Humboldt Park neighborhood and as a child had avoided riding her bike near the lagoon where corpses were found routinely. I frequently saw Kyle assert her own urban authenticity among fellow African Americans. Lest her targeted communities perceive her as someone who could not understand their own struggles, Kyle referenced her childhood in Altgeld Gardens, a public housing development on Chicago's south side.[29]

Although Butterfield was white and middle class and had grown up in a farming community, she had lived in Chicago for decades and drew authority from her urban living as well. In casual conversations I heard her mention that she had lived for many years as a single mother in Humboldt Park, where she had learned to duck when she heard gunshots outside her window. In sermons she would mention that she lived on the south side of Chicago, and at a clergy conversation she spoke about her experiences as being part of an interracial (white-Latino) couple living in a black community.[30] Her assertions of urban authenticity must have been effective, as her conversation with a colleague conveyed. Prior to a lunchtime presentation that Butterfield gave for Faith in Place participants in 2010, we were discussing our connections to Chicago. Butterfield mentioned that she had felt out of place when she lived in Washington, D.C., and now, she said, "I will never leave Chicago, except in a box." "Where'd you grow up in Chicago?" asked Greg, a seminary professor who had known Butterfield for years. Butterfield responded, to Greg's enormous surprise, that she had grown up in central Illinois. "So you're a convert?" he asked, incredulous that she had not been an urbanite her entire life. "Yes," Butterfield replied, "and I have all the zeal of a convert."[31] Faith in Place's move across city space undermined its grassroots image, but its leaders could reference their life experiences to reassert the organization's dedication to grassroots problems in the inner city.

A NEW ERA FOR FAITH IN PLACE

In its early years, Faith in Place offered religious environmental programming to a mostly white audience characteristic of other mainstream environmental groups. But through symbolic measures such as its human-centered religious message, its office locations, its youth program, and staff members' biographies, Faith in Place conveyed the image of a grassroots organization in tune with the needs of the inner city. As the organization increasingly achieved its diversity goals by distancing its work from mainstream environmentalism, however, it began to resemble mainstream groups in significant ways. In addition to Faith in Place's new downtown office, its growing commitment to policy work, a defining characteristic of mainstream environmentalism, marked Faith in Place's shift away from grassroots environmental efforts.[32]

When Butterfield first began organizing for Faith in Place in 1999, her primary goal was to get people involved and to convince them to change their daily habits through direct, individual contact. But she gradually introduced policy work as Faith in Place matured. "Personal change has a distressingly low impact, so advocacy is increasingly a large part of what we do," Butterfield explained to a group of environmental educators visiting Faith in Place.[33] To that end in 2008, Faith in Place began offering an annual workshop titled "Faithful Citizenship" to engage participants with environmental policy issues. It began collaborating with the Illinois Environmental Council to participate in a statewide Environmental Lobby Day that year, and staff members also began to participate in a National Lobby Day in conjunction with the annual meeting of Interfaith Power and Light. With her growing focus on policy, Butterfield provided updates on current environmental legislation during staff meetings, and the organization periodically sent e-mails asking participants to contact their legislators to support environmental policies. When Faith in Place hired Brian Sauder as central Illinois organizer in 2010, they took advantage of his proximity to the state capitol and assigned him a policy role as well. As policy director Sauder made regular visits to the state capitol during legislative sessions and developed "rapid response team" initiatives to involve more Faith in Place participants in lobbying efforts.

In 2011, Faith in Place entered new political territory by generating its own piece of legislation and recruiting sponsors to support it. The bill, the Fracturing Chemical Disclosure Act (SB 664), would require companies that used the natural gas drilling method of hydraulic fracturing, commonly known as "fracking," to disclose the chemicals they pumped into the earth. Sauder recruited sponsors for the bill in Springfield, and Faith in Place organizers extensively recruited participants to lobby for the bill through postcards and phone calls. The fracking bill passed in the Illinois State Senate in April 2011 and moved forward to the House the following month. While it did not pass the House, the bill represented a new era of sophisticated policy work at Faith in Place. While still cultivating partnerships and promoting lifestyle changes among individuals at neighborhood churches, Faith in Place had joined the league of mainstream environmental organizations that saw policy work as a top goal.

Changing Leadership

If the growing resources, financial stability, and policy priorities of Faith in Place under Butterfield's leadership led the organization to resemble mainstream organizations, those characteristics became even more pronounced after Butterfield decided to leave the organization in 2013.[34] Faith in Place's board selected Brain Sauder, previously the central Illinois organizer and policy director, to fill Butterfield's role.[35] Having recently completed an MBA in general management, Sauder projected a polished, professional appearance and brought fund-raising strengths, policy experience, and distinctive vision to his leadership role at Faith in Place. While continuing Butterfield's projects to increase environmental awareness in diverse religious communities, Sauder shifted the organization in significant ways.

Most visibly, gender dynamics under Sauder's leadership led the organization in a decisively mainstream direction. Whereas grassroots environmentalism is associated with female leaders, especially those who identify as housewives and mothers, mainstream environmentalism is associated with bureaucracy, staff expertise, and male leadership.[36] With professional experience as an attorney, and holding two terminal degrees, Butterfield was a far cry from the image of a humble housewife more often associated with grassroots leaders.[37] Yet she did lend a feminine identity to the organization throughout her time at Faith in Place, hiring an exclusively female staff in the organization's first ten years and recruiting mostly women to the board of directors.[38] The female staff attracted a predominately female constituency as well, with women outnumbering men among Faith in Place participants by a margin of 2:1.[39]

In addition to the sheer dominance of women at Faith in Place, Butterfield's leadership style lent the organization distinctively feminine characteristics. A consulting group captured the organization's feminine qualities during a board retreat in 2008.[40] "If Faith in Place were a person, what would s/he look like?" the consultants asked. "She is not authoritative. She is a leader from the margins. She makes assumptions of leadership that [are] empowering to others," board members responded.[41] Elaborating on the matters that "fire up" the organization, board members added that Faith in Place "cares more about the process than outcome. [It] doesn't mean to control," and said the process entailed "making better people."[42] Contrasting Faith in Place with descriptors such as "authoritative" and "controlling" that are commonly associated with men, the board members captured Faith in Place's feminine qualities under Butterfield's leadership.

Butterfield's feminine leadership characteristics also were evident in her fund-raising appeals. She always appeared uneasy with the fund-raising aspects expected of her role, and when asking for financial support in newsletters she pointed out that Faith in Place made direct appeals only twice each year. Even those appeals were not especially direct. "If you're someone who makes year-end gifts to non-profits you love, please consider making a donation to us," Butterfield timidly requested in one newsletter.[43] In another she offered a tender nudge at the end of a paragraph about upcoming activities: "Ok, we're also going to remind you that if you still have your spring appeal envelope at home this would be a great time to send us a contribution."[44] Employing a transformational leadership style often associated with women, Butterfield was trying to gently develop consensus in order to get the work done.[45] Avoiding direct confrontation and competitive values more often associated with male leaders, she employed the conditional mood when she asked people to donate *if* they were inclined to make donations, and in the request she assumed that Faith in Place was just one nonprofit among many that the newsletter's readers might support.

The first e-newsletter that Faith in Place sent out after Butterfield's departure offered a striking contrast. "It's time to step up!" the subject line declared, announcing a host of new activities and opportunities for participants to deepen their commitment and "embrace" Faith in Place. Two months later a large "Donate Now" button began to be featured prominently on Faith in Place's website and in the body of every e-mail. If Butterfield's approach to fund-raising was sheepish, Sauder embraced the position's fund-raising goal directly. This shift in tone mapped predictably onto a shift in the gender composition of the organization's top leadership.

Sauder appeared more confident in his embrace of the fund-raising role, and his leadership in many ways amplified Faith in Place's shift in the direction of mainstream environmental groups. By 2015 Sauder had hired four additional men to work at Faith in Place. Women still dominated on the staff, holding twelve of the seventeen positions, but the board of directors in 2015 included only one woman. With a growing budget and staff, the organization necessarily developed a degree of bureaucracy. The seventeen staff members in 2015 were housed in three separate offices, a major change from the time when I had met the four women who ran Faith in Place in 2006. With four directors and a coordinator who oversaw workers for their own particular projects, Faith in Place had developed a degree of professionalism that was a far cry from the "all hands on deck" appearance I observed at Faith in Place in its early years. The first time I visited Faith in Place I noticed that the executive director answered the phone and was familiar with the intimate details of every project. By 2015 there were plenty of lower staff members to attend to daily projects while the executive director could focus on fund-raising and the organization's broader vision. With a white man as executive director, a sophisticated and direct approach to fund-raising, and a growing staff that necessarily entailed a degree of bureaucracy, Faith in Place had shifted to align more with mainstream environmental organizations.

Participants

In the area of racial dynamics, however, Faith in Place differed. The "Green Ceiling" report found that minorities constituted no more than 16 percent of the staff and board positions of major American environmental institutions in 2014 and rarely occupied the most powerful positions.[46] By contrast, Faith in Place's seventeen staff members in 2015 included four African Americans and two Latinas. Of the six staff members with "director" or "coordinator" in their titles, only two were white. While Faith in Place's executive director was white, the majority of its other leaders were not.

Faith in Place also countered the "almost exclusively white" image of mainstream environmentalism in terms of its membership. A 2014 analysis of the organization's supporters indicated that approximately 19 percent of Faith in Place's nearly five thousand members were African American, while 4.3 percent were Hispanic and 1.4 percent were Asian. With the addition of two staff members dedicated to Latino outreach in 2014, the proportion of Hispanic participants would likely grow. The "Green Ceiling" report was unable to offer precise numbers about minority membership in mainstream environmental groups because the organizations did not track racial characteristics of their members. But on the basis of the survey responses of the organization's leaders—according to which only 7 of the 103 conservation and preservation organizations that participated indicated they had any minority members—the report concludes that "very few" minorities participated in the groups studied.[47] With nearly 25 percent of Faith in Place participants representing communities of color, the organization exhibited significant diversity in comparison to mainstream environmental groups.

Faith in Place was not unique among environmental organizations for developing programs to address the concerns of minorities, but it did address their concerns in distinctive ways. Diversity measures in organizations such as the Sierra Club included environmental justice projects designed to reduce the impact of environmental racism in minority communities.[48] At Faith in Place, programs designed for minority audiences sought to extend beyond environmentalism's narrow focus on justice issues, expressing Kyle's insistence that minority communities were more than mere victims of environmental problems. By 2015 Faith in Place offered two programs, La Fe y la Energía (Spanish for "Faith and Energy") and Monarchs, Migrations, Birds, and Me, designed specifically to advance environmentalism in particular communities. Whereas the former simply offered a Spanish translation of an established Faith in Place program, the latter was specifically designed to connect with the particular stories that brought minority communities to Chicago. Kyle further transformed Faith in Place's daily operations as she sought to create a culture more welcoming of African Americans. In terms of financial operations, Kyle insisted that congregations must directly receive a portion of the grant funds that Faith in Place secured to work in their communities. She also pointed out and sought to overcome factors such as financial barriers and cultural expectations that excluded African Americans from Faith in Place programs. Through these and related efforts, Faith in Place attracted minority communities to environmental activities such as nature restoration, energy conservation, and policy advocacy, more often associated with mainstream environmentalism's predominately white audiences.

FAITH AND THE ECO-DIVIDE

Summing up the history of American environmentalism between 1945 and 1998, historian Hal Rothman indicated a lack of diversity as one of the failures of the environmental movement. Although environmentalism had achieved remarkable results in the areas of cleaner air and rivers, protected status for endangered species, and widespread support as a popular movement, he suggested, the environmental movement "never entirely shed its privileged-class origins."[49] Environmentalism's limitations, moreover, "were the function of the perspectives that most environmental leaders shared and of the class from which they emanated."[50] While Faith in Place's diversification efforts focused on measures of race and ethnicity more directly than concerns about class, their environmental efforts defied Rothman's assertion of the movement's main failure. Drawing leaders and participants from populations historically uninvolved with environmentalism, Faith in Place expanded the range of perspectives that environmental coalitions advanced.

Faith in Place's environmentalism related to the work of other groups in conflicting ways. In some aspects it had come to resemble other mainstream environmental groups that inherited the legacy of Progressive Era conservationism. The main activities it offered by 2015 involved opportunities for conservation work, outdoor enjoyment, and policy advocacy. Yet Faith in Place developed this agenda with attention to overcoming the eco-divide. During my fieldwork I encountered white participants who envisioned minority communities as environmental victims in need of help, as comments by Marcus and Todd conveyed. They were interested in Faith in Place in part because they understood the organization as advancing environmental justice work. But even as Faith in Place's diverse coalition appealed to some participants based on a desire to achieve social justice, the organization concertedly developed its programming in distinction to mainstream environmentalism's narrow focus on environmental justice as the only way to attract minorities. Instead, its programming grew from Kyle's insistence that minority communities could embrace active environmental agendas beyond immediate concerns of daily survival. Faith in Place enacted specific measures to broaden the organization's appeal: providing free transportation, sharing grant money, and helping communities understand their own stories in the context of a broader ecological whole. It distanced its work from mainstream environmentalism even as it increasingly embraced a mainstream environmental agenda, and it downplayed its role in environmental justice campaigns even as ideas about justice for minority communities appealed to many of its supporters. Positioning itself as an authoritative religious voice representing the voices of all communities of faith, Faith in Place in fact represented the concerns of a particular segment of progressive, modern religious groups. But in spite of these contradictions, Faith in Place successfully advanced its primary goal of overcoming the eco-divide.

Conclusion

In this book I set out to understand how attitudes and assumptions about religion, race, ethnicity, and class have shaped the "greening" of American religion. In the decades following Lynn White Jr.'s famous condemnation of Western Christianity for its role in the modern environmental crisis, scholars and religious leaders have sought to reevaluate and reinterpret traditional religious teachings to cultivate positive environmental ethics. While constructive religion-and-ecology scholarship has offered resources to show how and why religious communities ought to "go green," this work has uncovered complex factors that have shaped religious environmentalism as it is actually lived among contemporary urban Americans. Through my analysis of participants at Faith in Place, I demonstrated that environmental innovations in American religions have developed for reasons that extend far beyond direct expressions of religious teachings and faith.

Faith in Place originated with a vision of creating a religiously and racially diverse coalition. While its early diversification efforts concentrated on recruiting Muslims, that priority shifted as the organization focused instead on involving African Americans. Environmental historians have offered several reasons for the absence of African Americans among environmental coalitions, including mainstream environmentalism's wilderness-focused agenda and its predominately white leadership. Faith in Place directly tackled those issues as it prioritized human concerns and hired outreach staff from minority communities. As a result it built a coalition with 25 percent minority representation, in an era when other environmental organizations were trying to diversify but remained "predominately white."[1]

From the beginning of her time at Faith in Place, Veronica Kyle insisted that African Americans needed to become involved for reasons that transcended a narrow focus on environmental justice. Through Bible studies, weatherization projects, and community gardens, she developed a different narrative as she insisted that African Americans could cultivate positive relationships with nature. While this rhetoric worked to attract African Americans, however, ideas about aiding the black underclass continued to attract white supporters to the work of Faith in Place. The organization developed particular programs to attract particular communities, ranging from Taqwa Eco-Foods to build relationships with Muslims to green jobs initiatives that connected with the concerns of African Americans. Faith in Place leaders did not see a need to develop particular programming for white Protestants because they seemed to come on their own. But the visible presence of certain minority groups at Faith in Place contributed to the organization's appeal for others, as symbolic connections with African Americans and Muslims fed into constructions of fantasy and desire among some of Faith in Place's white Protestant supporters.

While Faith in Place was noteworthy for the racial diversity of its coalition, its promise of religious diversity and interfaith dialogue was advanced much more in theory than in practice. Despite the visible presence of minority religious groups in Faith in Place's promotional materials and on its website, it remained predominately Protestant in its coalition, programming, and outlook. Advancing a liberal Protestant theological disposition couched in the language of religious universalism, the organization's leaders offered normative understandings of religion. The organization celebrated only those expressions of religious diversity that adhered to its modern religious expectations. Strategic decisions to hire outreach staff for African American and Latino communities, but not for recruiting religious minority groups, indicated that the organization was not particularly concerned with increasing its religious diversity.

The disjunction between Faith in Place's particular theological outlook and the universal religious values it purported to represent was emblematic of an issue not just among religious environmental activists but also in a particular branch of religion-and-ecology scholarship that has situated environmental values at the heart of every religion.

Religious environmental ideology has spread through liberal American religious culture in tandem with another celebrated liberal religious ideal—pluralism—as a set of self-evident truth claims about what is inherently good. If all religions are green, then the implication is that religious adherents who are not green are not properly interpreting or following their own religions. While recognizing some outward aspects of religious difference, constructive religion and ecology scholarship offers normative assumptions that all religions teach the same thing. Its views of the proper way to observe all religions, in turn, support the religious environmental work of organizations like Faith in Place.

Scholars such as Tomoko Masuzawa, Talal Asad, and Robert Orsi have noted the Protestant assumptions that underpin supposedly detached, scholarly accounts of religion within the academy, pointing to enduring power structures that such scholarship enacts.[2] Kocku von Stuckrad makes a similar point about scholarship in religion and ecology when he writes, "Although there may be good reasons for advocating the environmentally positive currents in religious traditions . . . this hidden agenda often leads to an ultimately colonializing attempt of 'improving' religions that are deemed ecologically inferior."[3] In keeping with that point, this work has sought to critically examine the power structures, dynamics, and implications of enforcing particular religious ecological outlooks. At Faith in Place, I discovered, earth stewardship was considered not just an ethic within, but the defining feature of, every religion. Its religious environmental teachings demanded that religious outlooks must bend to meet the earth's pressing needs. Those who maintained more conservative understandings of their inherited religious worlds, such as the understanding Sheikh Karimi advanced when he defended the practice of animal sacrifice, were written off as advancing "bad" religion.

Even as I have pointed out the theological assumptions that supported Faith in Place's work, some might examine my research and conclude that religion did not play a significant role in my interlocutors' environmental attitudes and ecological "conversions." In the previous chapters I identified some participants who already held deep environmental commitments prior to initiating religious environmental work. For them interfaith environmentalism was a happy synergy, but religious values did not especially motivate their environmental concerns. The organization's religious message, moreover, offered generalized statements about religious requirements to advance social justice, but the ideas it conveyed as "the teachings of faith" could just as easily have been advanced by any other secular environmental group. If "religion" per se was not the decisive motivating factor for most Faith in Place participants, and the organization's religious message was so general that it could work just as easily in a secular environmental group, then perhaps religion was not particularly relevant in this organization.

Such an interpretation would fail to appreciate the complex relationships between religion and the other practices of daily life, and the insider perspectives of religious environmentalists who did understand their environmental commitments as fundamental components of their religious worlds. It would also direct attention to the wrong question, asking how religion *caused* environmental attitudes and behaviors rather than focusing on ways that religious outlooks and environmental perspectives might shape each other. Even though some participants joined Faith in Place because of environmental commitments they had already cultivated in other areas of their lives, they described their environmental commitments variously as expressions of their faith awakenings and spiritual growth. Some congregational leaders hoped that the environmental programming could revitalize their churches and appeal to new, younger audiences. The creation of ecological rituals such as solar panel dedication ceremonies and "bike to worship" events, and Butterfield's resolve to understand environmental behaviors as fundamental components of religious life through her insistence that changing a lightbulb could be an "act of worship," also point to ways that environmental priorities are contributing to changing religious forms.

Whether or not "religion" per se was the decisive motivating factor that *caused* environmental conversions among Faith in Place participants, it is significant that its supporters chose to enact their environmentalism through an expressly religious organization as opposed to a secular environmental group. Butterfield explained that religious environmentalism was different from its secular counterpart because it was more hopeful and because it emphasized kindness for all. In terms of ecological ethics, her organization advanced a distinctive, moderate outlook designed to attract participants on the basis of their traditional understandings of faith. Through these and other measures Faith in Place appealed to those who identified as "people of faith," and they helped participants understand environmental behaviors as ways of aligning their practices with their beliefs.

Faith in Place participants may not have engaged in environmental behaviors because of great awakenings inspired by reading scripture or experiencing the divine. But that does not mean that their environmental and religious worlds were unrelated. The hermeneutic of lived religion directs attention to the complex relationships and interactions between religion, daily practices, and the material circumstances of everyday life. Through this work I have examined some of those complex relationships. I have shown how religious environmental commitments derive from a complex web of motivations that involves religious values, racial assumptions, and a host of other factors. Faith in Place participants came to understand environmental values as an important component of religious life and religious values as essential to supporting their environmental commitments. While the exact nature of those values may have varied among different individuals and groups, Faith in Place's work clearly contributed to changing forms of environmentalism and represented a new way of being religious in American life.

Notes

INTRODUCTION

1. Hoop houses are an eco-friendly alternative to a greenhouse. Consisting of a row of metal hoops covered by heavy greenhouse plastic, hoop houses create warmth and extend the growing season by several weeks. They trap natural heat from the sun and do not require the intense energy input of a greenhouse.

2. Environmental activist Van Jones, the founder and former president of Green for All and former special adviser for green jobs at the White House Council on Environmental Quality, writes and talks extensively about the eco-divide.

3. Roger S. Gottlieb, *A Greener Faith: Religious Environmentalism and Our Planet's Future* (Oxford: Oxford University Press, 2006); Arne Kalland, "The Religious Environmentalist Paradigm," in *The Encyclopedia of Religion and Nature*, ed. Bron Taylor (London: Continuum International, 2006).

4. For example, in a presentation titled "So You Want Allies among People of Faith? Tips for Working with Religious Congregations," Faith in Place's development director stated, "All religions share a common responsibility to care for the Earth" (Faith in Place, internal document, April 2007). Green Faith, an interfaith environmental organization based in New Jersey, similarly states on its website, "Our work is based on beliefs shared by the world's great religions—we believe that protecting the earth is a religious value, and that environmental stewardship is a moral responsibility." Green Faith, "About Green Faith: Mission and Areas of Focus," n.d., accessed April 17, 2016, www.greenfaith.org/about/mission-and-areas-of-focus.

5. For more on the white, affluent legacy of American environmentalism, see Robert Gottlieb, *Forcing the Spring: The Transformation of the American Environmental Movement*, 2nd ed. (Washington, DC: Island Press, 2005); Robert D. Bullard, "Anatomy of Environmental Racism and the Environmental Justice

Movement," in *Confronting Environmental Racism: Voices from the Grassroots*, ed. Robert D. Bullard (Boston: South End Press, 1993), 15–40; Frederick Buttel and William L. Flinn, "Social Class and Mass Environmental Beliefs: A Reconsideration," *Environment and Behavior*, no. 10 (September 1978): 433–50; Riley E. Dunlap, "Public Opinion on the Environment in the Reagan Era: Polls, Pollution, and Politics," *Environment* 29 (1987): 6–11, 31–37; Paul Mohai, "Public Concern and Elite Involvement in Environmental Conservation," *Social Science Quarterly* 66 (December 1985): 820–38; Paul Mohai, "Black Environmentalism," *Social Science Quarterly* 71 (April 1990): 744–65; Paul Mohai and Bunyan Bryant, "Is There a 'Race' Effect on Concern for Environmental Quality?," *Public Opinion Quarterly* 62, no. 4 (1998): 475–505; Carl Anthony, "Why African Americans Should Be Environmentalists," *Race, Poverty and the Environment* 1, no. 1 (1990): 5–6; Hal K. Rothman, *The Greening of a Nation? Environmentalism in the United States since 1945* (Fort Worth, TX: Harcourt Brace College, 1998).

6. Robert Booth Fowler, *The Greening of Protestant Thought* (Chapel Hill: University of North Carolina Press, 1995); Katharine K. Wilkinson, *Between God and Green: How Evangelicals Are Cultivating a Middle Ground on Climate Change* (New York: Oxford University Press, 2012), 15.

7. Mary Evelyn Tucker and John Grim, "Intellectual and Organizational Foundations of Religion and Ecology," in *Grounding Religion: A Field Guide to the Study of Religion and Ecology*, ed. Whitney Bauman, Richard Bohannon, and Kevin J. O'Brien (New York: Routledge, 2011), 81–95.

8. Roger Gottlieb, *Greener Faith*; Mallory McDuff, *Sacred Acts: How Churches Are Working to Protect Earth's Climate* (Gabriola Island, British Columbia: New Society, 2012); Mallory D. McDuff, *Natural Saints: How People of Faith Are Working to Save God's Earth* (Oxford: Oxford University Press, 2010).

9. Kocku von Stuckrad, "Finding Data: Some Reflections on Ontologies and Normativities," *Journal for the Study of Religion, Nature, and Culture* 1, no. 1 (2007): 39–46; Bron Taylor, "Religious Studies and Environmental Concern," in B. Taylor, *Encyclopedia*, 1373–79; Bron Taylor, "Editor's Introduction: Toward a Robust Scientific Investigation of the 'Religion' Variable in the Quest for Sustainability," *Journal for the Study of Religion, Nature and Culture* 5, no. 3 (2011): 252–63; Eleanor Finnegan, "What Traditions Are Represented in Religion and Ecology? A Perspective from an American Scholar of Islam," in *Inherited Land: The Changing Grounds of Religion and Ecology*, ed. Whitney Bauman, Richard Bohannon, and Kevin J. O'Brien (Eugene, OR: Pickwick Publications, 2011), 64–79.

10. Henry Martinez, "Earth Care in the Christian Tradition: Resources by Denomination," 2010, Web of Creation, Lutheran School of Theology at Chicago, www.webofcreation.org/images/stories/downloads/earth-care%20by%20denomination.pdf.

11. See the website for the Forum on Religion and Ecology at Yale at http://fore.research.yale.edu/.

12. Pope Francis, "Laudato Si: On Care for Our Common Home," Encyclical Letter on Climate Change and the Environment, 2015, http://w2.vatican.va

/content/francesco/en/encyclicals/documents/papa-francesco_20150524_enciclica-laudato-si.html.

13. Sally G. Bingham, *Love God, Heal Earth* (Pittsburgh, PA: St. Lynns Press, 2009); Scott C. Sabin and Kathy Ide, *Tending to Eden: Environmental Stewardship for God's People* (Valley Forge, PA: Judson Press, 2010); J. Matthew Sleeth, *Serve God, Save the Planet: A Christian Call to Action* (Grand Rapids, MI: Zondervan, 2007); Steven Bouma-Prediger, *For the Beauty of the Earth: A Christian Vision for Creation Care* (Grand Rapids, MI: Baker Academic Press, 2001); *Green Bible*, New Revised Standard Version, ed. Michael G. Maudlin and Marlene Baer (New York: HarperCollins, 2008); *Renewal*, dir. Marty Ostrow and Terry K. Rockefeller (Fine Cut Productions, 2008); "Ethical Eating," *Religion and Ethics Newsweekly*, PBS, July 16, 2010, transcript at www.pbs.org/wnet/religionandethics/2010/07/16/july-16-2010-ethical-eating /6630/; *When Heaven Meets Earth: Faith and Environment in the Chesapeake Bay*, dir. Jeffrey Pohorski, prod. Susan Emmerich (SkunkFilms, 2011).

14. Two of the three goals of the Buddhist Peace Fellowship are to "raise humanitarian, environmental, and social justice concerns among Buddhist communities" and to "bring a Buddhist perspective to contemporary peace, environmental, and social justice movements." Buddhist Peace Fellowship, "Mission," n.d., accessed January 12, 2012, www.bpf.org/about-us/mission-statement.

15. Green Faith, "About Green Faith."

16. For more on Green Faith's certification and leadership programs, see http://Green Faith.org/.

17. Lynn White Jr., "The Historical Roots of Our Ecologic Crisis," *Science* 155, no. 3767 (1967): 1203–7; Bron Taylor, introduction to B. Taylor, *Encyclopedia*, xiv.

18. White was not the first person to advance such a thesis, but he did so in the late 1960s, when a sense of environmental alarm was growing in America amid a wider political awakening, so his argument fell on attentive ears. Perry Miller's *Errand into the Wilderness* and Roderick Nash's *Wilderness and the America Mind* also made the case that Christianity led to antienvironmental attitudes, prior to the publication of White's thesis. Perry Miller, *Errand into the Wilderness* (Cambridge, MA: Belknap Press of Harvard University Press, 1956); Roderick Nash, *Wilderness and the American Mind* (1967; New Haven, CT: Yale University Press, 2001). Roderick Nash's *The Rights of Nature* also points out that Walter Lowdermilk, Joseph Sittler, and Richard Baer all critiqued Christianity for contributing to the environmental crisis prior to Lynn White's groundbreaking essay. Roderick Nash, *The Rights of Nature: A History of Environmental Ethics* (Madison: University of Wisconsin Press, 1989). For more on the intellectual roots of the field, see B. Taylor, introduction to B. Taylor, *Encyclopedia*, xv; Bron Raymond Taylor, "Environmental Ethics," in B. Taylor, *Encyclopedia*, 599.

19. White left a loophole for the creation of a "green" Christianity by suggesting that, while Christianity had been interpreted as anthropocentric, this interpretation was not necessarily "correct."

20. White, "Historical Roots," 1207.

21. J. Baird Callicott, *In Defense of the Land Ethic: Essays in Environmental Philosophy* (Albany: State University of New York Press, 1989); J. Baird Callicott and Roger T. Ames, *Nature in Asian Traditions of Thought: Essays in Environmental Philosophy* (Albany: State University of New York Press, 1989). But geographer Yi Fu Tuan challenged this line of thinking, pointing out that China's environmental record was poor long before it had significant contact with Western culture. Yi Fu Tuan, "Discrepancies between Environmental Attitude and Behavior: Examples from Europe and China," *Canadian Biographer* 12 (1968): 176–91.

22. Jay B. McDaniel, *Of God and Pelicans: A Theology of Reverence for Life* (Louisville, KY: Westminister/John Knox Press, 1989); Dieter T. Hessel, *After Nature's Revolt: Eco-Justice and Theology* (Minneapolis: Fortress Press, 1992).

23. Arthur Dahl, "World Wide Fund for Nature (W.W.F.)," in B. Taylor, *Encyclopedia*, 1770. The five leaders were Buddhist, Christian, Hindu, Jewish, and Muslim.

24. Ibid. Additional declarations were made by Baha'is (1987), Sikhs (1989), Jains (1991), and Daoists of China (1995).

25. Steven C. Rockefeller, and John Elder, *Spirit and Nature: Why the Environment Is a Religious Issue: An Interfaith Dialogue* (Boston: Beacon Press, 1992), 2; Bill Moyers, "Spirit and Nature," *Bill Moyers' Journal*, PBS, 1991, video and transcript at http://billmoyers.com/content/spirit-nature/.

26. The religions represented at the Harvard Conferences include Judaism, Christianity, Islam, Jainism, Hinduism, Buddhism, Confucianism. Daoism, Shinto, and "indigenous religions."

27. Yale Divinity School, invitation to conference, "Renewing Hope: Pathways of Religious Environmentalism," February 28–March 2, 2008, n.d., accessed April 17, 2016, www.yale.edu/divinity/news/071128_news_renewing .shtml.

28. Michael Hogue et al., "Chicago Religious Environmentalisms," panel, Religion and Ecology Group, annual meeting of the American Academy of Religion, Chicago, November 2, 2008.

29. McDuff, *Natural Saints.*

30. Faith in Place, "Who We Are," n.d., accessed June 2013, www.faithinplace .org/who-we-are (has since been updated).

31. Clare Butterfield, "Book Proposal for *Faith in Place, Faith in Practice: A Field Guide to Bringing Congregations into Right Relationship with the Earth*," April 30, 2007, 30.

32. The first of Faith in Place's "Ten Tips" for organizing environmental ministries, summarized in an introductory talk that staff members presented to new congregations, was "Connect green efforts to your faith." When elaborating this point, staff members emphasized the importance of connecting environmental values to the central worship life of the church so that the environment was on people's minds throughout the year (field notes, August 26, 2008).

33. GuideStar, "Faith in Place," GuideStar Exchange Charting Impact Report, Faith in Place internal document, last updated June 26, 2013.

34. Patrick Curry, *Ecological Ethics: An Introduction* (Malden, MA: Polity Press, 2006), 47.

35. For more on radical environmentalism, see John Davis, *The Earth First! Reader: Ten Years of Radical Environmentalism* (Salt Lake City, UT: Peregrine Smith Books, 1991); Christopher Manes, *Green Rage: Radical Environmentalism and the Unmaking of Civilization* (Boston: Little, Brown, 1990); Bill Devall and George Sessions, *Deep Ecology* (Salt Lake City, UT: G.M. Smith, 1985). Additionally, Bron Taylor analyzes the religious/spiritual elements of radical environmentalism in Bron Taylor, *Dark Green Religion: Nature Spirituality and the Planetary Future* (Berkeley: University of California Press, 2010).

36. Rebecca Kneale Gould, *At Home in Nature: Modern Homesteading and Spiritual Practice in America* (Berkeley: University of California Press, 2005).

37. Religions of the World and Ecology, series editors Mary Evelyn Tucker and John Grim (Cambridge, MA: Harvard University Press, 1997–2002).

38. There are, of course, notable exceptions to this general statement. See, for example, David L. Haberman, *River of Love in an Age of Pollution* (Berkeley: University of California Press, 2006); David L. Haberman, *People Trees: Worship of Trees in Northern India* (New York: Oxford University Press, 2013); Dianna Bell, "Understanding a 'Broken World': Islam, Ritual, and Climate Change in Mali, West Africa," *Journal for the Study of Religion, Nature and Culture* 8, no. 3 (2014): 287–306; Elizabeth Allison, "Waste and Worldviews: Garbage and Pollution Challenges in Bhutan," *Journal for the Study of Religion, Nature and Culture* 8, no. 4 (2014): 405–28.

39. Roger Gottlieb, *Greener Faith*, xi.

40. McDuff, *Natural Saints*, 112–13.

41. Field notes, November 5, 2009.

42. Field notes, December 2, 2009.

43. Field notes, June 4, 2009.

44. Field notes, October 29, 2009.

45. Robert Orsi, "Everyday Miracles: The Study of Lived Religion," in *Lived Religion in America: Toward a History of Practice,* ed. David Hall (Princeton, NJ: Princeton University Press, 1997), 6–7.

46. Ibid., 9.

47. Voter Activation Network, "An In-Depth Analysis of Faith in Place Supporters," Faith in Place, internal document, 2014.

48. Ann Braude, "Women's History *Is* American Religious History," in *Retelling U.S. Religious History,* ed. Thomas A. Tweed (Berkeley: University of California Press, 1997), 87–107; Lori D. Ginzberg, *Women and the Work of Benevolence: Morality, Politics, and Class in the Nineteenth-Century United States,* Yale Historical Publications (New Haven, CT: Yale University Press, 1990); Karen Warren, ed., *Ecofeminism: Women, Culture, Nature* (Bloomington: Indiana University Press, 1997); Nicholas Freudenberg and Carol Steinsapir, "Not in Our Backyards: The Grassroots Environmental Movement," *Society and Natural Resources* 4, no. 3 (1991): 235–45.

49. Clare Butterfield, interview, February 18, 2010.

50. In this way they supported the findings of a study of women's leadership in the movement for immigrant rights. A feminist consciousness served as a "vital resource" for the female leaders in this movement, Milkman and Terriquez found, but the women expressed that consciousness primarily behind

closed doors. Ruth Milkman and Veronica Terriquez, "'We Are the Ones Who Are Out in Front': Women's Leadership in the Immigrant Rights Movement," *Feminist Studies* 38, no. 3 (2012): 723–52.

51. Field notes, July 24, 2007.

52. Field notes, June 17, 2009.

53. Field notes, November 3, 2009. The dominance of women at Faith in Place did fade over time, a shift I discuss in chapter 7. Brian Sauder, the staff member hired for the central Illinois position, became the organization's executive director after Butterfield stepped down in 2013.

54. See the Girls in Green website at www.girlz-rule.org/girsingreen.html.

55. Field notes, December 12, 2009.

56. Field notes, February 19, 2010.

57. Dorceta E. Taylor, "The State of Diversity in Environmental Organizations: Mainstream NGOs, Foundations, Government Agencies," Report, Green 2.0, 2014, 4, www.diversegreen.org/the-challenge/. The environmental organizations included 191 conservation and preservation organizations, seventy-four government environmental agencies, and twenty-eight environmental grant-making foundations. In May 2015, Green 2.0, the working group that commissioned the study, applauded the Sierra Club for hiring Aaron Mair as the organization's first African American president. Green 2.0, "Green 2.0 Congratulates Aaron Mair, First African American Elected as President of the Sierra Club," press release, May 18, 2015, www.diversegreen.org/press-release-green-2–0-congratulates-aaron-mair-first-african-american-elected-as-president-of-the-sierra-club/.

58. Among the conservation and preservation groups with annual budgets over $1 million, 90 percent of the presidents were men.

59. D. Taylor, "State of Diversity," 4.

60. Dorceta E. Taylor, "The Green Insiders' Club: Highlights from 'The State of Diversity in Enviornmental Organizations,'" Green 2.0, 2014, www.diversegreen.org/the-challenge/.

61. Guidestar, "Faith in Place."

62. Mark Stoll, "Religion and African American Environmental Activism," in *"To Love the Wind and Rain": African Americans and Environmental History,* ed. Dianne G. Glave and Mark Stoll (Pittsburgh, PA: University of Pittsburgh Press, 2006), 150–63; Anthony, "Why African Americans"; Barbara Lee and Van Jones, "Want to Win the Climate Fight? Engage Communities of Color," *Huffington Post*, April 22, 2015, updated June 22, 2015, www.huffingtonpost.com/rep-barbara-lee/want-to-win-the-climate-f_b_7120006.html.

63. The "Green Ceiling" report acknowledges that it does not examine power structures based on religion, and it calls on future research to focus on that aspect. D. Taylor, "State of Diversity," 15.

64. For more on the United States as a secularized Protestant culture, see Tracy Fessenden, *Culture and Redemption: Religion, the Secular, and American Literature* (Princeton, NJ: Princeton University Press, 2007).

65. Charles Taylor contends that belief in God is still possible in the immanent frame, but belief in the supernatural is only one option among many and is "frequently not the easiest to embrace." Charles Taylor, *A Secular Age* (Cambridge, MA: Belknap Press of Harvard University Press, 2007), 3.

66. Talal Asad, *Formations of the Secular: Christianity, Islam, Modernity, Cultural Memory in the Present* (Stanford, CA: Stanford University Press, 2003); C. Taylor, *Secular Age; see also* Winnifred Fallers Sullivan, *Prison Religion: Faith-Based Reform and the Constitution* (Princeton, NJ: Princeton University Press, 2009); Fessenden, *Culture and Redemption;* W. Clark Gilpin, "Secularism: Religious, Irreligious, and Areligious," Religion and Culture Web Forum, March 2007, https://divinity.uchicago.edu/sites/default/files/imce/pdfs/webforum/032007/secularism.pdf; Craig J. Calhoun, Mark Juergensmeyer, and Jonathan VanAntwerpen, *Rethinking Secularism* (Oxford: Oxford University Press, 2011).

67. Craig J. Calhoun, Mark Juergensmeyer, and Jonathan VanAntwerpen, introduction to Calhoun, Juergensmeyer, and VanAntwerpen, *Rethinking Secularism,* 6; Fessenden, *Culture and Redemption.* As a guiding question Fessenden asks: "How have specific forms of Protestant belief and practice come enduringly to be subsumed under the heading of 'Christian'—to the exclusion of non-Protestant and differently Protestant ways of being Christian—and how, in many cases, does 'Christian' come to stand in for the 'religious' to the exclusion of non-Christian ways of being religious?" The answer, she contends, lies partly in "the ability of a Protestantized conception of religion to control the meanings of both the religious *and* the secular" (4).

68. Field notes, July 17, 2008.

69. Clare Butterfield, Veronica Kyle, Shireen Pishdadi, and Brian Sauder are the actual names of Faith in Place staff members. The names of all other informants mentioned throughout the text are pseudonyms.

70. Field notes, April 14, 2010.

71. James Clifford, "Introduction: Partial Truths," in *Writing Culture: The Poetics and Politics of Ethnography,* ed. James Clifford and George Marcus (Berkeley: University of California Press, 1986), 1–26; Ruth Behar and Deborah A. Gordon, eds., *Women Writing Culture* (Berkeley: University of California Press, 1995).

1. PEOPLE, NOT POLAR BEARS

1. Faith in Place, "Ten Tips Talk for Congregations," in "Seminarian Speakers Bureau Training," internal document, January 2010.

2. The Sierra Club says its mission is "to explore, enjoy, and protect the wild places of the earth; to practice and promote the responsible use of the earth's ecosystems and resources; to educate and enlist humanity to protect and restore the quality of the natural and human environment; and to use all lawful means to carry out these objectives." Sierra Club, "Sierra Club Policies," accessed July 20, 2013, www.sierraclub.org/policy/.

3. Geoffrey Johnson, "Green Awards 2007 Honorees," *Chicago Magazine,* May 26, 2007, www.chicagomag.com/Chicago-Magazine/April-2007/Green-Awards-Honorees/index.php?cparticle=4&siarticle=3#artanc.

4. Stoll, "Religion"; D. Taylor, "State of Diversity."

5. Faith in Place, "Ten Fruitful Years: Faith in Place Ten Year Report," internal document, 2009, 6.

6. Center for Neighborhood Technology, "One Creation, One People, One Place," July 1, 1998, www.cnt.org/publications/one-creation-one-people-one-place-a-statement-of-the-interreligious-sustainability.

7. Lowell W. Livezey and Elfriede Wedam, "Faith in Place (originally Interreligious Sustainability Project) Evaluation Report," Faith in Place, internal document, 2003.

8. Ibid.

9. Clare Butterfield, interview, December 18, 2010.

10. For example, historian Mark Stoll writes, "Despite early national and international recognition of the necessary connection between social justice and the environment, almost twenty years of American environmental activism has narrowed the gap between environmentalist and African American concerns very little, if at all." Stoll, "Religion," 152.

11. For a review of this literature, see Matthew Whittaker, Gary M. Segura, and Shaun Bowler, "Racial/Ethnic Group Attitudes toward Environmental Protection in California: Is 'Environmentalism' Still a White Phenomenon?," *Political Research Quarterly* 58, no. 3 (2005): 436.

12. Carolyn Merchant, *American Environmental History* (New York: Columbia University Press, 2007); Robert Gottlieb, *Forcing the Spring*.

13. Henry Vance Davis, "The Environmental Voting Record of the Congressional Black Caucus," in *Race and the Incidence of Environmental Hazards: A Time for Discourse,* ed. Bunyan Bryant and Paul Mohai (Boulder, CO: Westview Press, 1992), 55–63; Hawley Truax, "Beyond White Environmentalism: Minorities and the Environment," *Environmental Action* 21, no. 4 (January/February 1990): 19–31.

14. Joseph E. Taylor and Matthew Klingle, "Environmentalism's Elitist Tinge Has Roots in the Movement's History," *Grist,* March 9, 2006, http://grist.org/politics/klingle/; Caroline Beaton, "Is Environmentalism Elitist?," *Elephant Journal,* December 12, 2014, www.elephantjournal.com/2014/12/is-environmentalism-elitist/; Louis Sahagun, "History in a New Light: Rethinking Muir," *Los Angeles Times,* November 13, 2014.

15. Although Muir was self-educated, other Sierra Club founders had prestigious educational backgrounds. Rothman, *Greening of a Nation?,* 17.

16. Ibid., 34.

17. Robert Gottlieb, *Forcing the Spring*.

18. This includes the Water Quality Control Act (1965), the Wild and Scenic Rivers Act (1968), and the Clean Air Act (1970).

19. These activists were influenced by deep ecology, a concept developed in the early 1970s by Norwegian philosopher Arne Naess.

20. The report found that a community's racial composition was the single most significant factor in predicting the locations of hazardous waste facilities and concluded that it was "virtually impossible" for this distribution to be a matter of chance. Martin V. Melosi, "Environmental Justice, Ecoracism, and Environmental History," in Glave and Stoll, *"To Love the Wind,"* 127.

21. Eileen Maura McGurty, *Transforming Environmentalism: Warren County, PCBs, and the Origins of Environmental Justice* (New Brunswick, NJ: Rutgers University Press, 2007), 5.

22. Dorceta E. Taylor, "Green Insiders' Club"; Paul Mohai, "Dispelling Old Myths: African American," *Environment: Science and Policy for Sustainable Development* 45, no. 5 (2003): 10–26; Kerry Ard and Paul Mohai, "Hispanics and Environmental Voting in the US Congress," *Environmental Practice* 13, no. 4 (2011): 302–13; Whittaker, Segura, and Bowler, "Racial/Ethnic Group Attitudes."

23. Livezey and Wedam, "Faith in Place," 11.

24. Butterfield recounted this history to a group of environmental education master's students who visited Faith in Place's office in 2009 (field notes, December 3, 2009).

25. Butterfield, "Book Proposal," 18. Butterfield insists that "environmental refugees" should not be banished from their congregations' environmental initiatives but that they should play roles that are behind the scenes. Discussing this issue with a group of seminarians, Butterfield said: "There might be people who've been working on this for a long time, and people no longer listen to them. These people might be in the group you're talking to. Love them, support them, but don't make them the spokesperson" (field notes, August 26, 2008).

26. Clare Butterfield, interview, February 18, 2010.

27. Clare Butterfield, "Notes for Workshop, February 1, 2004," Faith in Place, internal document, 2004.

28. Faith in Place, "Introduction to Faith in Place," internal document, October 5, 2006.

29. Curry, *Ecological Ethics*.

30. Field notes, August 26, 2008.

31. Clare Butterfield, "A Moral Climate: Sermon for Prairie Circle Unitarian Universalist Congregation," Faith in Place, internal document, June 22, 2008.

32. Daishi, interview, July 21, 2010.

33. See the website at www.350.org. The number 350 refers to the parts per million of carbon dioxide that climate scientists say is the safe limit for humanity. According to the 350.org website (accessed May 3, 2016), the current level of carbon dioxide in the earth's atmosphere is 400 ppm.

34. Daishi, interview, July 21, 2010.

35. For more on the Lutheran School of Theology at Chicago's Earth Year, see their announcement, "LSTC Declares 2009–2010 'Earth Year,'" April 21, 2009, www.lstc.edu/communications/news/?a=article&id=229.

36. Field notes, January 22, 2010.

37. Margaret, interview, July 14, 2010.

38. Field notes, July 6, 2006.

39. Faith in Place, "Ten Fruitful Years."

40. Mark R. Warren, *Dry Bones Rattling: Community Building to Revitalize American Democracy* (Princeton, NJ: Princeton University Press, 2001), 42–43.

41. Butterfield, "Book Proposal," 15.

42. Ibid., 4.

43. By 2015 Faith in Place had made an updated version of these tips available on its website: "Ten Tips for Your Green Team," accessed April 18, 2016, www.faithinplace.org/sites/www.faithinplace.org/files/assets/10_Tips_Full-Sheet_smallerfile.pdf.

44. Field notes, August 26, 2008.

45. Butterfield, "Book Proposal," 13.
46. Megan, interview, July 22, 2011.

2. RELIGIOUS ENVIRONMENTALISM IN THE CITY

1. Nash, *Wilderness*.
2. Victor Rubin, "The Roots of the Urban Greening Movement," in *Growing Greener Cities: Urban Sustainability in the Twenty-First Century,* ed. Eugenie Ladner Birch and Susan M. Wachter (Philadelphia: University of Pennsylvania Press, 2008), 187–206.
3. David Dodman, "Blaming Cities for Climate Change? An Analysis of Urban Greenhouse Gas Emissions Inventories," *Environment and Urbanization* 23, no. 2 (2009): 185–201; David Owen, "Green Manhattan," *New Yorker,* October 18, 2004, 111.
4. Tom Daniels, "Taking the Initiative: Why Cities Are Greening Now," in Birch and Wachter, *Growing Greener Cities,* 11–27; Rubin, "Roots." Additionally, Peter Berg and Planet Drum Foundation offered some of the earliest manifestations of the green city movement. Peter Berg, Beryl Magilavy, and Seth Zuckerman, *A Green City Program for San Francisco Bay Area Cities and Towns* (San Francisco: Planet Drum Books, 1989).
5. However, the city's recycling system remained highly ineffective, a blight on Daley's environmental record. Mick Dumke, "Why Can't Chicago Recycle?," *Chicago Reader,* July 27, 2010.
6. Julia Kennedy, Peter Haas, and Bill Eyring, "Measuring the Economic Impacts of Greening: The Center for Neighborhood Technology Green Values Calculator," in Birch and Wachter, *Growing Greener Cities,* 326–45.
7. Community-supported agriculture is a system in which local farmers sell a number of "shares" of their harvest to the public. Subscribers purchase a season-long share of the harvest and receive a box of seasonal produce each week of the growing season. This arrangement is considered advantageous for small farmers, who can greatly benefit from the cash flow early in the season. It's also considered advantageous for consumers because they receive fresh, healthy vegetables and can develop relationships with the people who grow their food.
8. Taqwa Co-op, "About Us," Faith in Place, internal document, 2003.
9. The board made this decision on the basis of the recommendation of a consulting group that analyzed Faith in Place's operations in 2008. The consulting group noted that Taqwa ran at a deficit (it would take Faith in Place six years to pay off the debt at a rate of $500/month, according to the report), and they were not optimistic that there was a market for expanding the co-op beyond the families already involved. Eric Friedenwald-Fishman and Soudary Kittivong-Greenbaum, "Faith in Place: Findings and Recommendations," Metropolitan Group, December 17, 2008, Faith in Place, internal document, 2.
10. Clare Butterfield, interview, January 26, 2011.
11. The Good Loaf made only communion loaves for Protestants, and not communion wafers for Catholics, because Faith in Place did not want to create competition for Catholic sisters who sold wafers as an income source.

12. "Winter Farmers Markets," Faith in Place, accessed March 15, 2014, http://org2.democracyinaction.org/o/6265/p/salsa/web/common/public/content?content_item_KEY=8942.

13. Field notes, June 18, 2009.

14. Clare Butterfield, "Another Invitation for You," e-mail to Faith in Place Clergy Group, September 8, 2010.

15. Butterfield, "Book Proposal," 38–39.

16. Faith in Place ended the youth program in order to focus on other priorities after its coordinator left the organization in 2013.

17. Weatherization can include low-cost measures, such as covering windows and using caulk to fill in holes, and measures that cost significantly more, such as having insulation installed professionally, replacing doors or thermostats, and repairing furnaces. Weatherization makes buildings more comfortable and is "green" because it reduces energy use—for example, when heated air stays inside the house, furnaces do not have to be used as much.

18. This project was part of the Delta Institute Weatherization Program, which offered free weatherization services to middle-income families. Because they wanted to recruit a diverse constituency of home owners who would receive their services, they hired Faith in Place to help with their outreach.

19. Field notes, September 12, 2009.

20. Robert A. Orsi, *Gods of the City: Religion and the American Urban Landscape*, Religion in North America (Bloomington: Indiana University Press, 1999), 53.

21. Ibid., 52–53; see also George Chauncey, *Gay New York: Gender, Urban Culture, and the Makings of the Gay Male World, 1890–1940* (New York: Basic Books, 1994).

22. A 2012 report by the Manhattan Institute for Policy Research noted that racial separation in American neighborhoods declined significantly between 1890 and 2010, but Chicago remains the nation's most segregated city. Edward Glaeser and Jacob Vigdor, *The End of the Segregated Century: Racial Separation in America's Neighborhoods, 1890–2010* (New York: Manhattan Institute for Policy Research, January 2012), https://www.manhattan-institute.org/html/end-segregated-century-racial-separation-americas-neighborhoods-1890–2010–5848.html.

23. At a staff meeting, Butterfield asked Kyle to encourage members of the churches she'd been working with to attend an upcoming Faith in Place workshop, because "it's critical to pull people into the larger group" (field notes, June 17, 2009.

24. For example, in 2009 the development director proposed to hold a workshop at the Sikh gurdwara in Palatine because "it's a powerful place, and people will want it on their mental map" (field notes, December 15, 2009).

25. Deconstruction is the practice of carefully taking buildings apart rather than demolishing them with a wrecking ball or bulldozer. Then pieces are salvaged for reuse in future building projects.

26. These examples were offered through Faith in Place's "Three Thursdays in June" series in 2008.

27. An analysis of Faith in Place's database in 2014 indicated the organization had 4,474 supporters. Voter Activation Network, "In-Depth Analysis."

28. Orsi, *Gods of the City*.

29. Ibid., 13; Lee Clark Mitchell, *Witnesses to a Vanishing America: The Nineteenth-Century Response* (Princeton, NJ: Princeton University Press, 1981).

30. Peter Schmitt notes that in 1899 *Webster's Dictionary* cites John Burroughs's definition of Arcadia as a "scene of simple pleasure and untroubled quiet." He adds that "as a place it lay somewhere on the urban fringe, easily accessible and mildly wild." Peter Schmitt, *Back to Nature: The Arcadian Myth in Urban America*, 2nd ed. (Baltimore: John Hopkins University Press, 1990), xix.

31. Faith in Place, "Interreligious Sustainability Project Curriculum for Congregations in the Chicago Region: Curriculum 4," internal document, 2000.

32. Ibid., 6.

33. Daniels, "Taking the Initiative," 22.

34. Field notes, July 15, 2009. "It All Flows Downstream" event at the Field Museum.

35. Field notes, May 28, 2008.

3. PATHS LEADING TO FAITH IN PLACE

1. Faith in Place commissioned the analysis from the Voter Activation Network.

2. The largest concentration of Protestants identified themselves merely as "Christian." I am not including them in the ranking of Protestant denominations because presumably they belonged to particular Protestant denominations that they did not specify when providing their contact information to Faith in Place. I am including Unitarians as a Protestant denomination, although not all Unitarians would agree with that categorization. The relationship of Unitarian Universalism to Protestant Christianity is complex, and some Unitarians do not identify themselves as Christian. The movement is rooted in Reformed Protestant Christianity, although Unitarian Universalists now recognize both Jewish and Christian teachings as well as the teachings of various "world religions" and humanism as official sources. Unitarian Universalism is characterized by theological diversity, and worship style varies greatly among different congregations, with some identifying more strongly with Christianity than others. In this work I characterize Unitarian Universalism as a Protestant denomination because of its historical roots and theological outlook. John C. Godbey, "Unitarian Universalist Association," in *Encyclopedia of Religion,* ed. Lindsay Jones (Detroit, MI: Macmillan Reference USA, 2005); Andrew M. Hill, "Unitarians," in *Encyclopedia of Christianity,* ed. Erwin Fahlbusch, Jan Milic Lochman, and John Mbiti (Grand Rapids, MI: William B. Eerdmans, 2008).

3. Gavin, interview, February 18, 2010; Kate, interview, February 10, 2010.

4. The LVC is a national volunteer service program that places volunteers, often recent college graduates, in full-time positions at nonprofit organizations.

Groups of four to seven volunteers live together in intentional communities and receive a small living stipend for their services.

5. Lauren, interview, February 16, 2010.

6. This Bible study is the topic of chapter 4.

7. Anita, interview, April 7, 2010.

8. Jessica, interview, March 15, 2010.

9. Carol Mueller, "The One Thing All Religions Have in Common Is Responsibility for Caring for the Earth," *Lutheran*, August 2009, www.thelutheran.org/article/article.cfm?article_id=8337.

10. Danielle, interview, February 25, 2010.

11. Paul was not the only participant who seemed to look to Faith in Place almost as a replacement for his own home congregation. Butterfield told me that some Faith in Place participants seemed to consider her as their personal pastor, relying on her for support and pastoral calls that were more commonly addressed by the leaders of their own congregations. Butterfield said this was "tricky ethically" because she didn't want to "tread on somebody else's turf" (field notes, June 22, 2007).

12. Paul, interview, February 9, 2010.

13. Marcus, interview, June 17, 2010.

14. It is probably not a coincidence that this is precisely how Faith in Place leaders promoted their work. I discuss Faith in Place's religious message in chapter 6.

15. The estimate of two thousand viewers is based on Faith in Place's records. The organization asked the 144 participating conversations to collect the names and contact information of those who attended the event.

16. Jerry, interview, July 6, 2010.

17. David A. Snow and Doug McAdam, "Identity Work Processes in the Context of Social Movements: Clarifying the Identity/Movement Nexus," in *Self, Identity, and Social Movements*, ed. Sheldon Stryker, Timothy J. Owens, and Robert W. White, Social Movements, Protest, and Contention (Minneapolis: University of Minnesota Press, 2000), 41–67; Roberta Garner, *Contemporary Movements and Ideologies* (New York: McGraw-Hill, 1996); Marcy Darnovsky, Barbara Epstein, and Richard Flacks, eds., *Cultural Politics and Social Movements* (Philadelphia: Temple University Press, 1995); Roger V. Gould, *Insurgent Identities: Class, Community, and Protest in Paris from 1848 to the Commune* (Chicago: University of Chicago Press, 1995); Debra Friedman and Doug McAdam, "Collective Identity and Activism: Networks, Choices, and the Life of a Social Movement," in *Frontiers in Social Movement Theory*, ed. A.D. Morris and C.M. Mueller (New Haven, CT: Yale University Press, 1992), 153–76.

18. See Shannon Elizabeth Bell and Yvonne A. Braun, "Coal, Identity, and the Gendering of Environmental Justice Activism in Central Appalachia," *Gender and Society* 24, no. 6 (2010): 795.

19. Snow and McAdam, "Identity Work Processes," 48.

20. Ibid. Snow and McAdam define social networks as "people who not only are linked together structurally in some fashion or another but also share

common social relations, a common lifestyle, and a common fate and who therefore are likely to share a common identity" (48).

21. I discuss Jayla and Mrs. Weldon in greater length in chapter 4.

22. Snow and McAdam, "Identity Work Processes," 45.

23. Field notes, March 9, 2008.

24. Friedenwald-Fishman and Kittivong-Greenbaum, "Faith in Place," 16.

25. Field notes, January 22, 2008.

26. Ruth Frankenberg, *White Women, Race Matters: The Social Construction of Whiteness* (Minneapolis: University of Minnesota Press, 1993), 157.

27. In keeping with this observation, theologian Thandeka describes white shame as a defining feature of whiteness. Thandeka, *Learning to Be White: Money, Race, and God in America* (New York: Continuum, 2007), 12–13.

28. Robert Bullard, "Decision Making," in *Faces of Environmental Racism: Confronting Global Justice,* 2nd ed., ed. Laura Westra and Bill Lawson (Lanham, MD: Rowman and Littlefield, 2001), 6.

29. Kate, interview, February 10, 2010.

30. Anita, interview, April 7, 2010.

31. Field notes, August 26, 2008.

32. Field notes, May 4, 2010.

33. Mrs. Weldon, interview, May 17, 2010.

34. Mrs. Kinkaid, interview, April 6, 2010.

35. Nazneen, interview, May 24, 2010.

36. See, for example, this book's introduction.

37. Snow and McAdam, "Identity Work Processes"; Ralph H. Turner and Lewis M. Killian, *Collective Behavior,* 2nd ed. (Englewood Cliffs, NJ: Prentice-Hall, 1972); Louis A. Zurcher and David A. Snow, "Collective Behavior: Social Movements," in *Social Psychology: Social Perspectives,* ed. Morris Rosenberg and Ralph H. Turner (New York: Basic Books, 1981), 447–82; Ralph H. Turner and Lewis M. Killian, *Collective Behavior,* 3rd ed. (Englewood Cliffs, NJ: Prentice-Hall, 1987).

38. I have chosen to replace the garden's real name with the "Purple Radish Garden" to respect the privacy of the garden participants.

39. Unitarian Universalist Association of Congregations, "Our Unitarian Universalist Principles," accessed March 12, 2011, www.uua.org/beliefs/6798.shtml.

40. Unity Temple's senior pastor, interview, August 12, 2010. After conducting an environmental audit, the church bought a dishwasher and banned disposable paper products from the building. They replaced all of their incandescent lighting with energy-efficient compact fluorescent bulbs and installed a geothermal heating and cooling system in the church's office.

41. The class, called Menu for the Future, was one of nine discussion courses created by the Northwest Earth Institute (NWEI). Although the class was hosted at Unity Temple, the curriculum was not specifically designed for religious congregations. Intended for groups at workplaces, schools, neighborhoods, community centers, and faith communities, NWEI courses include a workbook with readings and discussion guides for self-facilitated small groups.

42. While five of the women identified as Unitarian and belonged to Unity Temple, the sixth identified as Catholic and became involved with the garden by

chance. After hearing about Unity Temple's Menu for the Future course from a friend, she inquired about participating and was welcomed to join the class and the garden that developed from it.

43. Marilyn, interview, September 29, 2010.

44. Doris, interview, September 14, 2010.

45. Marilyn, interview, September 29, 2010.

46. Jean, interview, April 13, 2010.

47. Jean, interview, April 13, 2010.

48. Marilyn, interview, September 29, 2010.

49. Andrea, "The [Radishes, pseud.] Are Busy," *Galaxy Café Newsletter* [pseud.], June 2010.

50. The Purple Radishes' use of language about religion and spirituality replicated a discourse popular in early twenty-first-century America. The two concepts were used without much precision both in popular conversations and in scholarly analyses, but in general "spirituality" was defined in contrast to the institutions, clergy, and traditions of religion. Courtney Bender, *Heaven's Kitchen: Living Religion at God's Love We Deliver* (Chicago: University of Chicago Press, 2003); Courtney Bender, *The New Metaphysicals: Spirituality and the American Religious Imagination* (Chicago: University of Chicago Press, 2010); Wade Clark Roof, *Spiritual Marketplace: Baby Boomers and the Remaking of American Religion* (Princeton, NJ: Princeton University Press, 1999); R. Stephen Warner, "Toward a New Paradigm for the Sociological Study of Religion in the United States," *American Journal of Sociology* 98 (1993): 1044–93.

51. Teresa, the group's only Catholic, expressly did not understand the garden as related to her religion, a topic I discuss in chapter 6.

52. Anthropologist Clifford Geertz describes the "really real" as a wide reality that corrects and completes the realities of everyday life. A defining concern of religious perspectives is to accept those wider realities. Clifford Geertz, *The Interpretation of Cultures* (New York: Basic Books, 1973).

53. Doris, interview, September 14, 2010.

54. Marilyn, interview, September 29, 2010.

55. Andrea, interview, September 14, 2010.

56. For more on "intuitive gardening," see Machaelle Small Wright and Perelandra Ltd., *Perelandra Garden Workbook: A Complete Guide to Gardening with Nature Intelligences,* 2nd ed. (Jeffersonton, VA: Perelandra, 1993).

57. Andrea, interview, September 14, 2010.

58. Jean, interview, April 13, 2010.

59. Ibid.

60. Ibid.

61. Doris, interview, September 14, 2010.

62. Andrea, interview, September 14, 2010.

63. Mosque leaders highlighted their environmental projects as they worked on what anthropologist Karen Brodkin would call their ethnoracial assignments. Whereas individuals construct their own ethnoracial identities in the context of the categories others place them in, ethnoracial assignment, Brodkin writes, "is about popularly held classifications and their deployment by those with national power to make them matter economically, politically, and socially

to the individuals classified." Karen Brodkin, *How Jews Became White Folks and What That Says about Race in America* (New Brunswick, NJ: Rutgers University Press, 1998), 3.

64. Alexandra Salomon, "Bridgeview Mosque Gets Solar Panel," WBEZ, Chicago Public Radio, August 1, 2008; Heidi Stevens, "Remarkable Woman: Clare Butterfield," *Chicago Tribune*, April 6, 2012; "Lt. Governor Quinn Honors 26 Residents with Environmental Hero Awards," SCARCE, December 30, 2008, www.scarceecoed.org/about-us/awards/81-lt-governor-quinn-environmental-hero-award.html.

65. Glenn R. Simpson and Amy Chozick, "Obama's Muslim-Outreach Adviser Resigns," *Wall Street Journal*, August 6, 2008.

66. Rany Jazayerli, "On Mazen Asbahi," *FiveThirtyEight: Politics Done Right*, August 8, 2008, www.fivethirtyeight.com/2008/08/perspective-on-mazen-asbahi.html.

67. Field notes, February 27, 2011.

68. Interestingly, Abdul-Matin goes to great lengths in his book to establish himself as an American. He writes: "I am an American whose roots go back to the Revolutionary War, and this book is therefore inevitable centered on people and places in North America. . . . I am simply presenting the perspective I know from being born and raised in the United States, and I hope these domestic examples will resonate with people living in other countries as well." Ibrahim Abdul-Matin, *Green Deen: What Islam Teaches about Protecting the Planet* (San Francisco: Berrett-Koehler, 2010), xxii.

69. Dr. Tahir Haddad, interview, February 3, 2011.

70. Ibid.

71. Sheikh Eshaal Karimi, interview, June 4, 2010.

72. See, for example, Seyyed Hossein Nasr, *The Encounter of Man and Nature: The Spiritual Crisis of Modern Man* (London: Allen and Unwin, 1968); Mawil Y. Izzi Dien, "Islamic Environmental Ethics, Law, and Society," in *Ethics of Environment and Development*, ed. J. Ronald Engel and Joan Gibb Engel (London: Bellhaven Press, 1990), 189–98. Although Haddad and Karimi offered viewpoints that aligned with constuctive "Islam and ecology" scholarship, both men indicated that they developed these ideas straight from Islamic sources, not from secondary literature. Karimi, moreover, indicated that he rarely read material about Islam written in English.

73. Dr. Tahir Haddad, interview, February 3, 2011.

74. Sheikh Eshaal Karimi, interview, June 4, 2010.

75. Dr. Tahir Haddad, interview, February 3, 2011.

76. Ibid.

4. FOOD AND ENVIRONMENT AT AN AFRICAN AMERICAN CHURCH

1. Field notes, October 27, 2009.
2. Snow and McAdam, "Identity Work Processes," 48.
3. Carl Anthony, quoted in Stoll, "Religion," 151.
4. Ibid., 152.

5. Ibid.

6. Robert D. Bullard, *Unequal Protection: Environmental Justice and Communities of Color* (San Francisco: Sierra Club Books, 1994); McGurty, *Transforming Environmentalism*; Melosi, "Environmental Justice"; Warren, *Ecofeminism*.

7. Field notes, February 26, 2010.

8. Jennifer Halteman Schrock, *Just Eating? Practicing Our Faith at the Table,* Presbyterian Hunger Program, Food and Faith Initiative, 2005, http://practicingourfaith.org/pdf/Just%20Eating%20Participant%20Book.pdf.

9. Ibid., 2.

10. Jennifer Halteman Schrock, *Just Eating? Practicing Our Faith at the Table: African American Congregation Adaptation,* Presbyterian Hunger Program, Food and Faith Initiative, 2005, www.pcusa.org/resource/justeatingaacadaptation/.

11. Wilson Jeremiah Moses, *Afrotopia: The Roots of African American Popular History* (New York: Cambridge University Press, 1998), 6.

12. The one woman who was not a college graduate was in the process of finishing her degree and has since begun graduate studies.

13. Bible study group member, interview, May 17, 2010.

14. Field notes, July 2, 2009.

15. Bible study group member, interview, April 6, 2010.

16. Jayla, interview, June 12, 2010.

17. See chapter 7 of this work for a discussion of these types of stereotypes among Faith in Place participants.

18. Field notes, April 22, 2010.

19. Field notes, July 2, 2009.

20. Mary E. Pattillo, *Black on the Block: The Politics of Race and Class in the City* (Chicago: University of Chicago Press, 2007).

21. Jayla, interview, June 16, 2010.

22. Field notes, July 2, 2009.

23. Several food theorists have written about ways that women transmit culture and show love to family and community members through food. For example, see Anne Bower, ed., *African American Foodways: Explorations of History and Culture* (Urbana: University of Illinois Press, 2007).

24. Anita Walters, interview, April 7, 2010.

25. Literary theorist Doris Witt suggests that if the writers of the Harlem Renaissance who were "committed to portraying what Du Bois termed the Talented Tenth . . . [had] depicted characters engaged in the act of eating, the food would probably not have been the down-home 'chicken and chitlins' typically associated with the migrating black masses." Doris Witt, "From Fiction to Foodways: Working at the Intersections of African American Literary and Culinary Studies," in *African American Foodways: Explorations of History and Culture,* ed. Anne Bower (Chicago: University of Illinois Press, 2007), 111.

26. Ibid., 115.

27. R. Marie Griffith, *Born Again Bodies: Flesh and Spirit in American Christianity* (Berkeley: University of California Press, 2004), 157.

28. Marvalene Hughes makes a similar argument about large body sizes in her discussion of black women and soul food. A black woman who serves food,

Hughes writes, "takes pride in watching her consumers literally gorge themselves until the fatty tissue forms and finds a permanent resting and growing place. Plumpness is a symbol of the wonderful job she is performing. Bigness represents health and prosperity." Marvalene H. Hughes, "Soul, Black Women, and Food," in *Food and Culture: A Reader,* ed. Carole Counihan and Penny Van Esterik (New York: Routledge, 1997), 272–80.

29. Griffith, *Born Again Bodies,* 135.

30. Anita Walters, interview, April 7, 2010. Emphasis added.

31. Field notes, July 2, 2009.

32. Veronica Kyle, interview, July 14, 2010.

33. Field notes, August 13, 2009.

34. Mrs. Weldon, interview, May 17, 2010.

35. Etta Madden and Martha Finch, introduction to *Eating in Eden: Food and American Utopias,* ed. Etta Madden and Martha Finch (Lincoln: University of Nebraska Press, 2006), 14.

36. Veronica Kyle, interview, July 12, 2010.

37. Algernon Austin, *Achieving Blackness: Race, Black Nationalism, and Afrocentrism in the Twentieth Century* (New York: New York University Press, 2006), 66.

38. See MOVE's website at http://onamove.com/.

39. Field notes, August 13, 2009.

40. Schrock, *Just Eating? Practicing Our Faith at the Table,* 25–32.

41. Anita Walters, interview, April 7, 2010.

42. Field notes, July 16, 2009.

43. Mrs. Kinkaid, interview, April 6, 2010.

44. Anita Walters, interview, April 7, 2010.

45. Ibid.

46. Field notes, August 20, 2009.

47. Mrs. Kinkaid, interview, April 6, 2010.

48. Field notes, July 16, 2009.

49. Anita Walters, interview, April 7, 2010.

50. Field notes, July 16, 2009.

51. Anita Walters, interview, April 7, 2010.

52. Ibid.

53. Ibid.

54. Mrs. Kinkaid, interview, April 6, 2010.

55. Field notes, August 13, 2009.

56. Ibid.

57. Schrock, *Just Eating?* (African American congregation adaptation).

58. Environmental activist Van Jones, the founder and former president of Green for All and former special adviser for green jobs at the White House Council on Environmental Quality, writes and talks extensively about the eco-divide.

59. Field notes, August 20, 2009.

60. John L. Jackson, *Harlem World: Doing Race and Class in Contemporary Black America* (Chicago: University of Chicago Press, 2001), 4.

61. Austin, *Achieving Blackness*; Moses, *Afrotopia.*

62. Austin, *Achieving Blackness*, 170.

63. Pattillo, *Black on the Block*, 113.

64. For more on ways lower-class repertoires are used to convey legitimacy, see J. Martin Favor, *Authentic Blackness: The Folk in the New Negro Renaissance,* New Americanists (Durham NC: Duke University Press, 1999).

65. Field notes, August 20, 2009.

66. Mrs. Weldon, interview, May 17, 2010.

67. Ibid.

68. Jayla, interview, June 16, 2010.

69. Jayla, interview, June 28, 2010.

70. Mrs. Kinkaid, interview, April 6, 2010.

71. Jayla, interview, June 28, 2010.

72. Jayla, interview, June 16, 2010.

73. Anita Walters, interview, April 7, 2010.

74. Field notes, May 4, 2010.

75. Faith in Place, e-news, August 11, 2011.

5. FINDING RACIAL DIVERSITY WITH RELIGIOUS PLURALISM

1. In my volunteer work with Faith in Place, I took an active role in soliciting silent auction donations for the annual fund-raiser. In that capacity, I procured many of the items for the interfaith section. However, my solicitations were based on items Faith in Place had offered in previous years, and I always worked under the direction of Faith in Place's deputy director.

2. As of 2014, 81 percent of Faith in Place's supporters identified as Protestants. For more details, see chapter 3 of this work.

3. Butterfield, "Moral Climate." Emphasis added.

4. Passages came from Hebrew Bible and Midrash, the New Testament, the Quran and Hadith, the Vedas, and the Baha'u'llah. Some examples are "See to it that you do not destroy My world, for there is no one to repair it after you" (Midrash Ecclesiastes Rabbah 7); "The world is green and beautiful and God has appointed you his stewards over it" (The Prophet Mohammed [PBUH]); "O God, scatterer of ignorance and darkness, grant me your strength. May all beings regards me with the eye of a friend, and I all beings! With the eye of a friend may each single being regard all others" (Sukla Yajur, Veda XXXVI).

5. All of the seminaries in Chicago are Christian, so this composition of seminarians is inevitable.

6. Field notes, January 22, 2008.

7. Paul, interview, February 19, 2010.

8. Ibid.

9. Faith in Place participant, interview, February 16, 2010.

10. Kate McCarthy, *Interfaith Encounters in America* (New Brunswick, NJ: Rutgers University Press, 2007), 86.

11. Anita Walters, interview, April 7, 2010.

12. After I completed my fieldwork in 2011, Faith in Place did add a Jewish staff member by hiring a volunteer from the Jewish Service Corps, AVODAH, but

they did not continue the relationship with AVODAH after the first volunteer completed her year of service.

13. Clare Butterfield, interview, January 26, 2011.

14. Rabbi, interview, February 14, 2011.

15. Clare Butterfield, interview, January 26, 2011.

16. Field notes, March 25, 2010.

17. Sociological studies confirm Butterfield's suggestion that conservative Christians avoid interfaith activity. See Nancy Tatom Ammerman, *Pillars of Faith: American Congregations and Their Partners* (Berkeley: University of California Press, 2005), and McCarthy, *Interfaith Encounters*.

18. Sarah M. Pike, *New Age and Neopagan Religions in America* (New York: Columbia University Press, 2004), 15.

19. Unitarian Universalist Association of Congregations, "Paganism: Theological Diversity in Unitarian Universalism," n.d., accessed September 15, 2011, www.uua.org/beliefs/welcome/6678.shtml.

20. Pike, *New Age*, 21.

21. Field notes, August 15, 2007.

22. Field notes, June 2, 2007.

23. Clare Butterfield, interview, January 26, 2011.

24. Her uneasiness was not unfounded. In a study of ecologically activist Catholic sisters, Sarah McFarland Taylor found that many of the sisters' detractors criticized them for supporting New Age or pagan ideas, even as the sisters strove to distance themselves from those associations. Sarah McFarland Taylor, *Green Sisters: A Spiritual Ecology* (Cambridge, MA: Harvard University Press, 2007), 271.

25. Clare Butterfield, interview, January 26, 2011.

26. Field notes, February 10, 2009.

27. Courtney Bender and Pamela E. Klassen discuss similar cases of "hybridity" in "Introduction: Habits of Pluralism," in *After Pluralism: Reimagining Religious Engagement,* ed. Courtney Bender and Pamela E. Klassen (New York: Columbia University Press, 2010), 13–15. See also Bender, *New Metaphysicals,* and Pamela E. Klassen, *Spirits of Protestantism: Medicine, Healing, and Liberal Christianity* (Berkeley: University of California Press, 2011).

28. Clare Butterfield, interview, January 26, 2011.

29. One Latina, Monica, already worked for Faith in Place as the director of the youth program. The staff occasionally called on Monica to try to make connections with Spanish-speaking congregations and religious leaders, but her primary focus was on the youth program. In 2013 Faith in Place hired two outreach workers to recruit in Latino communities.

30. Faith in Place, "Faith in Place Strategic Plan," approved by the Board April 16, 2009, internal document, 9–10.

31. Field notes, December 3, 2009.

32. Clare Butterfield, interview, January 26, 2011.

33. R. Stephen Warner, "Changes in the Civic Role of Religion," in *Diversity and Its Discontents: Cultural Conflict and Common Ground in Contemporary American Society,* ed. Neil J. Smelser and Jeffrey C. Alexander (Princeton, NJ: Princeton University Press, 1999), 236.

34. Field notes, October 3, 2010.

35. Clare Butterfield, interview, January 26, 2011.

36. Faith in Place, "2004 Communications Plan," internal document, 2004; Faith in Place, "2004 Notes from Conference Call for IPLs," internal document, 2004.

37. Kevin Schultz shows how tri-faith partnerships lent moral authority to national causes in Kevin Michael Schultz, *Tri-faith America: How Catholics and Jews Held Postwar America to Its Protestant Promise* (New York: Oxford University Press, 2011), 26–27, 179–84.

38. Field notes, June 17, 2009. Faith in Place recruited an African American woman to join the board later that year.

39. This observation is confirmed in D. Taylor, "State of Diversity."

40. For more on Blacks in Green, see their website at www.blacksingreen .org/.

41. Margaret, interview, July 14, 2010.

6. FAITH IN PLACE'S RELIGIOUS MESSAGE

1. I discuss the Purple Radishes in greater detail in chapter 3.

2. Field notes, October 12, 2010.

3. Teresa, interview, October 13, 2010. My interview with Teresa took place in 2010, five years before Pope Francis released his historic encyclical on the environment. It would be interesting to learn whether the encyclical changed Teresa's ideas about the relationship between religion and environmental concern.

4. Faith in Place, "So You Want Allies."

5. Faith in Place, "Introduction."

6. Faith in Place leaders offered the connections between environmental devastation and poor communities as self-evident. While I frequently heard them declaring that environmental degradation hurts poor people "first and the worst," they rarely elaborated or offered supporting evidence for this contention. When they did elaborate, they most frequently referenced the marginalized populations who were stranded in the Superdome after Hurricane Katrina.

7. I discuss ways Americans have associated environmentalism with elitism in chapter 1. See also Taylor and Klingle, "Environmentalism's Elitist Tinge"; Dorceta E. Taylor, "Women of Color, Environmental Justice, and Ecofeminism," in *Ecofeminism: Women, Culture, Nature*, ed. Karen J. Warren (Bloomington: Indiana University Press, 1997), 38–81.

8. Field notes, September 13, 2009.

9. Field notes, August 26, 2008.

10. Faith in Place, "One-Page Description," internal document, 2006.

11. Clare Butterfield, "Script for Multi-congregational Workshop," presentation notes for Cool Congregations gathering, Oak Park, IL, March 22, 2009, Faith in Place internal document.

12. Ibid.

13. She said: "In the three Abrahamic traditions there is an understanding of the human on the earth in a special position. The Hebrew and Christian

scriptures refer to this position in one place as 'dominion.' But they do so in a way that makes it pretty clear, if you think about it, that we are not here to exploit, but to mirror in our relationship to the rest of life God's relationship to us. It is not one of slavery, of exploitation, of using up, but one of love and care and responsibility. Though I am much less familiar with the Quran, I know that the human responsibility to bring forth food from the earth, for example, is treated as an exalted occupation in that sacred tradition. These relationships are meant to be relationships of celebration of the earth's bounty, of God's generosity, and of our special position as stewards." Clare Butterfield, "Notes for Workshop, February 1, 2004," Faith in Place, internal document, 2004.

14. Ibid. Emphasis added.

15. Clare Butterfield, "Script for Multi-congregational Workshop."

16. Although an intern worked on this project one summer, I never saw this resource materialize.

17. This model ignores the messy possibility that some interpretations of religion may not be so "green." For example, in "Ecological Buddhism?" Ian Harris argues that Buddhism is not "green" at all, because it began as a world-denying religion. Ian Harris, "Ecological Buddhism?," in *Worldviews, Religion, and the Environment,* ed. Richard C. Foltz (Belmont, CA: Thomson Wadsworth, 2003), 171–81.

18. Clare Butterfield, interview, January 26, 2011.

19. R. Steven Warner also demonstrates this emphasis on personal salvation in contrast to the mainline focus on social justice. See R. Stephen Warner, *New Wine in Old Wineskins: Evangelicals and Liberals in a Small-Town Church* (Berkeley: University of California Press, 1988).

20. Ammerman, *Pillars of Faith*, 4, 18, 121.

21. Ibid., 30–31.

22. Faith in Place, "Faith in Place Strategic Plan."

23. Butterfield, "Script for Multi-congregational Workshop."

24. Clare Butterfield, "Introduction and Conversation on Big Questions," speech presented at Faithful Citizenship Workshop, Jewish Reconstructionist Congregation, Evanston, IL, March 9, 2008; Faith in Place, "2009 New Brochure text," internal document; Faith in Place, "Why Should Your Congregation Take the Earth Stewardship Pledge?," internal document, 2006.

25. Faith in Place, "Earth Stewardship 4-Page Brochure," internal document, 2005.

26. Clare Butterfield, "Notes for Food Summit Workshop," Faith in Place, internal document, November 7, 2003.

27. Keane clarifies that he is describing modernity as an idea, not necessarily a clearly identifiable set of historical forces (*Christian Moderns: Freedom and Fetish in the Mission Encounter*, The Anthropology of Christianity [Berkeley: University of California Press, 2007], 48). But he insists that even as an idea modernity has played a powerful role in history, serving as a standard for how people ought to think and act. Having developed alongside and in relationship to the Protestant Reformation, aspects of modernity share affinities with and derive from aspects of Protestant Christianity, Keane explains. Modern religion relies on assumptions that some Protestant and secular traditions share. It

involves recognizing the capacity of humans to think and act for themselves and assigns moral value to the quest for human freedom.

28. Ibid., 5.

29. Keane acknowledges conceptual problems with defining modernity. The concept, he writes, "is certainly a word in danger of meaning everything and nothing" (ibid., 47). But he contends that we *can* make an indisputable empirical claim about modernity as an idea, that modernity "has a pervasive and powerful role in the popular imagination wherever we look" (48). In *Christian Moderns,* he analyzes that sense of modernity as a pervasive idea. It is that sense that I employ as well.

30. Ibid., 6.

31. Faith in Place, "Faith in Place Strategic Plan," 9.

32. Gary Dorrien, *The Making of American Liberal Theology: Crisis, Irony, and Postmodernity, 1950–2005* (Louisville, KY: Westminister John Knox Press, 2006).

33. Butterfield, "Book Proposal," 43.

34. Ibid., 9.

35. Clare Butterfield, "A Big Enough Box: A Six-Part Adult Education Curriculum on Ecology, Emergence, Theologies of God," unpublished manuscript, 2007, 18.

36. Robert Orsi, "Popular Theodicies," in *Religion and American Cultures: An Encyclopedia of Traditions, Diversity, and Popular Expressions,* ed. Gary Laderman and Luís D. León (Santa Barbara, CA: ABC-CLIO, 2003), 527–34.

37. Roger E. Olson, *The Journey of Modern Theology: From Reconstruction to Deconstruction* (Downers Grove, IL: IVP Academic, 2013), 398–420.

38. Clare Butterfield, "Already Here: The Emergence of God in the Modern Congregation," unpublished manuscript, 2009, 93.

39. Alfred North Whitehead, *Process and Reality* (1929; repr., London: Free Press, 1978), 35.

40. Phillip Clayton, *Mind and Emergence: From Quantum Physics to Consciousness* (Oxford: Oxford University Press, 2005).

41. Clayton describes this phenomenon in ibid., 77.

42. Butterfield, "Already Here," 4–5; Clayton, *Mind and Emergence.*

43. Clare Butterfield, "April Brownbag Discussion Series," presentation notes, April 28, 2010, Faith in Place internal document.

44. Ibid.

45. Keane, *Christian Moderns,* 47–51.

46. Dorrien, *Making of American Liberal Theology,* 3.

47. Clare Butterfield, "Conversation Cafe Notes for Introduction," September 13, 2009.

48. Faith in Place, "Faith in Place Strategic Plan."

49. "Introduction and Conversation."

50. Butterfield refused to ever purchase or drink Coca-Cola products because she found the practices of that company in developing countries abhorrent. For that reason, there was an informal ban on Coke products within Faith in Place's office.

51. Field notes, June 22, 2009.

52. Lauren, interview, February 16, 2010.
53. Gavin, interview, February 18, 2010.
54. Keane, *Christian Moderns*, 61.
55. Butterfield, "Moral Climate."
56. Butterfield, "Book Proposal."
57. Lauren, interview, February 16, 2010.
58. Danielle, interview, February 25, 2010.
59. Butterfield, "Book Proposal," 44.
60. Olson, *Journey of Modern Theology*, 30.
61. Ibid., 22.
62. Ibid., 21.
63. Field notes, March 19, 2010.
64. For example, VIVA! (Vegetarians International Voice for Animals) has initiated campaigns protesting the practice. See Juliet Gellatley, "Going for the Kill Report: Viva! Report on Religious Slaughter," n.d., accessed May 6, 2016, www.viva.org.uk/going-kill-report.
65. Field notes, March 18, 2010.

7. FROM GRASSROOTS TO MAINSTREAM

1. Faith in Place, "Spring into Climate Action with Faith in Place," E-newsletter, April 7, 2015.
2. Radical environmentalism sometimes is discussed as a third branch but does not receive attention in these particular typologies, with the exception of Robert Gottlieb's. Debra J. Salazar, "The Mainstream-Grassroots Divide in the Environmental Movement: Environmental Groups in Washington State," *Social Science Quarterly* 77, no. 3 (1996): 624–43; Bell and Braun, "Coal, Identity"; Freudenberg and Steinsapir, "Not in Our Backyards"; Robert Gottlieb, *Forcing the Spring*.
3. Freudenberg and Steinsapir, "Not in Our Backyards."
4. D. Taylor, "State of Diversity." See this work's introduction for a fuller discussion of this report.
5. McGurty, *Transforming Environmentalism*.
6. J. Taylor and Klingle, "Environmentalism's Elitist Tinge."
7. Faith in Place, "History," n.d., accessed November 13, 2010, www.faithinplace.org.
8. Field notes, July 6, 2006.
9. Faith in Place, "Who We Serve: Youth and Educators," n.d., accessed March 15, 2012, www.faithinplace.org/who-we-serve/Youth+and+Educators.
10. Orsi, *Gods of the City*, 9.
11. Ibid., 10.
12. Ibid., 6.
13. Faith in Place, "Interreligious Sustainability Project Curriculum." Emphasis added.
14. Ibid.
15. Kari Lydersen and Carlos Javier Ortiz, "More Young People Are Killed in Chicago Than Any Other American City," *Chicago Reporter*, January 25, 2012.

16. Field notes, January 22, 2008.

17. Marcus, interview, June 17, 2010. The term *food desert* refers to areas where residents lack access to healthy foods.

18. Field notes, February 5, 2010.

19. Field notes, October 27, 2009.

20. Faith in Place, "Earth Stewardship 4-Page Brochure," internal document, 2005; Veronica Kyle, "Letter re: Weatherization to Chicago Department of Environment," Faith in Place, internal document, October 30, 2009.

21. Friedenwald-Fishman and Kittivong-Greenbaum, "Faith in Place," 1.

22. Faith in Place, "Revised Goals and Objectives for Faith in Place," internal document, February 2, 2005.

23. Faith in Place, "Faith in Place Strategic Plan," 6–7. The 2009 strategic plan did include a reference to grassroots organizing in the section on policy. Describing the new policy director position, the plan said: "That staff member will be charged with leadership of all grassroots lobbying during the session and revert to role as outreach to downstate/rural congregations during rest of year" (12).

24. Field notes, June 13, 2007.

25. Field notes, June 28, 2007.

26. Clare Butterfield, "We're Moving!," *Faith in Place Newsletter*, Spring 2009.

27. Field notes, June 22, 2009.

28. Field notes, December 3, 2009.

29. Kyle also used her own childhood experiences to challenge stereotypes about the "inner city." On multiple occasions I heard Kyle tell the story of attending her sociology class as an undergraduate at the University of Iowa. One day the professor offered a case study of Altgeld Gardens, but Kyle thought his depiction was completely wrong. So she and another girl from her neighborhood stood up and taught the class for the next week, telling their peers how life *really* was in "the projects" (field notes, March 25, 2010).

30. Butterfield, "Moral Climate"; field notes, January 22, 2008.

31. Butterfield, "April Brownbag Discussion Series."

32. Salazar, "Mainstream-Grassroots Divide."

33. Field notes, December 3, 2009.

34. Butterfield had never intended to stay at Faith in Place until she reached the age of retirement.

35. Board member Henrietta Saunders assumed the role of interim executive director between October 2013 and June 2014 so that Sauder could complete his graduate studies before moving to Chicago.

36. Freudenberg and Steinsapir, "Not in Our Backyards"; Bell and Braun, "Coal, Identity."

37. Butterfield held a law degree from the University of Illinois and a Master of Divinity degree from Meadville Lombard Theological School when she started Faith in Place. In 2008 she also earned a Doctor of Ministry degree from the Chicago Theological Seminary.

38. Female leadership on the board reached a pinnacle in 2009, when the board consisted of eight women and three men. Between 2009 and 2012 women

held three of the four executive positions on the board as well, including board chair.

39. Voter Activation Network, "In-Depth Analysis."

40. The Ford Foundation, a major funder of Faith in Place, hired the Metropolitan Group to assess Faith in Place's resource development and infrastructure and to offer guidance on improving those, in 2008.

41. Friedenwald-Fishman and Kittivong-Greenbaum, "Faith in Place," 16.

42. Ibid., 17.

43. Clare Butterfield, Faith in Place e-news, December 4, 2007.

44. Clare Butterfield, Faith in Place e-news, July 6, 2010.

45. Alice G. Eagly and Linda L. Carli, "The Female Leadership Advantage: An Evaluation of the Evidence," *Leadership Quarterly* 14, no. 6 (2003): 807–34; Steven H. Appelbaum, Lynda Audet, and Joanne C. Miller, "Gender and Leadership? Leadership and Gender? A Journey through the Landscape of Theories," *Leadership and Organization Development Journal* 24, no. 1/2 (2003): 43–51.

46. D. Taylor, "State of Diversity," 4.

47. Ibid.

48. McGurty, *Transforming Environmentalism*, 5.

49. Rothman, *Greening of a Nation?*, 209.

50. Ibid., 210.

CONCLUSION

1. D. Taylor, "State of Diversity."

2. Tomoko Masuzawa, *The Invention of World Religions: Or, How European Universalism Was Preserved in the Language of Pluralism* (Chicago: University of Chicago Press, 2005); Talal Asad, *Genealogies of Religion: Discipline and Reasons of Power in Christianity and Islam* (Baltimore: John Hopkins University Press, 1993); Robert A. Orsi, *Between Heaven and Earth: the Religious Worlds People Make and the Scholars Who Study Them* (Princeton, NJ: Princeton University Press, 2005).

3. Stuckrad, "Finding Data," 43.

Bibliography

Abdul-Matin, Ibrahim. *Green Deen: What Islam Teaches about Protecting the Planet*. San Francisco: Berrett-Koehler, 2010.

Allison, Elizabeth. "Waste and Worldviews: Garbage and Pollution Challenges in Bhutan." *Journal for the Study of Religion, Nature and Culture* 8, no. 4 (2014): 405–28.

Ammerman, Nancy Tatom. *Pillars of Faith: American Congregations and Their Partners*. Berkeley: University of California Press, 2005.

Anthony, Carl. "Why African Americans Should Be Environmentalists." *Race, Poverty and the Environment* 1, no. 1 (1990): 5–6.

Appelbaum, Steven H., Lynda Audet, and Joanne C. Miller. "Gender and Leadership? Leadership and Gender? A Journey through the Landscape of Theories." *Leadership and Organization Development Journal* 24, no. 1/2 (2003): 43–51.

Ard, Kerry, and Paul Mohai. "Hispanics and Environmental Voting in the US Congress." *Environmental Practice* 13, no. 4 (2011): 302–13.

Asad, Talal. *Formations of the Secular: Christianity, Islam, Modernity*. Cultural Memory in the Present. Stanford, CA: Stanford University Press, 2003.

———. *Genealogies of Religion: Discipline and Reasons of Power in Christianity and Islam*. Baltimore: John Hopkins University Press, 1993.

Austin, Algernon. *Achieving Blackness: Race, Black Nationalism, and Afrocentrism in the Twentieth Century*. New York: New York University Press, 2006.

Beaton, Caroline. "Is Environmentalism Elitist?" *Elephant Journal*, December 12, 2014. www.elephantjournal.com/2014/12/is-environmentalism-elitist/.

Behar, Ruth, and Deborah A. Gordon, eds. *Women Writing Culture*. Berkeley: University of California Press, 1995.

Bell, Dianna. "Understanding a 'Broken World': Islam, Ritual, and Climate Change in Mali, West Africa." *Journal for the Study of Religion, Nature and Culture* 8, no. 3 (2014): 287–306.

Bell, Shannon Elizabeth, and Yvonne A. Braun. "Coal, Identity, and the Gendering of Environmental Justice Activism in Central Appalachia." *Gender and Society* 24, no. 6 (2010): 794–813.

Bender, Courtney. *Heaven's Kitchen: Living Religion at God's Love We Deliver.* Chicago: University of Chicago Press, 2003.

———. *The New Metaphysicals: Spirituality and the American Religious Imagination.* Chicago: University of Chicago Press, 2010.

Bender, Courtney, and Pamela E. Klassen. "Introduction: Habits of Pluralism." In *After Pluralism: Reimagining Religious Engagement,* edited by Courtney Bender and Pamela E. Klassen, 1–30. New York: Columbia University Press, 2010.

Berg, Peter, Beryl Magilavy, and Seth Zuckerman. *A Green City Program for San Francisco Bay Area Cities and Towns.* San Francisco: Planet Drum Books, 1989.

Bingham, Sally G. *Love God, Heal Earth.* Pittsburgh, PA: St. Lynns Press, 2009.

Birch, Eugenie Ladner, and Susan M. Wachter, eds. *Growing Greener Cities: Urban Sustainability in the Twenty-First Century.* Philadelphia: University of Pennsylvania Press, 2008.

Bouma-Prediger, Steven. *For the Beauty of the Earth: A Christian Vision for Creation Care.* Grand Rapids, MI: Baker Academic Press, 2001.

Bower, Anne, ed. *African American Foodways: Explorations of History and Culture.* Urbana: University of Illinois Press, 2007.

Braude, Ann. "Women's History *Is* American Religious History." In *Retelling U.S. Religious History,* edited by Thomas A. Tweed, 87–107. Berkeley: University of California Press, 1997.

Brodkin, Karen. *How Jews Became White Folks and What That Says about Race in America.* New Brunswick, NJ: Rutgers University Press, 1998.

Bullard, Robert D. "Anatomy of Environmental Racism and the Environmental Justice Movement." In *Confronting Environmental Racism: Voices from the Grassroots,* edited by Robert D. Bullard, 15–40. Boston: South End Press, 1993.

———. "Decision Making." In *Faces of Environmental Racism: Confronting Global Justice,* 2nd ed., edited by Laura Westra and Bill Lawson. Lanham, MD: Rowman and Littlefield, 2001.

———. *Unequal Protection: Environmental Justice and Communities of Color.* San Francisco: Sierra Club Books, 1994.

Buttel, Frederick, and William L. Flinn. "Social Class and Mass Environmental Beliefs: A Reconsideration." *Environment and Behavior,* no. 10 (September 1978): 433–50.

Butterfield, Clare. "Already Here: The Emergence of God in the Modern Congregation." Unpublished manuscript, 2009.

———. "April Brownbag Discussion Series." Presentation notes, April 28, 2010. Faith in Place, internal document.

———. "A Big Enough Box: A Six-Part Adult Education Curriculum on Ecology, Emergence, Theologies of God." Unpublished manuscript, 2007.

———. "Book Proposal for *Faith in Place, Faith in Practice: A Field Guide to Bringing Congregations into Right Relationship with the Earth.*" April 30, 2007.

———. "Conversation Cafe Notes for Introduction." September 13, 2009.

———. "A Moral Climate: Sermon for Prairie Circle Unitarian Universalist Congregation." Faith in Place, internal document, June 22, 2008.

———. "Notes for Workshop, February 1, 2004." Faith in Place internal document, 2004.

———. "Script for Multi-congregational Workshop." Presentation notes for Faith in Place workshop, Cool Congregations gathering, Oak Park, IL, March 22, 2009. Faith in Place internal document.

———. "We're Moving!" *Faith in Place Newsletter*, Spring 2009.

Calhoun, Craig J., Mark Juergensmeyer, and Jonathan VanAntwerpen. Introduction to *Rethinking Secularism*, edited by Craig J. Calhoun, Mark Juergensmeyer, and Jonathan VanAntwerpen. Oxford: Oxford University Press, 2011.

———. *Rethinking Secularism*. Oxford: Oxford University Press, 2011.

Callicott, J. Baird. *In Defense of the Land Ethic: Essays in Environmental Philosophy*. Albany: State University of New York Press, 1989.

Callicott, J. Baird, and Roger T. Ames. *Nature in Asian Traditions of Thought: Essays in Environmental Philosophy*. Albany: State University of New York Press, 1989.

Center for Neighborhood Technology. "One Creation, One People, One Place." July 1, 1998. www.cnt.org/publications/one-creation-one-people-one-place-a-statement-of-the-interreligious-sustainability.

Chauncey, George. *Gay New York: Gender, Urban Culture, and the Makings of the Gay Male World, 1890–1940*. New York: Basic Books, 1994.

Clayton, Phillip. *Mind and Emergence: From Quantum Physics to Consciousness*. Oxford: Oxford University Press, 2005.

Clifford, James. "Introduction: Partial Truths." In *Writing Culture: The Poetics and Politics of Ethnography*, edited by James Clifford and George Marcus, 1–26. Berkeley: University of California Press, 1986.

Curry, Patrick. *Ecological Ethics: An Introduction*. Malden, MA: Polity Press, 2006.

Dahl, Arthur. "World Wide Fund for Nature (W.W.F.)." In *The Encyclopedia of Religion and Nature,* edited by Bron Raymond Taylor. London: Thoemmes Continuum, 2006.

Daniels, Tom. "Taking the Initiative: Why Cities Are Greening Now." In Birch and Wachter, *Growing Greener Cities*, 11–27.

Darnovsky, Marcy, Barbara Epstein, and Richard Flacks, eds. *Cultural Politics and Social Movements*. Philadelphia: Temple University Press, 1995.

Davis, Henry Vance. "The Environmental Voting Record of the Congressional Black Caucus." In *Race and the Incidence of Environmental Hazards: A Time for Discourse*, edited by Bunyan Bryant and Paul Mohai, 55–63. Boulder, CO: Westview Press, 1992.

Davis, John. *The Earth First! Reader: Ten Years of Radical Environmentalism.* Salt Lake City, UT: Peregrine Smith Books, 1991.

Devall, Bill, and George Sessions. *Deep Ecology.* Salt Lake City, UT: G.M. Smith, 1985.

Dien, Mawil Y. Izzi. "Islamic Environmental Ethics, Law, and Society." In *Ethics of Environment and Development,* edited by J. Ronald Engel and Joan Gibb Engel, 189–98. London: Bellhaven Press, 1990.

Dodman, David. "Blaming Cities for Climate Change? An Analysis of Urban Greenhouse Gas Emissions Inventories." *Environment and Urbanization* 23, no. 2 (2009): 185–201.

Dorrien, Gary. *The Making of American Liberal Theology: Crisis, Irony, and Postmodernity, 1950–2005.* Louisville, KY: Westminister John Knox Press, 2006.

Dumke, Mick. "Why Can't Chicago Recycle?" *Chicago Reader,* July 27, 2010.

Dunlap, Riley E. "Public Opinion on the Environment in the Reagan Era: Polls, Pollution, and Politics." *Environment* 29 (1987): 6–11, 31–37.

Eagly, Alice G., and Linda L. Carli. "The Female Leadership Advantage: An Evaluation of the Evidence." *Leadership Quarterly* 14, no. 6 (2003): 807–34.

"Ethical Eating." *Religion and Ethics Newsweekly,* PBS, July 16, 2010. Transcript at www.pbs.org/wnet/religionandethics/2010/07/16/july-16–2010-ethical-eating/6630/.

Faith in Place. "Earth Stewardship 4-Page Brochure." Internal document, 2005.

———. "Faith in Place Strategic Plan." Approved by the Board April 16, 2009. Internal document.

———. "GuideStar Exchange Charting Impact Report." GuideStar form filled out by Faith in Place. Internal document, last updated June 26, 2013. www.guidestar.org/report/chartingimpact/546603535/faith-place.pdf.

———. "Interreligious Sustainability Project Curriculum for Congregations in the Chicago Region: Curriculum 4." Internal document, 2000.

———. "Introduction to Faith in Place." Internal document, October 5, 2006.

———. "One-Page Description [of Faith in Place]." Internal document, 2006.

———. "Revised Goals and Objectives for Faith in Place." Internal document, February 2, 2005.

———. "So You Want Allies among People of Faith? Tips for Working with Religious Congregations." Internal document, April 2007.

———. "Ten Fruitful Years: Faith in Place Ten Year Report." Internal document, 2009.

———. "Ten Tips for Your Green Team." Faith in Place website, accessed April 18, 2016. www.faithinplace.org/sites/www.faithinplace.org/files/assets/10_Tips_FullSheet_smallerfile.pdf.

———. "Ten Tips Talk for Congregations." In "Seminarian Speakers Bureau Training." Internal document, January 2010.

———. "Why Should Your Congregation Take the Earth Stewardship Pledge?" Internal document, 2006.

Favor, J. Martin. *Authentic Blackness: The Folk in the New Negro Renaissance.* New Americanists. Durham, NC: Duke University Press, 1999.

Fessenden, Tracy. *Culture and Redemption: Religion, the Secular, and American Literature*. Princeton, NJ: Princeton University Press, 2007.

Finnegan, Eleanor. "What Traditions Are Represented in Religion and Ecology? A Perspective from an American Scholar of Islam." In *Inherited Land: The Changing Grounds of Religion and Ecology*, edited by Whitney Bauman, Richard Bohannon and Kevin J. O'Brien, 64–79. Eugene, OR: Pickwick Publications, 2011.

Fowler, Robert Booth. *The Greening of Protestant Thought*. Chapel Hill: University of North Carolina Press, 1995.

Frankenberg, Ruth. *White Women, Race Matters: The Social Construction of Whiteness*. Minneapolis: University of Minnesota Press, 1993.

Freudenberg, Nicholas, and Carol Steinsapir. "Not in Our Backyards: The Grassroots Environmental Movement." *Society and Natural Resources* 4, no. 3 (1991): 235–45.

Friedenwald-Fishman, Eric, and Soudary Kittivong-Greenbaum. "Faith in Place: Findings and Recommendations." Metropolitan Group, December 17, 2008. Faith in Place internal document.

Friedman, Debra, and Doug McAdam. "Collective Identity and Activism: Networks, Choices, and the Life of a Social Movement." In *Frontiers in Social Movement Theory*, edited by A. D. Morris and C. M. Mueller, 153–76. New Haven, CT: Yale University Press, 1992.

Garner, Roberta. *Contemporary Movements and Ideologies*. New York: McGraw-Hill, 1996.

Geertz, Clifford. *The Interpretation of Cultures*. New York: Basic Books, 1973.

Gellatley, Juliet. "Going for the Kill Report: Viva! Report on Religious Slaughter." n.d. Accessed May 6, 2016. www.viva.org.uk/going-kill-report.

Gilpin, W. Clark. "Secularism: Religious, Irreligious, and Areligious." Religion and Culture Web Forum, March 2007. https://divinity.uchicago.edu/sites/default/files/imce/pdfs/webforum/032007/secularism.pdf.

Ginzberg, Lori D. *Women and the Work of Benevolence: Morality, Politics, and Class in the Nineteenth-Century United States*. Yale Historical Publications. New Haven, CT: Yale University Press, 1990.

Glaeser, Edward, and Jacob Vigdor. *The End of the Segregated Century: Racial Separation in America's Neighborhoods, 1890–2010*. New York: Manhattan Institute for Policy Research, January 2012. https://www.manhattan-institute.org/html/end-segregated-century-racial-separation-americas-neighborhoods-1890–2010–5848.html.

Glave, Dianne, and Mark Stoll, eds. *"To Love the Wind and the Rain": African Americans and Environmental History*. Pittsburgh, PA: University of Pittsburgh Press, 2006.

Godbey, John C. "Unitarian Universalist Association." In *Encyclopedia of Religion*, edited by Lindsay Jones, 9468–72. Detroit, MI: Macmillan Reference USA, 2006.

Gottlieb, Robert. *Forcing the Spring: The Transformation of the American Environmental Movement*. 2nd ed. Washington, DC: Island Press, 2005.

Gottlieb, Roger S. *A Greener Faith: Religious Environmentalism and Our Planet's Future*. Oxford: Oxford University Press, 2006.

Gould, Rebecca Kneale. *At Home in Nature: Modern Homesteading and Spiritual Practice in America*. Berkeley: University of California Press, 2005.

Gould, Roger V. *Insurgent Identities: Class, Community, and Protest in Paris from 1848 to the Commune*. Chicago: University of Chicago Press, 1995.

Green Bible. New Revised Standard Version. Edited by Michael G. Maudlin and Marlene Baer. New York: HarperCollins, 2008.

Griffith, R. Marie. *Born Again Bodies: Flesh and Spirit in American Christianity*. Berkeley: University of California Press, 2004.

Haberman, David L. *People Trees: Worship of Trees in Northern India*. New York: Oxford University Press, 2013.

———. *River of Love in an Age of Pollution*. Berkeley: University of California Press, 2006.

Harris, Ian. "Ecological Buddhism?" In *Worldviews, Religion, and the Environment*, edited by Richard C. Foltz, 171–81. Belmont, CA: Thomson Wadsworth, 2003.

Hessel, Dieter T. *After Nature's Revolt: Eco-Justice and Theology*. Minneapolis: Fortress Press, 1992.

Hill, Andrew M. "Unitarians." In *Encyclopedia of Christianity*, edited by Erwin Fahlbusch, Jan Milic Lochman, and John Mbiti. Grand Rapids, MI: William B. Eerdmans, 2008.

Hogue, Michael, David Rhoads, David Aftandilian, Robert Saler, and Clare Butterfield. "Chicago Religious Environmentalisms." Panel, Religion and Ecology Group, annual meeting of the American Academy of Religion, Chicago, November 2, 2008.

Hughes, Marvalene H. "Soul, Black Women, and Food." In *Food and Culture: A Reader*, edited by Carole Counihan and Penny Van Esterik, 272–80. New York: Routledge, 1997.

Jackson, John L. *Harlem World: Doing Race and Class in Contemporary Black America*. Chicago: University of Chicago Press, 2001.

Jazayerli, Rany. "On Mazen Asbahi." *FiveThirtyEight: Politics Done Right*, August 8, 2008. www.fivethirtyeight.com/2008/08/perspective-on-mazen-asbahi.html.

Johnson, Geoffrey. "Green Awards 2007 Honorees." *Chicago Magazine*, May 26, 2007. www.chicagomag.com/Chicago-Magazine/April-2007/Green-Awards-Honorees/index.php?cparticle=4&siarticle=3#artanc.

Kalland, Arne. "The Religious Environmentalist Paradigm." In *The Encyclopedia of Religion and Nature*, edited by Bron Taylor. London: Continuum International, 2006.

Keane, Webb. *Christian Moderns: Freedom and Fetish in the Mission Encounter*. The Anthropology of Christianity. Berkeley: University of California Press, 2007.

Kennedy, Julia, Peter Haas, and Bill Eyring. "Measuring the Economic Impacts of Greening: The Center for Neighborhood Technology Green Values Calculator." In Birch and Wachter, *Growing Greener Cities*, 326–45.

Klassen, Pamela E. *Spirits of Protestantism: Medicine, Healing, and Liberal Christianity*. Berkeley: University of California Press, 2011.

Kyle, Veronica. "Letter re: Weatherization to Chicago Department of Environment." Faith in Place internal document, October 30, 2009.

Lee, Barbara, and Van Jones. "Want to Win the Climate Fight? Engage Communities of Color." *Huffington Post*, April 22, 2015, updated June 22, 2015. www.huffingtonpost.com/rep-barbara-lee/want-to-win-the-climate-f_b_7120006.html.

Livezey, Lowell W., and Elfriede Wedam. "Faith in Place (Originally Interreligious Sustainability Project) Evaluation Report." Faith in Place internal document, 2003.

Lydersen, Kari, and Carlos Javier Ortiz. "More Young People Are Killed in Chicago Than Any Other American City." *Chicago Reporter,* January 25, 2012.

Madden, Etta, and Martha Finch. Introduction to *Eating in Eden: Food and American Utopias,* edited by Etta Madden and Martha Finch, 1–31. Lincoln: University of Nebraska Press, 2006.

Manes, Christopher. *Green Rage: Radical Environmentalism and the Unmaking of Civilization.* Boston: Little, Brown, 1990.

Martinez, Henry. "Earth Care in the Christian Tradition: Resources by Denomination." 2010. Web of Creation, Lutheran School of Theology at Chicago. www.webofcreation.org/images/stories/downloads/earth-care by denomination.pdf.

Masuzawa, Tomoko. *The Invention of World Religions: Or, How European Universalism Was Preserved in the Language of Pluralism.* Chicago: University of Chicago Press, 2005.

McCarthy, Kate. *Interfaith Encounters in America.* New Brunswick, NJ: Rutgers University Press, 2007.

McDaniel, Jay B. *Of Gods and Pelicans: A Theology of Reverence for Life.* Louisville, KY: Westminister/John Knox Press, 1989.

McDuff, Mallory D. *Natural Saints: How People of Faith Are Working to Save God's Earth.* Oxford: Oxford University Press, 2010.

———. *Sacred Acts: How Churches Are Working to Protect Earth's Climate.* Gabriola Island, British Columbia: New Society, 2012.

McGurty, Eileen Maura. *Transforming Environmentalism: Warren County, PCBs, and the Origins of Environmental Justice.* New Brunswick, NJ: Rutgers University Press, 2007.

Melosi, Martin V. "Environmental Justice, Ecoracism, and Environmental History." In Glave and Stoll, *"To Love the Wind,"* 120–32.

Merchant, Carolyn. *American Environmental History.* New York: Columbia University Press, 2007.

Milkman, Ruth, and Veronica Terriquez. "'We Are the Ones Who Are Out in Front': Women's Leadership in the Immigrant Rights Movement." *Feminist Studies* 38, no. 3 (2012): 723–52.

Miller, Perry. *Errand into the Wilderness.* Cambridge, MA: Belknap Press of Harvard University Press, 1956.

Mitchell, Lee Clark. *Witnesses to a Vanishing America: The Nineteenth-Century Response.* Princeton, NJ: Princeton University Press, 1981.

Mohai, Paul. "Black Environmentalism." *Social Science Quarterly* 71 (April 1990): 744–65.

——. "Dispelling Old Myths: African American." *Environment: Science and Policy for Sustainable Development* 45, no. 5 (2003): 10–26.

——. "Public Concern and Elite Involvement in Environmental Conservation." *Social Science Quarterly* 66 (December 1985): 820–38.

Mohai, Paul, and Bunyan Bryant. "Is There a 'Race' Effect on Concern for Environmental Quality?" *Public Opinion Quarterly* 62, no. 4 (1998): 475–505.

Moses, Wilson Jeremiah. *Afrotopia: The Roots of African American Popular History.* New York: Cambridge University Press, 1998.

Moyers, Bill. "Spirit and Nature." *Bill Moyers' Journal*, PBS, 1991. Video and transcript at http://billmoyers.com/content/spirit-nature/.

Mueller, Carol. "The One Thing All Religions Have in Common Is Responsibility for Caring for the Earth." *Lutheran*, August 2009. www.thelutheran.org /article/article.cfm?article_id=8337.

Nash, Roderick. *The Rights of Nature: A History of Environmental Ethics.* Madison: University of Wisconsin Press, 1989.

——. *Wilderness and the American Mind.* 4th ed. 1967. New Haven, CT: Yale University Press, 2001.

Nasr, Seyyed Hossein. *The Encounter of Man and Nature: The Spiritual Crisis of Modern Man.* London: Allen and Unwin, 1968.

Olson, Roger E. *The Journey of Modern Theology: From Reconstruction to Deconstruction.* Downers Grove, IL: IVP Academic, 2013.

Orsi, Robert A. *Between Heaven and Earth: The Religious Worlds People Make and the Scholars Who Study Them.* Princeton, NJ: Princeton University Press, 2005.

——. "Everyday Miracles: The Study of Lived Religion." In *Lived Religion in America: Toward a History of Practice,* edited by David Hall, 3–21. Princeton, NJ: Princeton University Press, 1997.

——. *Gods of the City: Religion and the American Urban Landscape.* Religion in North America. Bloomington: Indiana University Press, 1999.

——. "Popular Theodicies." In *Religion and American Cultures: An Encyclopedia of Traditions, Diversity, and Popular Expressions,* edited by Gary Laderman and Luís D. León, 527–34. Santa Barbara, CA: ABC-CLIO, 2003.

Owen, David. "Green Manhattan." *New Yorker*, October 18, 2004, 111.

Pattillo, Mary E. *Black on the Block: The Politics of Race and Class in the City.* Chicago: University of Chicago Press, 2007.

Pike, Sarah M. *New Age and Neopagan Religions in America.* New York: Columbia University Press, 2004.

Pope Francis. "Laudato Si: On Care for Our Common Home." Encyclical Letter on Climate Change and the Environment. 2015. http://w2.vatican.va /content/francesco/en/encyclicals/documents/papa-francesco_20150524_ enciclica-laudato-si.html.

Renewal. Dir. Marty Ostrow and Terry K. Rockefeller. Fine Cut Productions, 2008.

Rockefeller, Steven C., and John Elder. *Spirit and Nature: Why the Environment Is a Religious Issue: An Interfaith Dialogue*. Boston: Beacon Press, 1992.

Roof, Wade Clark. *Spiritual Marketplace: Baby Boomers and the Remaking of American Religion*. Princeton, NJ: Princeton University Press, 1999.

Rothman, Hal K. *The Greening of a Nation? Environmentalism in the United States since 1945*. Fort Worth, TX: Harcourt Brace College, 1998.

Rubin, Victor. "The Roots of the Urban Greening Movement." In Birch and Wachter, *Growing Greener Cities*, 187–206.

Sabin, Scott C., and Kathy Ide. *Tending to Eden: Environmental Stewardship for God's People*. Valley Forge, PA: Judson Press, 2010.

Sahagun, Louis. "History in a New Light: Rethinking Muir." *Los Angeles Times*, November 13, 2014.

Salazar, Debra J. "The Mainstream-Grassroots Divide in the Environmental Movement: Environmental Groups in Washington State." *Social Science Quarterly* 77, no. 3 (1996): 626–43.

Salomon, Alexandra. "Bridgeview Mosque Gets Solar Panel." WBEZ, Chicago Public Radio, August 1, 2008.

Schmitt, Peter. *Back to Nature: The Arcadian Myth in Urban America*. 2nd ed. Baltimore: John Hopkins University Press, 1990.

Schrock, Jennifer Halteman. *Just Eating? Practicing Our Faith at the Table*. Presbyterian Hunger Program, Food and Faith Initiative. 2005. http://practicingourfaith.org/pdf/Just%20Eating%20Participant%20Book.pdf.

———. *Just Eating? Practicing Our Faith at the Table: African American Congregation Adaptation*. Presbyterian Hunger Program, Food and Faith Initiative, 2005. www.pcusa.org/resource/justeatingaacadaptation/.

Schultz, Kevin Michael. *Tri-Faith America: How Catholics and Jews Held Postwar America to Its Protestant Promise*. New York: Oxford University Press, 2011.

Simpson, Glenn R., and Amy Chozick. "Obama's Muslim-Outreach Adviser Resigns." *Wall Street Journal*, August 6, 2008.

Sleeth, J. Matthew. *Serve God, Save the Planet: A Christian Call to Action*. Grand Rapids, MI: Zondervan, 2007.

Snow, David A., and Doug McAdam. "Identity Work Processes in the Context of Social Movements: Clarifying the Identity/Movement Nexus." In *Self, Identity, and Social Movements*, edited by Sheldon Stryker, Timothy J. Owens, and Robert W. White, 41–67. Minneapolis: University of Minnesota Press, 2000.

Stevens, Heidi. "Remarkable Woman: Clare Butterfield." *Chicago Tribune*, April 6, 2012.

Stoll, Mark. "Religion and African American Environmental Activism." In Glave and Stoll, *"To Love the Wind,"* 150–63.

Stuckrad, Kocku von. "Finding Data: Some Reflections on Ontologies and Normativities." *Journal for the Study of Religion, Nature, and Culture* 1, no. 1 (2007): 39–46.

Sullivan, Winnifred Fallers. *Prison Religion: Faith-Based Reform and the Constitution*. Princeton, NJ: Princeton University Press, 2009.

Taylor, Bron Raymond. *Dark Green Religion: Nature Spirituality and the Planetary Future*. Berkeley: University of California Press, 2010.

———. "Editor's Introduction: Toward a Robust Scientific Investigation of the 'Religion' Variable in the Quest for Sustainability." *Journal for the Study of Religion, Nature and Culture* 5, no. 3 (2011): 252–63.

———. "Environmental Ethics." In *The Encyclopedia of Religion and Nature*, edited by Bron Raymond Taylor. London: Thoemmes Continuum, 2006.

———. Introduction to *The Encyclopedia of Religion and Nature*, edited by Bron Taylor, vii–xxi. London: Continuum International, 2006.

———. "Religious Studies and Environmental Concern." In *The Encyclopedia of Religion and Nature*, edited by Bron Taylor, 1373–79. London: Continuum International, 2006.

Taylor, Charles. *A Secular Age*. Cambridge, MA: Belknap Press of Harvard University Press, 2007.

Taylor, Dorceta E. "The Green Insiders' Club: Highlights from 'The State of Diversity in Enviornmental Organizations.'" Green 2.0. 2014. www.diversegreen.org/the-challenge/.

———. "The State of Diversity in Environmental Organizations: Mainstream NGOs, Foundations, Government Agencies." Report, Green 2.0. 2014. www.diversegreen.org/the-challenge/.

———. "Women of Color, Environmental Justice, and Ecofeminism." In *Ecofeminism: Women, Culture, Nature*, edited by Karen J. Warren, 38–81. Bloomington: Indiana University Press, 1997.

Taylor, Joseph E., and Matthew Klingle. "Environmentalism's Elitist Tinge Has Roots in the Movement's History." *Grist*, March 9, 2006, http://grist.org/politics/klingle/.

Taylor, Sarah McFarland. *Green Sisters: A Spiritual Ecology*. Cambridge, MA: Harvard University Press, 2007.

Thandeka. *Learning to Be White: Money, Race, and God in America*. New York: Continuum, 2007.

Truax, Hawley. "Beyond White Environmentalism: Minorities and the Environment." *Environmental Action* 21, no. 4 (January/February 1990): 19–31.

Tuan, Yi Fu. "Discrepancies between Environmental Attitude and Behavior: Examples from Europe and China." *Canadian Biographer* 12 (1968): 176–91.

Tucker, Mary Evelyn, and John Grim. "Intellectual and Organizational Foundations of Religion and Ecology." In *Grounding Religion: A Field Guide to the Study of Religion and Ecology*, edited by Whitney Bauman, Richard Bohannon, and Kevin J. O'Brien, 81–95. New York: Routledge, 2011.

Turner, Ralph H., and Lewis M. Killian. *Collective Behavior*. 2nd ed. Englewood Cliffs, NJ: Prentice-Hall, 1972.

———. *Collective Behavior*. 3rd ed. Englewood Cliffs, NJ: Prentice-Hall, 1987.

Voter Activation Network. "An In-Depth Analysis of Faith in Place Supporters." Faith in Place, internal document, 2014.

Warner, R. Stephen. "Changes in the Civic Role of Religion." In *Diversity and Its Discontents: Cultural Conflict and Common Ground in Contemporary American Society*, edited by Neil J. Smelser and Jeffrey C. Alexander, 229–44. Princeton, NJ: Princeton University Press, 1999.

———. *New Wine in Old Wineskins: Evangelicals and Liberals in a Small-Town Church*. Berkeley: University of California Press, 1988.

———. "Toward a New Paradigm for the Sociological Study of Religion in the United States." *American Journal of Sociology* 98 (1993): 1044–93.

Warren, Karen, ed. *Ecofeminism: Women, Culture, Nature*. Bloomington: Indiana University Press, 1997.

Warren, Mark R. *Dry Bones Rattling: Community Building to Revitalize American Democracy*. Princeton, NJ: Princeton University Press, 2001.

When Heaven Meets Earth: Faith and Environment in the Chesapeake Bay. Dir. Jeffrey Pohorski. Prod. Susan Emmerich. SkunkFilms, 2008.

White, Lynn, Jr. "The Historical Roots of Our Ecologic Crisis." *Science* 155, no. 3767 (1967): 1203–7.

Whitehead, Alfred North. *Process and Reality*. 1929. Reprint, London: Free Press, 1978.

Whittaker, Matthew, Gary M. Segura, and Shaun Bowler. "Racial/Ethnic Group Attitudes toward Environmental Protection in California: Is 'Environmentalism' Still a White Phenomenon?" *Political Research Quarterly* 58, no. 3 (2005): 435–47.

Wilkinson, Katharine K. *Between God and Green: How Evangelicals Are Cultivating a Middle Ground on Climate Change*. New York: Oxford University Press, 2012.

Witt, Doris. "From Fiction to Foodways: Working at the Intersections of African American Literary and Culinary Studies." In *African American Foodways: Explorations of History and Culture*, edited by Anne Bower, 101–25. Chicago: University of Illinois Press, 2007.

Wright, Machaelle Small, and Perelandra Ltd. *Perelandra Garden Workbook: A Complete Guide to Gardening with Nature Intelligences*. 2nd ed. Jeffersonton, VA: Perelandra, 1993.

Zurcher, Louis A., and David A. Snow. "Collective Behavior: Social Movements." In *Social Psychology: Social Perspectives*, edited by Morris Rosenberg and Ralph H. Turner, 447–82. New York: Basic Books, 1981.

Index